How to **Preach & Teach**
the Old Testament
for All Its Worth

Also Available:

How to Read the Bible for All Its Worth
(Gordon D. Fee and Douglas Stuart)

How to Read the Bible Book by Book
(Gordon D. Fee and Douglas Stuart)

How to Read the Bible through the Jesus Lens
(Michael Williams)

How to Choose a Translation for All Its Worth
(Gordon D. Fee and Mark L. Strauss)

How to Read the Bible as Literature
(Leland Ryken)

A FOLLOW-UP TO *HOW TO READ THE BIBLE FOR ALL ITS WORTH*

How to Preach & Teach the Old Testament for All Its Worth

Christopher J. H. Wright

 ZONDERVAN®

ZONDERVAN

How to Preach and Teach the Old Testament for All Its Worth
Copyright © 2016 by Christopher J. H. Wright

First published by Langham Preaching Resources in the United Kingdom under the title
Sweeter than Honey.

This title is also available as a Zondervan ebook.

Requests for information should be addressed to:

Zondervan, 3900 *Sparks Dr. SE, Grand Rapids, Michigan 49546*

Library of Congress Cataloging-in-Publication Data

Names: Wright, Christopher J. H., 1947- author
Title: How to preach and teach the Old Testament for all its worth / Christopher J.H.
     Wright.
Description: Grand Rapids, MI : Zondervan, 2016. | Includes bibliographical
     references.
Identifiers: LCCN 2016008386 | ISBN 9780310524649 (softcover)
Subjects: LCSH: Bible. Old Testament — Homiletical use. | Bible. Old Testament —
     Sermons. | Preaching.
Classification: LCC BS1191.5 .W75 2016 | DDC 221.071 — dc23 LC record available at
     http://lccn.loc.gov/2016008386

Cover design: LUCAS Art & Design
Cover photo: Lightstock
Interior design: Matthew Van Zomeren and Kait Lamphere

Printed in the United States of America

HB 09.14.2023

To

Jonathan Lamb

in friendship and gratitude
who, as pioneer and director of the
Langham Preaching program 2002–2013,
enabled me to develop the substance of this book
through teaching it in many different countries.

Contents

Detailed Table of Contents

PART 1

WHY SHOULD WE PREACH AND TEACH FROM THE OLD TESTAMENT?

CHAPTER 1

God Has Spoken

Why should we bother to preach from the Old Testament? Many preachers hardly ever do. Many churches go on from year to year with nothing but sermons from the New Testament and maybe sometimes a psalm. And perhaps you say, "What's wrong with that? We are followers of Jesus Christ and we read about him in the New Testament. And there is plenty to preach from in the New Testament. What more do we need?"

And to be honest, the Old Testament is a difficult set of books. There is a lot of history, and we don't like history, especially when it's full of strange names. There is a lot of violence and war, and we don't like that either. And there is a lot of weird ritual stuff about priests and sacrifices, clean and unclean food, and strict rules with nasty punishments. How can such ancient customs possibly apply to us today? And it all seems to be about this one "chosen" nation, Israel, which doesn't seem very fair on the rest of the world. And since it all happened before Jesus, is it not now all outdated and irrelevant? Of course, there are a few good stories that you can preach a clear and simple message from, and some of the Psalms can be very encouraging for people's faith. But apart from that, trying to preach a sermon or teach a Sunday school class from the Old Testament is too exhausting for the pastor or Bible study leader and too confusing for the people. It's much easier to stick with what we know—the New Testament.

If that's how you feel, let me offer three reasons right away that should at least make you want to dig a bit deeper in trying to understand the Old Testament and learn how to preach and teach from it.

THE OLD TESTAMENT COMES TO US FROM GOD

If the president of your country or somebody very important like that gave you a personal gift, I think you'd take it home carefully and look after it very well. Maybe you'd put it on a shelf for everybody to see. Or suppose you give a really special gift to somebody you love more than anyone else. It's a very expensive gift, and you saved for years to buy it and give it. And then that person only looks at a small part of your gift and doesn't even bother to take the wrapping off most of it. They just put it to one side and forget about it. How would you feel? Well, God is more important than anyone in the universe, and he loves us so much that he gave his Son to save us. And it is this same God who gave us the whole Bible, including what we now call the Old Testament. What does God feel if we don't even bother to open most of his gift? He gave us these books; what does it say about us if we just ignore them year after year?

Sometimes we talk about the Bible as "the Scriptures," and of course we now include both the Old and New Testament in that. But at the time Jesus and Paul lived, when people talked about "the Scriptures" they meant the books that are now contained in what we call the Old Testament. For them, "the Scriptures" were God's greatest gift to his people (second only to the Lord Jesus Christ). They treasured them. They studied them lovingly and taught them to their children.

So Paul knew that his friend Timothy, whose mother and grandmother were Jewish, had learned the Scriptures (i.e., the Old Testament) from childhood, and he encouraged him to study them carefully and teach and preach them urgently and often. When Paul says "Holy Scriptures" and "all Scripture," he means the whole of what we call the Old Testament. Read what Paul says here about the Old Testament and notice the reasons Paul gives to Timothy for preaching and teaching from it.

> But as for you, continue in what you have learned and have become convinced of, because you know those from whom you learned it, and how from infancy you have known the Holy Scriptures, which are able to make you wise for salvation through faith in Christ Jesus. All Scripture is God-breathed and is useful for teaching, rebuking, correcting and training in righteousness, so that the servant of God may be thoroughly equipped for every good work.

> In the presence of God and of Christ Jesus, who will judge the living and the dead, and in view of his appearing and his kingdom, I give you this charge: preach the word; be prepared in season and out of season; correct, rebuke and encourage — with great patience and careful instruction.
>
> *(2 Tim 3:14–4:2)*

Paul says three things that we should take seriously.

First, the "Holy Scriptures" (and remember, he meant the Old Testament) are able to lead people to salvation through faith in Christ Jesus. They prepare the way for Jesus the Messiah and show how the same God who had so often saved his people in the past has now acted through Jesus to bring salvation to people everywhere. Paul knew this because he had spent his life bringing people to faith in Jesus, using the Old Testament to make his case and prove his point. So the Old Testament is not a "dead book." It contains salvation and points to the Saviour.

Second, the Scriptures of the Old Testament were "God-breathed." That word is often translated "inspired by God." But Paul did not mean that the authors were "inspired" in the kind of way we might speak of a beautiful work of art, a great piece of music, or a wonderful football player as "inspired." Paul meant that the words we now have in the writings of the Old Testament Scriptures were "breathed out" by God. That means that, although they were spoken and written by ordinary human beings like us, what was said and written down was as if it had come from the mouth of God.

Suppose you are a reporter and you go to a press conference arranged by the government. The spokesperson makes a statement. You immediately ask him or her, "What is your source for that statement?" The spokesperson says: "I have it from the mouth of the president [or the prime minister]." That means: "What I have told you carries the authority of the president." It's as if the president him- or herself said the words. You take them seriously.

So it is with the Scriptures — including the Old Testament. What we read is what God wanted to be said. So it carries his authority. Of course, that still leaves us to think hard about what the words *meant* for those who first heard them, and what the words *mean* for us today, and to work out *what we must do in response.* Yes, we have all that work to do, but we *must* do it, and it is *worth* doing, because these texts come from God himself.

Third, Paul says the Old Testament Scriptures are "useful." Then he gives a list of the kinds of ways that Scripture functions "usefully" ("teaching, rebuking, correcting and training in righteousness")— all of which are things that should happen within the church community to help people live now in the way God wants us to. This is why Paul immediately tells Timothy to "preach the word." It's not just that the Old Testament functioned in the *past* to lead people to faith and salvation in Christ. It's not something that we then leave behind once we have come to Christ. No. Because it comes from God and so carries the *authority* of God, it continues to be *relevant* for us. We can and should *use* the Old Testament for teaching and guidance for life—as Paul tells Timothy to do. Of course, once again, we have to be careful working out *how* the Old Testament is relevant to us. It certainly does not mean that we simply do everything it says, exactly as written. We shall think about that in later chapters. For the moment, all we need to agree is that the Old Testament has *authority* (because it comes from God), and that it has *relevance* (because it is "useful" for us in our lives).

THE OLD TESTAMENT LAYS FOUNDATIONS FOR OUR FAITH

Have you ever walked into a committee meeting toward the end and tried to join the conversation that people are having about some important topic near the bottom of the agenda? *You* don't know what everybody has said in the past hour, but those who are talking are *presupposing* all that has been said and agreed already. You could very easily misunderstand what someone says toward the end because you don't know all that went before. The people round the table don't have to repeat all that went before because they already know it. They take for granted all the earlier points that have been made already. But you weren't there. You could miss a great deal, and you might misunderstand a lot of the conversation, especially if the things agreed and decided in the earlier part of the agenda were very important.

If you read only the New Testament, it's like joining a meeting very late and missing the discussions that have happened and the decisions that have been made so far. That's because the New Testament *presupposes* all that God said and did within the story of the Old Testament and does not necessarily repeat it again. And that includes certain things that are essential truths of the biblical Christian faith. Here are some things that God teaches us about in the *Old* Testament, which are then assumed in the New and brought into relationship with Christ.

- *Creation.* Not just in Genesis 1 and 2 but in other places also (the Psalms, and some of the prophets), we learn the truth about our world. It is not an accident, or an illusion, or nothing but atoms. Everything that exists (apart from God) was created and ordered by the one living God. The whole of creation is continuously sustained by God, belongs to God, and brings praise and glory to God. God loves everything he has made. These are truths which the Old Testament teaches and the New Testament assumes.

- *God.* Whom do we mean when we use the word "God" in English (or its equivalent in any other language)? Whom did the writers of the New Testament mean when they spoke about *theos* (in Greek)? It might seem obvious, but it's a very important question because, of course, there are many "gods" and many concepts of "God" in the world— just as much then as now. So even for us to say that "Jesus is God" could be open to all kinds of confusion unless we are very clear about what we mean by the word "God." And the writers of the New Testament, of course, were very clear about it. They meant the God who reveals himself in the Old Testament, in the history, life, and worship of Old Testament Israel. They meant the God whose personal name is usually translated "the LORD" in English. They did not repeat all the ocean depths of revelation about this God that is there in the Old Testament Scriptures. They just assumed it. They knew whom they were talking about.

  So we need to read the Old Testament deeply in order to know the true God—the God whom we meet when he came to live among us in Jesus of Nazareth. Otherwise, if we don't, we could end up attaching Jesus to all kinds of wrong ideas of "god-ness" that we have absorbed from our own cultural or religious background.

- *Ourselves.* Who are we, and what does it mean to be human beings? Again, it is the Old Testament that teaches us the foundational truths about ourselves. We are creatures (not gods or angels). But God created us in his own image so that we could exercise his authority within the rest of creation, by using it well and by caring for it.

- *Sin.* What's gone wrong with the world? The world's religions and philosophies give many different answers to this question. The Old Testament makes it clear that we human beings rebelled against our Creator. We refused to trust his goodness and chose to disobey his command. The Old Testament shows how deep-rooted is our sin, affecting every part of our personality, every generation, every culture. Only when we know how big is the problem (from the Old Testament) can we understand the size of God's solution to it through Christ in the New Testament.

- *The plan of God.* Genesis 3 – 11 tells us what went wrong with the human race — at both individual and ethnic levels. The earth is cursed and nations are scattered. Genesis 12 tells us what God planned to do about the problem. When God called Abraham, it was in order to launch God's great plan of redemption that would take up the whole of the rest of the Bible, through to Revelation. God promised to turn the curse into blessing. He would do it through the people of Abraham first. But then, through Israel, he would bring blessing to all nations on earth and indeed ultimately restore the whole creation — a new heaven and a new earth (Isa 65:17 – 25). That is the great saving plan of God for the world (the world of nations and the world of nature) which was accomplished by Christ in the New Testament. The New Testament gives us God's final answer, but it is the Old Testament that tells us both the scale of the problem and the scale of God's promise. So we will understand the gospel in a far more full and comprehensive way when we see it first in the Old Testament.

So then, we need to study and to preach the Old Testament so that we understand these great foundational truths that God spent thousands of years teaching his people before he sent his Son into the world. If we only ever read and preach the New Testament, it is like wanting to live in the top storey of a house without having the foundation and lower storeys or wanting to enjoy the fruit of a tree while cutting out the roots and sawing up the trunk.

THE OLD TESTAMENT WAS THE BIBLE OF JESUS

The most important reason, however, why we need to really get to know the Old Testament is because it was the Bible of Jesus. Of course, we read *about* Jesus in the New Testament. But Jesus himself never read the New Testament! As noted earlier, for him, the Scriptures were the books that now form our Old Testament. And Jesus knew them very thoroughly indeed. He would have learned them first from Mary and Joseph, like any Jewish boy of his times. By the age of twelve he knew them so well he could sit in the Jerusalem temple for days discussing them with the adults who were theologians and scholars. Jewish boys at the time of Jesus used to memorize whole books of the Old Testament. If they were good at it (as Jesus clearly was), they would know whole sections (the Torah, books of the prophets) and qualify as a "rabbi"— teacher. And that's what they called Jesus. He knew the Scriptures as well as he knew his carpenter's tools.

When the time came for Jesus to begin his public ministry, after his baptism in the Jordan by John, he went into the wilderness alone for forty days and wrestled with the immense task that lay ahead of him. What was he doing all that time? Well, when Satan tempted him to take a different course from the one he knew he must take in obedience to his Father, he answered three times with quotations from the Scriptures. All three of the texts that Jesus quoted came from Deuteronomy 6 and 8. That suggests that he was thinking deeply about the implications of that whole section of Deuteronomy (1–11) for himself and his mission. And all through his ministry, right up to the cross and after his resurrection, Jesus insisted that the Scriptures must be fulfilled. His whole understanding of himself—his life, his mission, his future—was rooted in his reading of the Scriptures, the Old Testament.

Have you ever gone to the Holy Land or wanted to go there? Some people go there on pilgrimage because, they say (or the advertising brochures say), it will bring them closer to Jesus by walking in the land where he walked, seeing the hills he knew, sitting by the sea of Galilee, and so on. Well, it certainly does bring the Bible to life when you visit the land where so much of the action took place. Take the opportunity if you get it. But if you really want to get to know Jesus, to understand what filled his mind and directed his intentions, here's a better way than going on pilgrimage to Israel (and it will cost you a lot less!): read the Bible Jesus read. Read your Old Testament.

For these were the stories Jesus heard as a child. These were the songs Jesus sang. These were the scrolls that were read every week in his synagogue. These were the prophetic visions that had given hope to his people for generations. This is where Jesus discerned the great plan and purpose of God for his people Israel and through them for the world. This is where Jesus found the source texts that shaped who he was and what he had come to do.

Now of course, we remind ourselves, Jesus was the Son of God, and he had a very close and direct relationship with his Father God. Undoubtedly he understood himself and his mission in a form of divine consciousness. However, Luke tells us twice that Jesus grew up as a normal human child, growing in physical, mental, and spiritual capacity (Luke 2:40, 52). I think this must have included growth in understanding through the study of the Scriptures. At any rate, he certainly *used* the Old Testament Scriptures to explain himself to his disciples and help them to understand the meaning of his life, death, and resurrection for Israel and the world—not only during his lifetime but especially after his resurrection (Luke 24).

So, if Jesus did that, should we not follow his example? Should we not "preach Christ" in the way that Christ preached himself—that is, using the Scriptures? In the next two chapters we shall see how important the Old Testament is in understanding Jesus. We need the Old Testament to understand the story and the promise that Jesus fulfilled. And we need the Old Testament to understand who Jesus thought he was and what he had come to do.

QUESTIONS AND EXERCISES

1. What would you say to someone who dismisses the Old Testament, perhaps telling you not to bother preaching or teaching from it, because, they say, "We are New Testament Christians. We have Jesus. We do not need the Old Testament any more"?

2. Make a short list of the essential teachings of the Christian faith. How many of them are taught in the Old Testament? What would we *not* know (or not know clearly) if we did not have the Old Testament?

3. Prepare a sermon or a lesson on 2 Timothy 3:14–16. Make it clear that Paul was talking about the Old Testament Scriptures. Explain what he says about their source, authority, power, and usefulness. What will be your main point—the main thing that you will want your listeners to do as a result of your teaching?

CHAPTER 2

The Story and the Promise

The journey took them ten hours by road in a minibus! They were a group of pastors, and the journey they made was from Guayaquil on the Pacific coast of Ecuador up to the capital city, Quito, nearly 3,000 metres high in the mountains. They had come to participate in the Langham Preaching seminar in Quito, where I was one of the facilitators. When I heard about their long journey, I wanted to do my teaching well and make their journey worthwhile!

THE DESTINATION OF THE JOURNEY

Imagine you had stopped the minibus at some point along the way and asked the passengers, "Where are you going?" "To Quito!" they would have answered, cheerfully or wearily. You would have got the same answer whether you stopped and asked them near the start of the journey, or somewhere in the middle, or close to the end. The whole journey, from beginning to end, had the same destination—Quito. The road would have been winding. Maybe they had to make a few detours. Sometimes, in heavy traffic, it might have seemed they were not moving at all. Sometimes they might have stopped for a break and got out to admire the view. Maybe somewhere there was a landslide or roadblock and they had to turn around and go by a different route. But whatever happened on the journey, and however long and complicated it became, the destination was the same. And eventually they arrived at that destination. And the destination was the end of the journey.

The Old Testament is a journey that leads to a destination, and the destination is Jesus Christ. It was a very long journey, with many twists and turns, stops and starts. It was a journey that was interrupted and threatened by all kinds of bad things and bad people. It was a journey that involved a lot more people than would fit in a minibus, and a lot more miles than from Guayaquil to Quito. And it took not ten hours but twenty centuries! It was a journey that involved the history of a whole nation—Israel—set within the histories of many other nations. But no matter where you step into the journey—near the beginning, in the middle, or near the end—the direction is always the same. This is the story of God leading God's people towards God's Messiah, Jesus of Nazareth. That is the constant direction of movement. Jesus is the destination. *The Old Testament tells the story that Jesus completes.*

Have you ever wondered why Matthew starts his account of the gospel in the way he does? He says in his first verse that he wants to tell us about Jesus. So why does he not go straight on to 1:18—"This is how the birth of Jesus the Messiah came about"? Isn't that what we want to know? Why does he start with Abraham and then give us a whole list of fathers and sons for forty-two generations? Well, because all those names were part of the great story of the Old Testament. Some of them were kings in the line of David—and Jesus was the promised Son of David who would be the true King of Israel. All of them were descendants of Abraham—and Jesus would be the one through whom God's promise to bless all nations on earth through Abraham's people would be fulfilled.

So Matthew is telling the reader, "You want to know about Jesus? Good. But you won't understand Jesus unless you see that he comes as the end of the great story represented in his ancestry. Here is the journey that leads up to Jesus. Jesus is the destination of the great historical journey that started with Abraham. In order to make sense of Jesus, you need to understand that starting point and that journey first."

Thinking back to the journey that the pastors made, we could say this: the journey (from Guayaquil) only made sense because of its destination (Quito). If they had no destination, they would just have been driving around aimlessly for no reason. So the Old Testament, taken together as a whole story, makes sense only in the light of its destination—Jesus Christ. It is not just a mixed bag of stories. It is not just a children's storybook, with no connection or direction. (Unfortunately, that is how some people use the

Bible, and how some churches teach it. It's how a lot of Christians think of the Old Testament — just a bag of stories, and some of them not very nice.) No, the Old Testament is in fact one long and complex narrative with many smaller stories contained within it that ultimately leads to Jesus and makes sense when it arrives at its destination in him.

Did I say "long and complex"? Yes, indeed it is, and that's what makes people confused. It has so many different kinds of writing and so many small stories that it's easy to get lost. My father was lost once in the Amazon jungle. He was a missionary among several indigenous tribes there in the days before roads and aeroplanes opened it up, and he was travelling on foot. It was terrifying, he said. Under the tree canopy you cannot get oriented by the sun. At a river bank, if you have no compass, you cannot tell which direction the river is flowing. The Old Testament is vast and complex like the Amazon River. It is not like a neatly constructed aqueduct running in straight lines directly from one place to another. And yet, for all its twists and turns and tributaries, the Amazon is one great body of water, accumulating all the way from different sources, but all moving in one direction. Eventually it arrives at the Atlantic Ocean. That is its ultimate destination. And the Old Testament, with its many streams and tributaries, is all moving in one direction — toward Jesus Christ.

Not only must we see the Old Testament as a story that makes sense in the light of Jesus but also we have to understand Jesus in the light of the story that goes before. Jesus came into the world because of all that had happened in the story so far. That is why we need to read, understand, teach, and preach from the Old Testament. We do it for Christ's sake. It is his story. It was, we might say, his DNA.

THE PURPOSE OF THE JOURNEY

Supposing, when you stopped the minibus, after the passengers told you *where* they were going (to Quito, the destination), you then asked them a second question: "*Why* are you going to Quito?"

"Because," they would have answered, "the Langham Preaching seminar will be happening next week, and we want to be part of it." So their journey had not only a destination but also a *purpose*. There was an exciting event that would take place in Quito and they planned to be there for it. All through the long hours of the journey, they would have been thinking of what lay ahead and looking forward to it. The journey was worth making because of the good thing it was leading to. The journey was long but promising.

Indeed, in a sense their journey started long before they piled into the minibus. A long time earlier they had received a letter telling them about the seminar in Quito, calling them to come and participate, and promising that it would be a time of great teaching and fellowship. They would be greatly blessed and strengthened if they made the journey and participated in it. So their whole journey, their preparation, packing, travelling, and enduring all the discomforts and difficulties on the way—all of it was done in response to an invitation and a promise, and all of it was done in faith (trusting the promise of the organizers) and hope (looking forward to the good things the seminar would do for them in the future when they arrived).

The Old Testament is like that. It is not just a journey in time—a long sequence of one thing happening after another until eventually it comes to an end when Jesus arrives. It is also a journey with a purpose and point. The coming of Jesus was not just the end of the journey but the whole purpose of the journey. He was not only the destination but the *fulfilment*. Just like that letter that came to the pastors in Guayaquil promising them what was going to happen in Quito and motivating them to make their journey, so the Old Testament presents God's promise. And when Jesus came, God kept his promise. *The Old Testament declares the promise that Jesus fulfils.*

Let's go back to the first two chapters of Matthew. Five times Matthew tells us a story about when Jesus was an infant and immediately follows it with a reference back to the Old Testament. And each time he says that a text from the Old Testament has been fulfilled in some way. The table shows them all together. Take a moment to read Matthew's verses and then look up the Old Testament quotation alongside each one.

Matthew	Event	"Fulfilled"
1:22–23	Announcing his birth and name	Isaiah 7:14
2:5–6	Born in Bethlehem	Micah 5:2–4
2:14–15	Taken to Egypt	Hosea 11:1
2:16–18	Murder of boys in Bethlehem	Jeremiah 31:15
2:23	Growing up in Nazareth	uncertain

Why does Matthew do this? Well, first of all it's clear he is not simply quoting *predictions*.

- Only one of the Old Testament texts is really a straightforward prediction that is directly fulfilled by Jesus. That is the one from *Micah* saying that a future king of Israel would be born in Bethlehem.

- *Isaiah* was giving a sign to King Ahaz that a child would be born soon who would be given the name "Immanuel" ("God with us") because within that space of time the enemies who were threatening his kingdom of Judah (Israel and Syria) would be defeated. Matthew sees deeper messianic significance in the name ("Immanuel") and in the fact that the "young woman" who gave birth to Jesus was in fact a virgin at the time of conception and birth. (It was not a straightforward prediction—fulfilment since, in the event, they did not call Mary's son "Immanuel" but "Jesus." The significance lies in the *meaning* of the word "Immanuel." Jesus is indeed "God with us.")

- *Hosea* was not making any prediction for the future but referring to God bringing Israel up out of Egypt in the exodus in the past.

- *Jeremiah* was talking about the people of Judah in 587 BC going off into exile past the grave of Rachel and imagines her weeping (in her grave) for her suffering descendants. Jeremiah's very next verse, however, tells Rachel to dry her tears, for her children would return. The exile would come to an end.

- Matthew's final one is a bit of a puzzle since no text seems to say exactly the words "He will be called a Nazarene."

So what is Matthew doing, if most of the texts were not simple predictions? He is showing us that even in Jesus' infancy there were events in his life that call to mind the Old Testament Scriptures. He sees the *whole* Old Testament as a great *promise* from God. It all speaks about God's commitment to his people (and, through Israel, to the world as well). So even baby Jesus has an "exodus experience" that recalls God redeeming Israel out of Egypt. And the arrival of Jesus was like the ending of exile (ending Rachel's tears). And best of all, in Jesus, God truly came to be "with us." *The Old Testament declares the promise that Jesus fulfils.*

At this point it would be helpful to think briefly about the difference between a *prediction* and a *promise*. A prediction is fairly straightforward. I may predict that something will happen at some point in the future. If it does, my prediction comes true. If it does not, then either my prediction was wrong, or it remains unfulfilled as yet. Making a prediction can be about something completely external and unconnected to myself. It need not involve me at all. But if I make a *promise* to someone else, that is very different. I have committed myself to a relationship with that person, at least with regard to what I've promised them. It's not just a matter of whether my promise "comes true" or not. Rather, it's a matter of whether I can be trusted or not. My integrity is involved. My reputation is at stake. My word is being tested. A promise changes things.

When I was teaching at All Nations Christian College, I used to explain the difference between a prediction and a promise to my class like this. I would say, "I can *predict* that at least one of you men is going to marry one of these women by the end of this year." (That was a fairly safe prediction. It did happen every year that some students came to the college single and went away married!) "But as a prediction, it does not involve me personally in any way. But if one of you men and one of you women say to each other, on a very special day, 'I take you as my wife/husband, to have and to hold, to love and to cherish, for better, for worse, for richer, for poorer, in sickness and in health, forsaking all others, till death us do part'—that is not just a prediction. That is a *promise*, and it changes your life for ever."

A promise like that expresses a *long-term* commitment and intention. And that's another point. A prediction simply comes true (or not), and that's that. But a promise can go on being fulfilled over a very long time, in all kinds of new ways and new circumstances. I have been married for forty-four years. My wife and I made promises to one another in August 1970. We do not have to go on repeating them or changing them every time something new happens in life or in our family. The promise rolls on, expands, picks up fresh levels of commitment, and is "fulfilled" in all kinds of ways we could never have dreamed of on our wedding day.

So it is with the Old Testament. God declares his promise — way back in Genesis itself. Even in the garden of Eden, straight after Adam and Eve's sin, God affirms that the seed of the woman will eventually crush the serpent's head. But even more clearly, in Genesis 12:1 – 3, God promises that all nations on earth will be blessed through Abraham's descendants. That is such an important promise that Paul actually calls it "the gospel in advance" (Gal 3:8). It is not just a prediction. It is something God commits himself to. It is a promise God will keep because of his own integrity and trustworthy faithfulness. God has invested his own character in that promise.

From that point on, the whole Old Testament story is driven forward by that promise. The word "covenant" is used for the great promises that God made in the Bible. They come in a sequence and are connected to each other. You could say that God's great promise goes on being fulfilled and then "re-fuelled" for another part of the journey. You can trace the whole Bible story like a chain, with the links made up in the sequence of covenants — that is, with each covenant being a fresh renewal or expansion of God's promise.[1]

- Covenant with Noah
- Covenant with Abraham
- Covenant with Israel at Mount Sinai
- Covenant with David
- The new covenant, promised by the prophets and inaugurated by Jesus

So when we finally turn the page from Malachi to Matthew, the message is, "All that God promised is coming true!" So far

---

1. For a fuller description of these covenants, see my book, *Knowing Jesus through the Old Testament* (Downers Grove, IL: IVP Academic, 2nd ed., 2014).

we have only looked at Matthew 1–2, but when you read the rest of his Gospel you'll see he keeps making this point again and again. Luke does it even more excitingly in Luke 1. That chapter is simply dripping with echoes and quotes from the Old Testament Scriptures. Indeed, when Mary the mother of Jesus and Zechariah the father of John the Baptist sing their songs of rejoicing, they each celebrate how God has *"remembered."* They don't mean that God had forgotten up till then, but rather that God was now going to act to keep his great promises made ever since Abraham (1:54–55, 72–73). And at the end of his Gospel, Luke shows us Jesus helping his disciples to see that the whole Old Testament pointed to himself (Luke 24:25–27, 44–48).

So you see, it is not enough to say that the Old Testament contains some interesting messianic *predictions* that came true in Jesus (e.g., that he was born in Bethlehem). Rather, the Old Testament contains God's commitment, God's covenant, God's *promise* (which was first for Israel, but then for the whole world — all nations, as God said to Abraham).

In our next chapter, we will think about *who Jesus thought he was* and *what Jesus thought he had come to do*. But since Jesus himself answered both those questions by using the Old Testament Scriptures, we need to do the same. That is to say, if we want to understand fully what Jesus achieved, we need to understand fully what God promised to do (the promise he made in the Old Testament). And in order to understand what God promised to do, we need to understand the problem that God set out to solve (the problem described very early in the Old Testament). And in order to understand that problem, we need to go back to the very beginning. Let's do that right now.

THE STORY IN SYMBOLS[2]

Actually, the whole Bible (not just the Old Testament) is one great story. It has a beginning (creation), an ending (new creation — which is really a new beginning), and a middle (the long story of redemption in history, centred on Christ).

---

2. I owe this concept and the diagram to Chris Gonzalez and Tyler Johnson, who lead the Missional Pastors Training Network in Phoenix, Arizona, USA.

"The Bible is one single big story? I just don't get it," said a member of the church in Phoenix, Arizona, where Chris Gonzalez was pastoring. He was standing by her desk at work at that moment. On the spur of the moment, he grabbed a used envelope and on the back drew the symbols shown in the diagram, explaining them as he went along. "Here is the whole Bible story," he said, "right here on the back of an envelope."

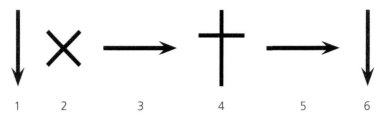

The Bible is like a drama with six acts, or stages.

Stage 1: Creation. The downward arrow points to the moment when God came down, as it were, and created the earth (Gen 1–2). Creation includes, of course, the whole space-time universe, but the Bible focuses on how God created the earth we live in. He created it to function perfectly, with its days and nights, its weather and seasons, and with all the fullness of earth, sea, and sky. He made it both as a place for us human beings to live, as the image of God on earth, and as the place where he could live with us. Creation was like a vast temple for God to dwell in, filling it with his glory and all the abundance of life.

Stage 2: Fall. The cross like an X indicates something wrong. And indeed it did go wrong. Genesis 3–11 describes how sin and evil entered the experience of human beings. We chose to rebel against God, to question God's goodness and reject God's authority. As a result the whole of our life on earth, and indeed the earth itself, is infected by our sin and its consequences.

Stage 3: Promise. In a world gone wrong (and going from bad to worse), God promised to put things right. In a world under curse, God promised blessing. God's promise to Abraham in Genesis 12 launched the whole of the rest of the Bible story, but especially the story of Israel in the Old Testament. God planned to bring blessing and salvation to the world *through* this people. This does not mean that Israel would somehow save the world. The Old Testament will show that, as a people, they were as sinful and in need of salvation as any other nation. What it means is that God would use Israel as the means by which he would bring salvation into the world—salvation which we know was accomplished only by Jesus, the Messiah of Israel. As we've been saying, the whole Old Testament is like a journey with a destination and a purpose, all leading to Jesus Christ. It is a story of promise and hope, even in the midst of continuing evil and sin.

Stage 4: Gospel. Here we have the centre of the whole Bible drama. In faithfulness to his promise to Israel, God sent Jesus as the Messiah of Israel and (therefore) the Saviour of the world. The gospel is the good news of all that God accomplished through the birth, life, teaching, death, resurrection, and ascension of Jesus of Nazareth. The symbol of the cross is intended here to include all that is there in the Gospel narratives (not just the cross of Calvary itself).

Stage 5: Mission. After the Gospels comes the book of Acts, describing how God poured out his Holy Spirit on the day of Pentecost, empowering the disciples of Jesus for their mission of bearing witness to him among all nations to the ends of the earth. The community of God's people that God had called into existence through Abraham (initially Old Testament Israel) now includes both Jews and Gentiles who trust in Jesus Christ. We could call Stage 5 the era of the church, but we should remember that the church did not start only in the New Testament. If we are "in Christ," then we are part of the people of Abraham (Gal 3). And the reason for our existence as God's people remains the same. Our mission is to participate in God's mission of bringing blessing to all nations on earth.

Of course, the New Testament does not tell the whole story right up to the second coming of Christ. It shows how God kept his promise to Old Testament Israel by sending Jesus and how Christ accomplished the salvation of the world through his death and resurrection. It is the task of the church, in the power of the Spirit, to bring the good news of that salvation to the ends of the earth, as Jesus commanded. That is where we fit in. We are part of the continuing story in Stage 5. We are partners in God's great project through our daily lives and work. We live in between Christ's finished work of redemption in Stage 4 and the time when Christ will return to bring in the Bible's final great scene—Stage 6.

Stage 6: New creation. The final arrow in the diagram sym-
bolizes the return of Christ. From the beginning, God's concern
was for the whole creation. Genesis 1–2 (the first two chapters of
the Bible) show how God created "in the beginning." Revelation
21–22 (the last two chapters) show how God will purge and restore
creation as the place where God will dwell with his redeemed
people from all nations and where all suffering, evil, sin, death,
and curse will be no more. This too had been promised back in the
Old Testament (Isa 65:17–25) and has already been accomplished,
in anticipation, through the death and resurrection of Jesus (Col
1:15–20). So although this is where the Bible story ends, it is not
really "the end of the world" but a new beginning. It will be the
end of the world of sin, evil, and rebellion against God, but it will
be the beginning of a new creation that will last forever.

Perhaps you are thinking that the final arrow should be pointing upwards, not downwards, to picture us going up to heaven.
But that is not how the Bible actually ends. It does not picture us
going off somewhere else but announces God coming down to
earth (Rev 21:1–5), transforming the earth itself into the city of
God. Other texts speak of the fire of God's judgment (2 Pet 3),
but that is not fire that obliterates creation altogether. Rather, it
is the fire that purges creation of all sin and evil so that it can be
cleansed, restored, and made fit for God to live in again with us
(which is what God announces—Rev 21:3). The meaning of the
name "Immanuel" applies as much to the second coming of Christ
as to his first coming. It means "*God* [coming here to be] *with us*,"
not "*us* [going somewhere else to be] *with God*".

PREACHING AND TEACHING WITHIN THE STORY

How does all this affect our preaching and teaching, particularly
from the Old Testament? It means that we now live and do our
preaching somewhere in Stage 5, but we are preaching from God's
Word given during the course of Stage 3 (the Old Testament),
in the light of what happened in Stage 4 (the Gospels), and in
anticipation of what will happen in Stage 6 (the new creation). Of
course, I am not suggesting that our sermons count on the same
level as the Bible itself! There are some preachers who sound as
if they think that. But we should be quite clear that the text of
the Bible is the unique and complete Word of God, with final

authority. Nothing we can say or preach stands on the same level, and we should never claim that the words we preach are, in themselves, the Word of God.

What I mean is that we as preachers and teachers, and the people we serve, do live *within the framework* of the whole Bible story. *We are participating in Stage 5 of the Bible drama*, which began on the day of Pentecost and will continue until Christ returns. Our preaching and teaching should aim to equip our listeners for their engagement in the world as God's people. That is their mission. That is what God has called them to be and do. *Our* mission is to strengthen them in that role and task. We Christians are people who are defined and shaped by what God did through Christ in Stage 4. And we live in this world in anticipation of Stage 6. That is the story we are living in — as Christians in general and as Bible teachers and preachers in particular.

When we think of ourselves as participating in the whole story of the Bible in this way, it also helps us to remember that when we preach and teach from the Old Testament, it is not just a lot of old stories, songs, and prophecies from ancient Israel — remote and distant from us. No, the Old Testament is Stage 3 of the one great single drama that we ourselves are now living in. They lived in Stage 3. We live in Stage 5. But we all live within the same great biblical story. *Their* story is part of *our* story. We are *together* the people of God. And what links them to us, and us to them, is Stage 4 — the gospel events. That was the fulfilment of their part of the story and the launching of our part of the story.

The Old Testament also contains, of course, Stages 1 and 2, creation and fall. And although they are definite moments in the great story, they do also define "where we are now." We still live within God's creation as responsible stewards of the resources of God's earth. And the whole human race still lives in sinful rebellion against God. So our preaching and teaching must also explain these realities and their implications. In particular, our preaching and teaching need constantly to show how the realities of sin and evil (in the world since Stage 2) drive us to see our need for God's solution to that fundamental problem (in the gospel of Stage 4). In the next chapter we will think in more detail about how our preaching and teaching of the Old Testament ought to lead people to Christ — in many different ways, but essentially because that is where the Old Testament itself leads.

To summarize this chapter, this is what we have seen:

- We compared the Old Testament to a journey that had not only a destination to reach but also a purpose to fulfil. Jesus is that destination. And Jesus fulfilled the purpose that God had declared in the Old Testament. That is, the Old Testament tells the story of Israel that Jesus completes, and the Old Testament declares God's promise to Israel that Jesus fulfils.

- Then we have seen that the Old Testament itself is part of the whole Bible story. That "big Bible story" has the gospel story of Jesus Christ right at its centre, and it concludes with the return of Christ and the new creation. We need to preach and teach in such a way that people not only come to understand the whole Bible story but also see their own place within it and live in the light of it.

QUESTIONS AND EXERCISES

1. How would you explain to someone that the Old Testament is not just full of *predictions* about Jesus, but rather declares the *promise* of God which Jesus fulfils?

2. Discuss the idea of the Bible being like a drama with six acts or stages. How helpful do you find that structure (and the symbols that go with it) for explaining "what the Bible is all about" to a) a new Christian believer, and b) somebody who is not yet a believer but is interested in the Christian faith?

3. Prepare one or a series of six sermons or lessons to illustrate each stage of the Six-Act Drama of the Bible. Carefully choose key texts that sum up each of the six great stages.

CHAPTER 3

Understanding Jesus through the Old Testament

In chapter 2 we compared the Old Testament to a journey that leads to Christ. All the time we are reading or preparing to preach or teach from the Old Testament we are looking forward, facing the direction of travel, thinking of where the whole journey leads. But when we arrive at the destination, what then? When we get to the Gospels and meet Jesus there, can we simply forget the journey and throw away the used ticket? Can we just ignore the Old Testament from now on, now that we have come to know Jesus himself? Well, not if we follow the example of Jesus himself, and of the four men who each gave us their account of the gospel, Matthew, Mark, Luke, and John. For Jesus and his followers (including also the Apostle Paul), *the Old Testament was essential* in order to understand the identity and mission of Jesus—that is, who Jesus was and what he came to do.

So our main point in this chapter is to stress a very important reason why we ought to preach and teach from the Old Testament: people need to know the Old Testament in order to understand Jesus—both as he understood himself and as his first followers explained him.[1]

---

1. For much more detail on how the Old Testament helps us understand Jesus, see my book *Knowing Jesus through the Old Testament* (Downers Grove, IL: IVP Academic, 2nd ed., 2014).

WHO DID JESUS THINK HE WAS?

Jesus raised a lot of questions in people's minds. Once, when he calmed the storm that had nearly swamped their boat, the disciples were so astonished that they asked bluntly, "Who is this? Even the wind and the waves obey him!" (Mark 4:41).

That was the right question. *Who is this man?*

Jesus was interested in how *other people* answered that question, so he asked his disciples, "Who do people say the Son of Man is?" (Matt 16:13). Apparently some people thought he was John the Baptist come back to life again after he had been murdered by Herod. But most people went much further back—to their Scriptures. Jesus reminded them of Elijah, or of Jeremiah, or one of the prophets. They were partly right, of course. Jesus was indeed a prophet, speaking the word of God to the people. He had healing power like Elijah. He had a message that brought him suffering and rejection, like Jeremiah. So when the people around Jesus tried to make sense of him and all he was doing and saying, they looked for answers in their Scriptures—the Old Testament.

Jesus was even more interested in how *his disciples* would answer the question, so he asked them, "But what about you? Who do you say I am?" (16:15). And Peter answered, "You are the Messiah." That means, the one anointed by God to carry out his purpose; the one who was to come in fulfilment of various Old Testament promises. And Jesus agreed with Peter's answer, saying that God had revealed it to him (v. 17). So Jesus knew that he was indeed that anointed one. However, he did not want his disciples to go about proclaiming that just yet (v. 20). Why not? It seems that many people had the idea that the Messiah, when he came, would lead them in a great military victory over their enemies. And that was not part of Jesus' plan at all. He saw his messiahship in very different terms—ones which were not so attractive to Peter (vv. 21–28).

And how did *God the Father* answer the question? Matthew, Mark, and Luke all record the baptism of Jesus. It was a wonderful moment in which the whole Trinity was involved. There is God the Son coming out of the river Jordan. There is God the Spirit, descending in the form of a dove. And there is God the Father, speaking in a voice from heaven. And how does that voice from God describe Jesus? Not in words that were completely new and fresh, never heard before. No; even God quotes the Scriptures.

"This is my Son, whom I love; with him I am well pleased" (Matt 3:16–17). There are at least two and possibly three Old Testament texts that are echoed in those words.

- *Isaiah 42:1.* "Here is my servant, whom I uphold, my chosen one in whom I delight." The Servant of the Lord in Isaiah would be the one who called Israel back to God and brought God's salvation to the ends of the earth. God is identifying Jesus as that one — his Servant/Son. Isaiah went on to describe how the Servant would suffer and die to accomplish God's will (Isa 53).

- *Psalm 2:7.* "You are my son; today I have become your father." These were words spoken by God to King David and his descendants who reigned after him. By the time of Jesus, there was no actual king in the line of David on the throne in Jerusalem. So the words of this psalm were already understood as applying to the Messiah, the future son of David who would be their true King. God is identifying Jesus as that one — "great David's greater son."

- *Genesis 22:2.* "Take your son, your only son, whom you love — Isaac ... Sacrifice him ..." Possibly the words of God the Father at the baptism of Jesus echo these instructions from God to Abraham. Jesus was indeed the "only son" whom the Father would be willing to sacrifice for the sins of the world.

Who then was this man stepping out of the Jordan after his baptism by John? According to his own Father, he was God's Servant and God's Son. He would carry out the mission of God and he would reign not only over Israel but over the nations of the earth (Ps 2:8). But first he would suffer rejection and death. And all of this is portrayed in terms drawn from the Old Testament. It was the Bible of Jesus that explained the identity of Jesus.

But how did *Jesus himself* answer the question? Well, as we have seen, Jesus accepted the title "Messiah/Christ" but chose not to publicize it too much because people had wrong ideas about what it meant. But his favourite way of speaking about himself was "*the Son of Man.*" Where did he get that term from, and what did it mean? Some people think it is just a kind of matching title to "Son of God"; that is, they think that the two terms — Son of God and

Son of Man — were just ways of saying that Jesus was both divine and human. Sometimes the words "son of man" did indeed just mean "a human being," but at other times it was much more than that.

In one of the visions of Daniel (Dan 7) he saw beasts coming up from the sea. They symbolized the rampaging evil of various empires that were to come. But then Daniel also saw God seated on his throne, sovereign over all those "beasts." Then Daniel saw another figure:

> ... one like a son of man, coming with the clouds of heaven. He approached the Ancient of Days [God on the throne] and was led into his presence. He was given authority, glory and sovereign power; all nations and peoples of every language worshipped him. His dominion is an everlasting dominion that will not pass away, and his kingdom is one that will never be destroyed.
>
> *(Dan 7:13–14)*

This "son of man" is an exalted figure who shares in the reign of God himself. So it's not surprising that when Jesus, during his trial, claimed to be the Son of Man as Daniel described, the chief priests immediately accused him of blasphemy (Mark 14:62–63). The point is that both Jesus and his judges understood the meaning of the title "Son of Man" from what the Old Testament Scriptures said. So if we want to understand who Jesus thought he was, we need to know the scriptural texts that he used to explain himself.

So did Jesus think he was God? Certainly he didn't just stand up and say, "Hello, folks, I am God." That would have got him stoned immediately. Actually, though, he did get rather close to it when he used the great revealed name of God from Exodus ("I am who I am"), and said to the Jewish leaders, "Before Abraham was born, I am!" And they did indeed try to stone him for blasphemy (John 8:58–59). That was a rare moment. But what Jesus more regularly did was to say and do things that the Old Testament said or promised about God, and then leave people to draw their own conclusions. For example,

- God had said he would send Elijah before God himself came to the people (Mal 3:1; 4:5). Jesus said that John the Baptist was that Elijah, sent to prepare the way for the Lord. But if John was Elijah, and Jesus came after John, then who was Jesus (Matt 11:11–15; 17:10–13)?

- God had promised that, when he came, the blind would see, the deaf hear, the lame walk, and so on (Isa 35:4–6). When John's disciples asked Jesus if he was the one who was to come, he told them, "Look around you. What is happening? Who is here?" (Matt 11:1–6).

- Jesus told certain individuals that their sins were forgiven. The people quite rightly asked, "Who can forgive sins but God alone?" (Matt 9:1–7; Luke 7:36–50). So who was Jesus claiming to be?

- Jesus said he was driving out demons "by the finger of God," as proof that the reign of God had come among the people—in the person and actions of Jesus himself (Matt 12:28; Luke 11:20).

- And after his resurrection he said, "All authority in heaven and on earth has been given to me" (Matt 28:18). That is how the Old Testament speaks about YHWH, the LORD God of Israel (Deut 4:39), but Jesus calmly applied the words to himself.

We could go on. Who was Jesus? Think of all the words or titles you can. Lord, Christ/Messiah, Saviour, Redeemer, King, Prophet, great High Priest, Son of God, Son of Man, Son of David, Lamb of God, Good Shepherd, Prince of Peace, Immanuel ... All of these and many more come from the Old Testament Scriptures. And they are not empty phrases, like the exalted titles that some boastful kings and presidents like to give themselves today. They describe essential aspects of what Jesus did or still does. So if we want to understand and explain Jesus using such words, we need to know how they are used in the Old Testament.

So then, even in order to understand what it means to say that Jesus was divine, that he was fully God as well as fully human, we need the Old Testament. For it is the Old Testament that reveals to us the God who became human and walked among us in the man Jesus of Nazareth.

WHAT DID JESUS COME TO DO?

Did Jesus come to start a new religion? That's what a lot of people think, isn't it? Question: Who was the founder of Christianity? Answer: Jesus. That makes it sound as if Jesus came along one day and said, "Listen, friends, we've had this Judaism thing long enough, and it seems to have failed. Here's a whole new religion I've thought of. Follow me instead and become Christians."[2] But, of course, he did not do that. In fact, to people who *thought* he was abolishing the Law and the Prophets (the scriptural foundation of Israel's faith) he said: "Don't think that! I have not come to abolish them, but to fulfil them."

Remember chapter 2, "The Story and the Promise"? Jesus knew the story he was in — the great story of Israel in the Old Testament Scriptures, and the promise of God that the story contains. And Jesus knew that he had come to keep that promise and to accomplish for the sake of the world what God had promised to do through Israel. Jesus came to finish the story that the Old Testament had begun.

Think back to those Bible story symbols in chapter 2. The Old Testament part of the story (Stages 1–3 of the whole Bible story) at its simplest goes like this:

- God created the good world and human beings in his own image to love and worship him, to use and care for creation, and to love and serve one another.

- We rebelled and disobeyed God, bringing judgment and death on ourselves, division and strife among nations, and the spoiling of creation.

- God called Abraham and promised to turn the curse into blessing for all nations, through his descendants, the people of Israel.

- But since Israel was a nation of sinners like the rest of humanity, those who were to be the bearers of God's cure also carried the disease itself. Israel showed itself to be as much in need of salvation as the rest of the nations.

- God's promise remained, however. The Old Testament points forward to One who would fulfil the mission of

---

2. Jesus never used the words "Christian" or "Christianity." Those were words that were invented later. "*Christianoi*" (meaning "people who keep on talking about Christ") was first used as a nickname for the followers of Jesus in Antioch in Syria. The word "Christian" is found in the New Testament only three times. The usual word was "disciples" — i.e., followers of Jesus, which is found more than two hundred times.

Israel, who would bear the sins of Israel and the world, and bring the good news of God's salvation to the ends of the earth. That's what Jesus came to do.

So Jesus came, as Israel's Messiah, to fulfil Israel's mission, and to keep God's promise for the sake of all nations. He announced the good news that the reign of God had begun. That was what Jesus called "the good news [gospel] of the kingdom." Jesus summoned people to repent and believe that good news about God's kingdom by trusting and following Jesus himself—the King.

The people knew about the kingdom of God from the Psalms and prophets. They were eagerly expecting God to come and begin his reign on earth. They thought of that as a future age to come. They imagined a whole new messianic era. John the Baptist and Jesus both announced that these hopes of their people were coming true at last. "The time is fulfilled! The kingdom of God is at hand!" That means that *God had arrived* in the person of Jesus himself. God was *putting things right* in a world gone wrong. God was *overcoming the power of Satan*, as Jesus demonstrated in his miracles. God was *bringing salvation* into the world through Jesus (whose name, like Joshua, means "The LORD is salvation").

But God was doing all of this *not* in the way some people expected. God's kingdom was *not* established by military power, contrary to those who wanted to overthrow and drive out the Roman forces. God's kingdom was *not* established by forcing everybody to be "good," like the Pharisees ("good" in their own terms). Rather, God's way was the way of Jesus. Or, to put it the other way round, the way of Jesus was God's way of keeping his promise to bring the blessing and salvation of the kingdom of God. That's what Jesus came to achieve.

Jesus lived a life of faithful obedience to God (whereas Israel had rebelled and disobeyed). Like Israel, Jesus was "tested in the wilderness," (forty days, for their forty years), but unlike Israel he chose to trust and obey his Father God. And he was obedient right to death. When Jesus died on the cross, God was taking upon himself, in the person of his Son, the judgment and consequences of sin—not only for Israel but for the whole world. And so, through the cross and resurrection, Christ won the victory over sin and over Satan and all evil powers. That's why he cried out "It is finished!"—that means, "It is accomplished!"

Then, after his resurrection, Jesus told his disciples that the way was now open for them to go and preach repentance and forgiveness of sins *in his name* to all nations — because, he said, "This is what is written." What he meant by that expression was that the Old Testament Scriptures had "programmed" not only what Jesus accomplished in his earthly life as the Messiah, through his death and resurrection, but also what Jesus would go on doing through the mission of the church (Luke 24:45 – 47; Acts 1:1). So Jesus says that we must read and understand the Old Testament Scriptures (as he taught his disciples), both in relation to the *Messiah* and what he did, and in relation to *mission* — what we are commissioned to do to the ends of the earth.

IS YOUR GOSPEL BIG ENOUGH?

So you see that we need the Old Testament not only to understand who Jesus was (as he understood himself) but also to understand fully what Jesus accomplished. We need this especially to avoid reducing the whole message of the Bible to a purely individualistic minimum.

It's very easy to reduce the Bible to something like this:

- I know I'm a sinner.
- But I believe that Jesus died to take my sins away.
- So I can be forgiven and go to heaven when I die.

For that sort of message you don't need the Old Testament at all (apart from maybe the story of the fall and a few verses about sin). You don't need much of the New Testament either, actually. All you need is just the story of Jesus' death and a few verses from Paul to explain it. Maybe that's why some pastors only ever preach from those very few texts. They've never seen the big picture, the whole story. And so they never preach from the rest of the Bible.

Now of course, those three points above are true — thank God — and I believe them too! But the Bible tells a far bigger story. Sin is not just something personal, and neither is salvation. The Bible tells the story of God's great project of restoring the whole of creation through Christ, healing the division of the nations, and bringing salvation at every level of human and creational need and loss. That is the Bible's "big story" of salvation. That was how the

Apostle Paul thought of salvation. It was for the whole creation, for the whole church, and for individual believers (in Col 1:15–23 that's the order he puts things in).

Put it another way round. What was the problem that God solved through the death and resurrection of Jesus Christ? Some people talk (and preach, and teach, and sing songs) as if the *only* problem is "me and my sin." That is a problem, of course. Without Christ I stand condemned as a sinner with no hope and no eternal future with God. Because of Christ and his death in my place, I can indeed know that God forgives me and that I can be sure of eternal salvation. Good news! I believe it! But if that is the *only* way we think and speak about the gospel, we make it entirely self-centred. It's all about me, my sin, and my salvation. But that is making the gospel far narrower than the Bible itself. And it is surely strange and wrong to be self-centred in thinking about the gospel, which is God's great plan for the whole of creation.

When we go back and read the Bible story from the beginning, what do we find? Think again of those six stages in the great Bible drama. The Bible starts with creation. Human life is lived on and from the earth that God has put us in (Stage 1). But when Adam and Eve disobeyed God (Stage 2), the consequences affected not only individual human relationships with God (as if the only problem was that Adam and Eve were individual sinners who needed to be forgiven). Creation itself suffered. "Cursed is the ground because of you" (Gen 3:17). *The whole creation* is affected by sin and evil, as Paul clearly affirms (Rom 8:18–22). Then the story goes on to show how sin corrupted *all human relationships in society*—in marriage, between brothers, in wider society, and through the generations of history. And finally, human sin and arrogance resulted in *the nations of humanity being divided and scattered* (Gen 11).

So then, putting Genesis 3–11 together, the problem facing God is not just that individuals are sinners who need salvation from judgment and death but also that human families, societies, nations, and cultures are broken and fighting and that the earth itself is suffering the effects of sin and evil. And because of *all* this, we are faced with the reality of God's ultimate judgment. That's a big problem! And that's why we have a big gospel!

Where does the gospel *start*? I used to ask that question in classes I taught in India, and somebody would always say, "In

Matthew." And I would respond, "Wrong! The gospel starts in Genesis!" That's what Paul says. Check it out in Galatians 3:8. It's true. Paul calls God's promise to Abraham "good news" God called Abraham and promised blessing—not just as personal blessing for him, but blessing for all families/nations on earth.[3] God was thinking not just about individuals but about nations and the earth. That's the good news of the biblical gospel. And we need the Old Testament to prepare us for it. Then we can see the truly glorious, cosmic, enormous scale of what God accomplished through the death and resurrection of Jesus Christ.

Where does the gospel *end* (if we can put it like that)? The Bible's great drama takes us right on to Stage 6, when the good news of God's great salvation project reaches its triumphant finale—mission accomplished. If you read Revelation 21–22 you will find lots of echoes of Genesis 3–11. God's ultimate solution matches the original problem at many points.

Think of the terrible results of sin described in Genesis 3–11 (Stage 2). Then think of the wonderful picture of life in the new creation (Stage 6).

The results of sin	The new creation
The earth is cursed.	There will be no more curse.
We live under sentence of death because of sin.	There will be no more death.
We were driven away from the presence of God.	God will come to dwell with us in a new heaven and earth, united as the "city of God."
We were denied access to the tree of life.	The tree of life will flourish beside the water of life in the "garden city."

---

3. In fact, God's promise goes back even further to Genesis 3:15, which is sometimes referred to as the "proto-evangelium"—the "first gospel"— since it gave Adam and Eve the good news that God would eventually crush the head of the serpent through someone descended from Eve.

Human life became full of violence, suffering, and tears.	There will be no more tears, mourning, crying, or pain because there will be no more sin, immorality, deceit, or oppression.
Nations are divided in confusion, strife, and conflict.	People of every tribe, nation, and language will be united in worship of God.
	"The leaves of the tree are for the healing of the nations" (that is, not only will individuals have eternal life, but human cultures and nations will be reconciled).

The whole Bible story of salvation—that is, the redemptive history that runs through Stage 3 (the Old Testament promise), Stage 4 (the gospel), and Stage 5 (the mission of the church)—is what fills the gap between the great rebellion (Stage 2) and the great restoration (Stage 6). Once we grasp this whole story, we can no longer think of "the gospel" only as the answer to my individual problem of sin and as the way I can "get to heaven." Rather, we come to see that "my personal salvation," precious as it is, fits within God's much bigger plan that includes the healing of the nations and the reconciliation of all creation to God.

That's what Christ came to do. That's what Christ achieved through his death and resurrection. That's what was included in his triumphant final words from the cross, "It is finished!"—meaning, "It is accomplished." What was accomplished? All that God had promised in the Scriptures of the Old Testament.

Let me ask you a question: Do you preach the gospel? I hope you would answer immediately: "Yes!" But then, in the light of what you've just read, do you preach the whole gospel from all that the Bible includes in its "good news"? Or have you narrowed the gospel down to a message of individual salvation only? And if you are honest enough to say that maybe the latter is what you have been doing—well, first of all, you are in a large company because very many Christians seem to do exactly that. However, are you willing to change? Would you agree that narrowing down the gospel in that way is dishonouring to the Lord? After all, it reduces the scope and importance of all that the Bible tells us that Jesus accomplished on the cross and announced through the power of his resurrection. I am sure that we all want to be faithful to the Bible and preach and teach the truth. But the sad thing is that what some people call "the pure gospel" is a truncated gospel that reduces the glorious message of the Bible as a whole.

We started this chapter thinking of that journey, like the pastors on the road from Guayaquil to Quito. When we read the Old Testament we should remember to face the direction of travel. It all leads to Jesus. So that is why we need the Old Testament in order to understand who Jesus was and what Jesus came to do—and what he did in fact accomplish in the gospel events. We read the Old Testament looking forward to Jesus. I hope this chapter has helped you to see how that works and how important it is for a proper biblical understanding of Jesus.

But when you reach your destination you can look back on the journey also. When the pastors were enjoying the Langham Preaching seminar in Quito, they might have thought back to the long journey beforehand. I hope they thought it was all worthwhile! They could have drawn the journey on a map and pointed out how every stop on the journey was connected along the line that eventually got to Quito. It was a journey that connected together and reached its destination. So does the Old Testament.

They could also hold up the teaching, notes, and books they received at the seminar (and the group photo!) and then compare all that abundance with the letter they got way back a long time beforehand inviting them to come. The letter was a promise of what would happen when they reached Quito. They came in faith that the promise would be fulfilled, and it was. And I like to hope that the fulfilment of the promise (the seminar in Quito and all they were given) was even better than anything they might have imagined during the journey itself. So they would always look back on that long journey in the light of the blessing they received at the end of it.

In the same way, the New Testament shows us how Jesus fulfilled all the promise of the Old Testament—and in wonderful and surprising ways that were far better than anything the Old Testament people could have imagined. They had faith in God's promise, and even if many of them didn't see the fulfilment, God did keep his promise (that's the message of Hebrews 11). So we can look back on the Old Testament journey in the light of what happened at the end of it.

That means, then, that when we are reading and preparing to preach from a passage from the Old Testament, we need to do two things. First of all, we need to think of ourselves "sitting in the text," like those pastors in the minibus, facing the direction of travel, looking forward to where the journey will eventually lead—to Christ. But, second, we need to look back at the text (which comes from Stage 3) in the light of what actually happened at the end of the journey—that is, in the light of Christ and the whole gospel story in Stage 4. We are reading and preaching these texts *as Christian believers and to Christian believers,* all of us now living within Stage 5. So we must "connect" the Old Testament texts to Jesus Christ. Or, as it is sometimes expressed, we should "preach Christ from the Old Testament."

In the next two chapters we shall think of some good ways to do that and a few wrong ways too.

QUESTIONS AND EXERCISES

1. Discuss your answers to the questions I asked in the paragraph starting with "Let me ask you a question" (p. 32). Be honest! What steps might you need to take to make your teaching and preaching of the gospel more fully biblical in content?

2. Make a list of some of the names or titles that we commonly use for Jesus. Where do they come from in the Old Testament? What do they teach us about who Jesus was and what he came to do?

3. Prepare a lesson or a sermon on the baptism of Jesus, focusing especially on the words of God the Father in Matthew 3:16–17. Show how God echoes words from Old Testament texts and use them to explain who Jesus truly was and what he had come to do.

CHAPTER 4

Don't Just Give Me Jesus

A nne Graham Lotz, daughter of Billy Graham, is a gifted evangelist and preacher. After a particularly stressful period in her life she wrote a poem and a book with the title *Just Give Me Jesus*. It is a wonderful poem describing Jesus in a great variety of ways, each section ending with the repeated, "Just give me Jesus."[1] She has also conducted many seminars and revival conferences with the same theme. Her point is, of course, that our Lord Jesus Christ is sufficient for everything that we may face in life, death and beyond. He is all we need for our salvation, and he is the source of all the grace, blessings, and strength that God gives us for our lives on earth and in the new creation.

So, it is a superb phrase to capture the sufficiency of Christ for all our personal and pastoral needs. But when it comes to preaching from the Old Testament, I'm afraid it really won't do. The preacher should not imagine that, when he preaches from the Bible, his congregation are sitting there saying, "Just give me Jesus." Preaching from the Old Testament is not just preaching *about* Jesus, though it should certainly lead people ultimately *to* Jesus.

I once got sent the advertising leaflet for a conference at which I was to speak. My subject was the Old Testament foundations for Christian mission. At its climax the leaflet said, "and the great thing about the Old Testament is that it's all about Jesus!" They were trying to be encouraging. But that is not what I would have written. For it isn't really true to say that quite so simply.

---

1. You can read the full poem at www.askeugene.wordpress .com/2010/11/24/give-me-Jesus/. It is important to stress that the chapter title "Don't just give me Jesus" applies only to preaching from the Old Testament and is not meant in any way as a criticism of Anne Graham Lotz and her ministries.

Maybe after reading the last two chapters of this book you might be thinking the same way as the conference leaflet. I've been stressing very much that we need to understand the Old Testament in the light of Christ (the Old Testament like a journey that leads to Christ and declares the promise that was fulfilled by Christ). So you might be thinking, "The Old Testament? It's all about Jesus."

But it isn't, not directly.

What I've been saying in the past two chapters is not that the Old Testament is "all about Jesus," but that it is a journey that leads to him. It all *points to* Christ. It is not all "*about* Christ."

Think again of those pastors on the minibus from Guayaquil to Quito. Yes, their whole journey was in the direction of Quito. Yes, Quito was the intended destination. Yes, they would have been thinking and talking about what lay ahead when they arrived in Quito. The whole focus of their journey was on Quito. But that does not mean that every time they looked out the window of the minibus they were seeing Quito. No, what they were seeing was scenery on the route to Quito. Maybe sometimes they even saw road signs that said "Quito 150 km." But even then, the sign was not Quito itself. It was a reassurance that they were going in the right direction. So if there had been a little child in the back who kept calling out, "Are we there yet?" the adults would have to answer, "No, not yet! Be patient. We will get to Quito soon."

Being on the road *to* Quito is not the same thing as being *in* Quito. In the same way, saying that the Old Testament leads *to* Christ is not the same thing as saying that it is *about* Christ.

Now, how does this affect our preaching and teaching of the Old Testament? Does it mean that, in spite of all I've said in the last two chapters, we can't preach about Christ from Old Testament texts after all? Not at all. In chapter 5 I will be saying that we certainly can, and indeed must, preach Christ from the Old Testament. And I will try to explain how we can go about doing that in a good and valid way. But first of all, we need to get some negative points out of the way in this chapter.

Unfortunately, there are some preachers who imagine that, no matter what text they are preaching from anywhere in the Bible, they have to make their message be about Jesus. They have taken the *truth* that the whole Bible is *centred and focused* on the Lord Jesus Christ and bears witness to him in many ways and then have turned it into a very simplistic method of interpretation in which every verse in the Old Testament somehow has to be "*about* Jesus." And they can make their preaching sound very clever when they do that. But there are all kinds of problems with that method. Here are some of them. Making every Old Testament text somehow be "about Jesus" can have the following bad effects.

THE DANGER OF IGNORING THE ORIGINAL MEANING OF THE TEXT

What is the first rule of exegesis—the first thing we must do when reading and understanding any Bible text? We must ask, "What *did* this text mean at the time it was written for the people who first heard or read it? What was the author talking about, and what was he *saying* about what he was talking about?" In other words, we work hard to understand the text in its own original context *before* we ask any other questions or make any application.[2]

But if you approach a text in the Old Testament with the assumption that "This must be about Jesus," you easily overlook all that the original author was actually trying to say. In fact, you end up putting a gag on the mouth of the original author, in order to make him say what you think his text must be about since it must be "all about Jesus." And that is a very bad thing to do to the Bible!

I once heard a preacher preach from the text of Amos 5:24: "But let justice roll on like a river, righteousness like a never-failing stream." He spoke for a few moments about Amos, but then he went on to say, "The only righteousness we can have is the righteousness of Christ." From there he moved to justification by faith. He might as well have been preaching from Romans. All that he said was true, of course. But it had nothing to do with what Amos said! And worse, it was *distorting* the text of Scripture. It was silencing all that Amos actually wrote in that passage about *doing* justice and ending exploitation, cheating, and oppression.

So that preacher, because he was so concerned to get Jesus into or out of his text, actually ignored the original meaning of the text itself. When Amos wrote those words he was *not* talking about Jesus. He was challenging the people of Israel to live as

---

2. If you have read Gordon Fee and Douglas Stuart's classic *How to Read the Bible for All Its Worth*, you will have learned this right at the start. It is *always* the first thing to do, every time we study any Bible passage.

God wanted them to. It *would* be possible to preach on that text in a way that *both* explains and applies fully what Amos meant *and* makes a link to Jesus Christ and the gospel. In the next chapter I'll suggest some ways we can do that properly. But just "jumping to Jesus" right at the start of the sermon is not the way to do it!

THE DANGER OF FANCIFUL INTERPRETATIONS

I participated in a Bible study for some time where a few of the participants were rather obsessed with the idea that any and every passage in the Old Testament must have Jesus in it somewhere. So they spent the whole time working out how that might be the case — and coming up with some very strange ideas. One of them noticed that there were thirteen Levites standing beside Ezra as he read the law in Nehemiah 8 and concluded that this must represent the twelve original disciples of Jesus plus Paul. So Ezra became Jesus teaching the people — and Nehemiah 8 turned out to be really all about Jesus! Once you let your imagination loose in that way, anything at all can become "about Jesus" in one way or another.

But that is an irresponsible way to treat the Bible. And if we teach that kind of thing, all we do is reinforce people's suspicion that the Bible is a book they could never understand for themselves. They think they need clever preachers and teachers who can bring out of any text all sorts of meanings "about Jesus" that they would never have thought of themselves. But the Bible is not a kind of game. Have you seen those "Where's Wally?" or "Where's Waldo?" picture books? They're full of complicated pictures, and somewhere hidden in each one is the character Wally (or Waldo), and it's a lot of fun trying to find him. But we should not treat the Old Testament like that, as if it were a "Where's Jesus?" picture book.

I agree with Dale Ralph Davis, who is also concerned about the bad side effects of wanting to get Jesus out of any and every text in the Old Testament. Here is what he writes about what Jesus said in Luke 24:25–27, 44–47:

> I think Jesus is teaching that *all parts* of the Old Testament testify of the Messiah in his suffering and glory, but I do not think Jesus is saying that *every* Old Testament passage/text bears witness to him. Jesus referred to the things written about him *in* the law of Moses, the prophets and psalms — he did not say that every passage

spoke of him (v. 44). Therefore, I do not feel compelled to make every Old Testament passage point to Christ in some way because I do not think Christ himself requires it ... [but] ... just because I don't think every Old Testament text is about Christ does not mean I oppose preaching Christ from Old Testament texts if he is legitimately to be seen there ... However, I am convinced that I do not honour Christ by forcing him into texts where he is not.[3]

THE DANGER OF OVERLOOKING OTHER BIG THINGS THAT GOD TEACHES

That might sound wrong. What could be "bigger" than Jesus? Well, nothing, of course. And it is true that we can connect all the great things that God revealed and taught in the Old Testament to Jesus. For example, the Old Testament begins (Bible Story Stage 1) with creation. And we know from the New Testament that all things in heaven and earth were created by Christ and for Christ (John 1:1–3; Col 1:15–20; Heb 1:3). Yes, but when the Scriptures talk about creation (not only in Gen 1–2 but in many other places, like Pss 19, 33, 104; Jer 10; Job 28, 38–41), they are talking about creation—not "about Jesus." We have a lot to learn from those texts about God, about the universe, about the earth, and about ourselves. So let us learn and teach and preach what the text says not what we read into it from later in the Bible.

Think of all the other great things that God reveals in the Old Testament:

- What it means to be human, made in the image of God;
- The fact of sin and the terrible consequences of evil;
- God's anger against injustice and oppression;
- God's love and faithfulness to his promises;
- God's sovereign rule over all nations and all history;
- The way God wants his people to worship him;
- The way God wants people to live and behave toward one another;
- God's plan for the restoration of the whole creation.

---

3. Dale Ralph Davis, *The Word Became Flesh: How to Preach from Old Testament Narrative Texts* (Fearn: Christian Focus, 2006), 135–38.

Of course, we can show how all these great themes eventually lead us to Christ (and we'll think about that below). But if we read great texts where God is teaching about *those* things, and all the time we are thinking, "This must be all about Jesus," we will miss all the richness and depth of what God is *actually* saying to us in those original texts. And that is not only sad—it is tragic. For it leaves people not understanding and applying so much of what is there in the Bible. Indeed, it distracts them away from listening to what God wants to say to them in those texts—and that is a seriously bad thing to do with the Bible.

Perhaps you are thinking of the Apostle Paul, who said, "we preach Christ crucified," and how he decided to "know nothing ... except Jesus Christ and him crucified" (1 Cor 1:23; 2:2). Some people think this means that Paul preached only about Jesus and the cross and nothing else. But that can't be true.

First of all, notice the context of both those verses. Paul was contrasting his style of preaching of the gospel with the fancy eloquence of the Greek philosophers. He did not bring clever arguments and skilled rhetoric like they did but simply the historical truth about Jesus with the power of the Holy Spirit. And second, Paul himself says that he taught his churches much more than only the story of the crucifixion. He reminded the leaders of the churches in Ephesus that during his years there, "You know that I have not hesitated to preach anything that would be helpful to you but have taught you publicly and from house to house," and "I have not hesitated to proclaim to you the whole will of God" (Acts 20:20, 27). That is, Paul's preaching was both *topical* (v. 20; addressing the needs and questions of the church) and *scriptural* (v. 27; explaining the whole "will of God"—which means the plan and purpose of God as revealed in the Scriptures—i.e., the Old Testament). All of this, of course, would have *centred* on Christ, but it was not just "*about*" Jesus." Rather, it would have been rich teaching from all over the Scriptures—especially when he was engaging with Jews. Paul spent thousands of hours during his two years at Ephesus lecturing and debating daily in the public lecture hall of Tyrannus. That must have been about more than the crucifixion alone!

THE DANGER OF FLATTENING THE BIBLE STORY AND REMOVING THE UNIQUENESS OF THE INCARNATION

When we talk about "Jesus in the Old Testament," it can have the effect of putting the whole Bible into the same time zone, as it were. It's as if everybody in the Old Testament were living at the same time as Jesus and "knew" him, prayed to him, even met him from time to time. Now again, of course, we agree that God the Son, the Second Person of the Trinity, has been eternally alive and active from before the creation of the world. So in that sense the God whom the saints of Old Testament times worshipped was the God whom *we* know as Father, Son, and Holy Spirit. So the divine person whom we meet as Jesus of Nazareth in the New Testament existed in Old Testament times as well. Sometimes he is spoken of as the "*pre-incarnate* Christ"—that is, God the Son *before* he took on human flesh through being conceived by the Holy Spirit in the womb of the virgin Mary.

God himself, of course, is invisible spirit. He cannot be seen in a physical sense in his essence as God. However, God did choose to take on a human appearance on several occasions in the Old Testament in order to speak to people—as when the LORD appeared to Abraham or to Moses and others. Some people suggest these were appearances of the Second Person of the Trinity—God the Son, the "pre-incarnate Christ," as I said. That may be so, but I don't think we have to insist on it. The Bible simply says "God, or the LORD, appeared." God made human beings in his own image. It was perfectly natural for God to take human form when he wanted to engage in conversation with someone in a direct way.

However, we must not ignore the way the Bible presents the great story of redemption—as a story that moves from one stage to the next. There is a crucial difference between Bible Story Stage 3 and Bible Story Stage 4. Only at Stage 4 did God step into human history in human flesh. Only at Stage 4 did God actually *become* human, from conception, through birth, infancy, childhood, youth, and adulthood. And only *then* did God, as man, take on the name "Jesus." "Jesus" is the name that was given to the son of Mary, Jesus of Nazareth. And we need to understand that something new and unique happened at the incarnation, when God became human, when the Word became flesh and dwelt among us. This was something that had *never happened before.* Jesus was not just another one of those appearances of God in human form that we read about sometimes in the Old Testament. Jesus was not "an appearance" at all—but a real, physical, human being like you and me.

As the Gospels make clear in their opening chapters, the birth of Jesus and his earthly life were the beginning of the new age of God's salvation. Those events heralded the coming of the kingdom of God. They were the fulfilment of all God had promised in the Old Testament. When Joseph and Mary named the baby "Jesus," Matthew says, it fulfilled the Immanuel prophecy. God, at last, had come to be "with us." When Jesus was born, a new world began.

So we really should not use the name "Jesus" before his birth, and talk about Jesus in the Old Testament. It is the name of the man Jesus, born in Bethlehem, crucified under Pontius Pilate, raised to life, ascended, and now seated at God's right hand as Lord. "Jesus," in that New Testament sense—the man Jesus— was simply "not around" in the Old Testament (though, of course, as I said, God the Son most certainly was!). So we should not read and preach the Scriptures of the Bible Story Stages 1–3 (the Old Testament) as if Stage 4 had already happened or as if the characters in the earlier stages already knew all that would happen at Stage 4 (even though they looked forward to it as they trusted God's promise).

THE DANGER THAT ALL YOUR PREACHING MAY SOUND THE SAME

I knew one church where several of those who preached took this view—that the whole Old Testament was "all about Jesus." They preached very well, but for me (and several others in the church), it always sounded the same. No matter where the Bible text came from, the sermon was *predictable.* We always ended up very quickly hearing about Jesus. And also, because they were very committed to evangelism, the sermons almost always ended up calling people to conversion and faith in Christ. In fact, some people say that all preaching should be evangelistic and end with an "altar call." I'm afraid I disagree, and so would the Apostle Paul, I think, judging by how he described his own preaching in Acts 20:20, 27.

Please don't misunderstand me. Of course I believe in the importance of evangelistic preaching and in telling people about Jesus and inviting them to put their faith in him. And there are many texts in the whole Bible that do exactly that, including all four Gospels, naturally. But there are many more texts throughout the Bible that do *not* do that. And if our preaching is supposed to be teaching people what the Bible actually says, we should do that—*preach what the Bible text says*, not what we can make it say by jumping quickly to Jesus and calling for conversion. Indeed, I would say that faithful preaching of the great variety of the Bible's teaching over time *will* lead people to a better understanding of Christ and what it actually means to trust him as Saviour and follow him as Lord. People will see Christ from many different angles and perspectives. And they will come to connect Jesus with the wonderful variety of God's revealed teaching in both Old and New Testaments.

Imagine for a moment that the Bible is a very large house. Some preachers are always standing at the front door, preaching about Jesus (from every text) and inviting people to come and admire the door and come through it into salvation and church membership. Now that is a good thing to do, and Jesus did say, "I am the door." We do need to preach the gospel in that way and call people to repentance and faith. But evangelistic preaching is not all there is. We should not always just stand at the front door. Why not invite people to come on in and show them the rest of the house? There is so much in the Bible, so much about God, about life, about what it's like to live with Jesus at the centre of life, the universe, and everything.

Why not plan your preaching so that over time you faithfully preach through many different parts of the Bible and teach people what is actually there? That is like offering guided tours of the rest of the Bible house. Then you can show people the wonderful riches that are in every room so that they long to come in and enjoy living there. In this way your preaching and teaching will have great variety. Yet at the same time, it will be clear that the only way into the house is through the door that is Christ.

QUESTIONS AND EXERCISES

1. Discuss how you would explain the difference between saying that the Old Testament points towards Christ and saying that every passage in the Old Testament is "all about Jesus."

2. Think about your own preaching and teaching over the years. It is of course good, right, and essential that we keep our eyes focused on Jesus Christ as the centre of our preaching. But are there parts of the Bible or themes of biblical teaching that you have hardly ever touched on? Make a list of these and reflect on (or discuss with your group) how you might plan to include them in your preaching and teaching in future—without forgetting about Christ!

CHAPTER 5

Connecting with Christ

L et's go back to our pastors in the minibus on the road from Guayaquil to Quito. It's a very scenic route. There are lots of places where they might stop to enjoy the view of the mountains and take photos. Now imagine one of the pastors showing his photos to his family after he gets home from the Langham Preaching seminar in Quito. As he goes through them one by one, what will he do? He will describe what's in each picture itself. Maybe he will point to a photo of a great mountain and tell them the name of it. Maybe he has a photo of a restaurant they stopped at on the way, and he will tell them the names of the others in the photo. Maybe he shows them a photo of the place where the road had been damaged by a landslide and they had to go round by another route. So he will talk about what is actually in each photo and put it in its own context. "That's when we stopped for lunch." "That's when we had to turn round and find another way." "That's my friend Ricardo when he got off the bus feeling sick." Every picture tells a story, as they say.

But as well as that, he would put the whole collection of photos in their wider context. They were all taken *on the journey to Quito for the purpose of attending the Langham Preaching seminar*. So he might say, "Here's a photo of us all getting on the minibus early in the morning *on our way to Quito*." Or he might show a big landscape from a mountain top and say, "Here we are looking *down towards Quito* in the far distance." So he will *make links* between the actual content of each photo and the destination and purpose of the journey they were travelling on. He may even show a photo of a road sign pointing to Quito. All the photos are of the journey and have their own specific content. But they are *linked* to what lay at the end of the journey. These particular photos could only be taken because they were on the road to Quito, not somewhere else. So the photos are *linked to each other* (it was all one single journey), and they are *all linked to the destination* (it was a journey to Quito, for the preaching seminar).

What he will *not* do is point out a photo that was taken while they were still on the journey and say, "Look at this one. That's Quito." He can't do that until he actually gets to Quito and has photos of the city itself.

Now think again of the Old Testament. We've seen that it is a journey that leads to Christ. And it is a journey full of all kinds of wonderful scenery. Imagine the contents of the Old Testament like an enormous photo album. When you pick out one of those photos (a particular text), what is your first task? You have to say *what is actually there in that text.* That means, as the very first rule of good exegesis, you observe what the text actually said (the content of the text) in its own context. You do all the work of studying and understanding the text itself. And when you come to preach it, that has to be your starting point. Your sermon has to major on explaining and applying what the original author wrote and meant. You must put the text into its own context (its place in the journey) and help people understand that. So, as we saw in the last chapter, you don't just "jump to Jesus" and ignore the main point of the text itself. That would be like one of the pastors showing a photo of the mountains on the journey and saying: "This photo was taken on the way to Quito, so let me just tell you about Quito."

However, because all these texts are connected together as part of the great journey that led to Jesus, you certainly can and should help your congregation to understand that by *making links* with Jesus and the New Testament gospel. There are several ways to do that, which we shall look at below. In this chapter it will be enough just to list these ways of making links, along with a few comments on each. When we come to Part 2 and think about how to preach and teach from different kinds of literature in the Old Testament, we can explain some of them in greater detail and give more examples. But before we look at some of the links between Old Testament texts and Christ, let's note a few quick points:

- The positive benefit of making such links in your teaching is that it helps your listeners regularly to *see the whole Bible for what it is*—a great story-journey in which the Old Testament leads to Christ and the New Testament leads on to the return of Christ and the new creation. They will begin to see the connections between the different parts and learn how to read it for themselves, looking for these links. They will learn to see themselves *within* the Bible story, reading it from the perspective of Stage 5.

- However, you should not turn the links into the main message. Concentrate on teaching what is in your text itself, but at relevant points show how the text connects to Christ and why that matters (which we will explain further below).

- Don't try to use every kind of link listed below in every sermon! Usually one is sufficient, or sometimes two that go well together.

MAKING LINKS WITH CHRIST THROUGH THE STORY

The first and most obvious way to link any Old Testament text to Christ is simply to point out how that text fits into a story that ultimately leads to Jesus. This is most obvious when we remember that the whole Old Testament is "BC"—Before Christ. But we can show that it is also "TC"—Toward Christ.

Making the story-link is fairly simple when you are preaching from an Old Testament narrative text. You can open up the background of the smaller story to show that it is part of the wider story of God and Israel and point out how that long story ultimately leads us to Christ. That needn't take long. A sermon is not a detailed history lesson. But it can be a moment to lift people's eyes up from merely thinking, "How does this single story apply to me?" to wondering, "What does it mean that this story is part of the bigger story that leads to Jesus?"

Example

Suppose your text is **Joshua 1**. You can point out how this comes after the earlier story of how God redeemed Israel out of Egypt and then led them and provided for them in the wilderness (Exodus to Deuteronomy). Now he is giving them the land he promised. So this is the next step in the long story that leads to Christ, through whom God has redeemed us from sin and provides us with an inheritance and "rest" even better than the land of Canaan, with reference to Hebrews 4. Now at that point, you need to concentrate on what Joshua 1 says and preach from that text. You don't jump straight to Jesus or Hebrews. But by mentioning them you show how *this* story (Joshua 1) fits into and prepares the way for *that* story (the New Testament).

Example

Suppose your text is from the book of **Ruth**. The writer ends the book by pointing out how the son of Ruth and Boaz became the grandfather of King David. Already, the book sets its own story in the wider story of Israel and the king who would come. So you can point out how Matthew connects this with Jesus by including Ruth in his genealogy (Matt 1:5–6), making Jesus "great David's greater Son."

It might seem harder to make a link through the whole Bible story if the text is from one of the other kinds of literature—such as the law, the prophets, or Psalms. But even then connections can be drawn. All such texts have their place within the history of Israel, and you can think backwards and forwards within that history.

Example

Suppose your text is **Psalm 96**. It celebrates the name, the salvation, the glory, and the mighty deeds of the LORD God of Israel. What did those words mean to an Old Testament Israelite? If you had asked that question to the writer or one of the singers, they would have told you the stories of Israel's history. God's name was revealed to Moses and Israel at Mount Sinai. God's salvation was experienced when he liberated them from Egypt. The glory of God filled the tabernacle in the wilderness and later the temple in Jerusalem. The mighty deeds of the LORD included his victories over his enemies and the gift of the land. But you can point out that the psalmist looks forward to "the nations," "all peoples," in "all the earth" singing "a new song" about these great things of God. How could that happen? For the psalmist, it had to be an act of faith and imagination. But we know that through the Lord Jesus Christ, the name, the salvation, the glory, and the mighty deeds of the LORD God of the whole Bible story are being proclaimed among nations all over the world. The psalm itself points forward from the story that lies *behind* it, to the story that lies *ahead* of it.

With a text from the law, you can point out how even within the law itself (e.g., in **Deuteronomy 29–30**) it is recognized that Israel would fail to obey God—just as we do. So although the law was like a "schoolmaster" and we have much to learn from it, it points us through our sin and failure to the Lord Jesus Christ. The law also leads us to Christ (we will think much more about this later).

MAKING LINKS WITH CHRIST THROUGH THE PROMISES

This is a link that often fits together very well with the storylink above. That's because, as we saw in chapter 2, the journey of the Old Testament story not only had a *destination* (Jesus Christ) but also a *purpose* (all that God promised in the Old Testament and then accomplished in the New Testament). So wherever possible we should show how an Old Testament text is connected in some way to that promise. It may be a direct connection, as when the text itself contains an element of promise or speaks of God's future purpose. Or it may be indirect, as when the text simply assumes God's promise as a kind of background awareness. Remember the way Matthew draws from various Old Testament texts, some direct and others indirect, and sees all of them fulfilled in Jesus? That is how the rest of the New Testament also sees the Old Testament. As a whole it constitutes God's great promise regarding the whole creation and all peoples.

Direct connections would include passages such as Genesis 12, 15, 17, and so on, where God makes his promise to Abraham (it is actually recorded five times in Genesis); God's promises to Israel in Egypt (Exod 6:6–8); his promises to David (2 Sam 7); and passages in the prophets about the future restoration of Israel after exile. All of these point forward to Christ and are echoed often in the New Testament itself.

Indirect connections take more time to think about and find. Remember, for example, that the whole story of *Israel as a people* is a story of God's promise. Israel as a people only existed because of God's promise to bring blessing to all nations through them. Paul quotes Genesis 12:3 and calls it "gospel" in Galatians 3:8. So in theory, whenever you are handling a text about Israel you should be aware of the background promise of God—*even though* so often the text will be showing how Old Testament Israel *failed* to live up to their calling and frustrated God's purpose for them. That failure in itself is an indirect pointer to the One who would come and fulfil Israel's mission, in perfect obedience, then suffering, death, and resurrection. Israel's failure provides an indirect but very powerful link to Christ.

There may be other hints in a given text. Look for *covenant* language that is a reminder of God's promise, for example, when the text speaks of "your God" or "my people." That points to the relationship that ultimately becomes ours in the new covenant through Christ. Or when God promises to be "with" someone, or with his people. Ultimately God is "with us" through our Immanuel, Jesus. The hope and expectations of the psalmists, that God would deliver them, rest on God's faithfulness to his promises, and that in turn points to his greatest faithfulness of all, in Christ. So look out for ways that the text assumes the underlying story of God's promise, and think how that can link to the fulfilment of all God's promises in Christ.

The key thing to bear in mind is that *the Bible as a whole is a story of redemptive fulfilment.* That is, God made his great promise to bring blessing and salvation to the world of broken, sinful humanity and spoiled creation. The Old Testament is constantly moving forward to see how God will eventually fulfil that promise and redeem the world. And the New Testament shows that God has done so through the Lord Jesus Christ. Paul put it most simply when he said to the Jews in the synagogue in Pisidian Antioch: "We tell you the good news [gospel]: what God promised our ancestors he has fulfilled for us, their children, by raising up Jesus" (Acts 13:32–33).

Example

Suppose, again, that your text is **Joshua 1**. Here's how I began a sermon I preached on that chapter (at the start of a series on the book of Joshua). I began by asking people to notice how the first three verses mention several important things: (a) the death of Moses; (b) "all these people" —i.e., Israel, the people of God; and (c) the promise of God. I then asked them to turn back a page in their Bibles to see that the death of Moses comes in Deuteronomy 34. And there too we read about God's promise and God's people. Deuteronomy 34:4 refers to God's promise to Abraham. That sends us spiralling even further back to Genesis. And so immediately we see where this book of Joshua fits in the story of the Bible. It comes immediately after the Pentateuch (Genesis–Deuteronomy), and we need to know the story so far that is contained in those five books. God created the world good, but human sin and rebellion has spoiled everything. But in Genesis 12 God promised Abraham that through him and his people he would turn that curse to blessing that would come to all nations. God also promised Abraham that he would give his descendants this land. And that is what God is about to do in this book of Joshua. But we need to see that the story of Joshua and the land is not complete in itself. It is one step along the journey that leads to Christ, and to the inheritance we have in him. Indeed, the promised land not only points to what we now have in Christ (Eph 2:19–25; Heb 4:1–11; 12:22–24; 1 Pet 1:4) but ultimately to the new heaven and new earth, the new creation in which God will dwell with his people for ever (Rev 21–22). So I helped people look backwards from the text and forwards from the text.

It only took a few minutes to make those points near the beginning of my sermon (and to return to them at the end to bring out some implications for how we should now live). As soon as I had set the chapter in that wider context in relation to God's promise and God's people in the great Bible story, I concentrated on what God actually said to Joshua and preached the message of those great verses. So my aim was to *preach the text*, and to *link the text to Christ* by way of the whole story of God's promise and its fulfilment.

When we look in Part 2 at preaching from the prophets, we will think in more detail about the "three horizons" of Old Testament texts. Horizon 1 is the Old Testament period itself—what the text was talking about in its own context. Horizon 2 is the Christ-horizon, specifically the Gospels and Acts. Horizon 3 is the return of Christ and the new creation. For now, it is enough just to keep these horizons in mind. When studying any Old Testament text for preaching and teaching, it is always worth asking, "Where does this text *fit* within the wider context of what God promised right at the start of the story? And where does this text *point* in relation to the fulfilment of God's promise through Christ—whether at his first or second coming?"

MAKING LINKS WITH CHRIST THROUGH SIMILARITIES

"God is always Godding!" I remember the excitement of the woman who exclaimed those words—actually inventing a word! She had quite recently become a Christian and belonged to our homegroup. She was thrilled at the ways God was active in her life.

God was simply doing for her what God regularly and repeatedly does—and has been doing throughout history. God is consistent.

It's not that God simply repeats himself. Rather, God acts in ways that are *characteristic*. When somebody we know does something that we recognize as the way they always act, something very characteristic of them, we smile and say, "That's just typical!" Or, "Typical John!" They are acting "true to type." It's what we've come to expect from that person. Once you get to know somebody well, you can see patterns and similarities in the way they behave. My wife tells me I always stand the same way to clean my teeth; that I arrange things in the same order every day for breakfast; that (left to myself) I'd wear the same clothes all the time. It's just me. Typical. Creature of habit.

Well, God is not a creature, of course, and he does not exactly have "habits." But God certainly acts in typical ways, so that those who knew him well in Bible times began to recognize God's ways. They saw the patterns and similarities between how God acted at one time and then another. They saw what he did in the exodus, and they knew he could do the same thing again—for Israel (in restoring them after defeat or exile) and indeed for individuals (suffering injustice or danger). They heard what God did to Sodom and Gomorrah, and it became a picture of other terrible moments of God's judgment, including on Jerusalem in the end. They knew God had provided for the Israelites for a generation in the wilderness, so they trusted that God could do the same for those in serious need, even in exile. They also knew God had been testing the Israelites in the wilderness and saw the same kind of testing at later periods of history, as to whether they would trust and obey him or not.

Now those who encountered Jesus in the New Testament clearly saw all kinds of ways in which the God they knew so well from their Old Testament Scriptures was "Godding" again. They point out significant correspondences between things in the Old Testament and what God had now done in and through Jesus Christ. And they used those Old Testament things in order to explain many aspects of the meaning of Christ's birth, life, death, resurrection, and ascension.

Another word for that kind of explanation is "analogy." An analogy is where you use one well-known thing to explain some new thing that has some similarities. They are not exactly the same, but you can see *correspondences* between them. In the Bible we find analogies drawn between Jesus Christ and events, persons, institutions, themes, and images that are found in the Old Testament. The table shows a few examples in each of those categories. There are many more, of course, but this gives some idea of what I mean. Some of them will be familiar to you, I'm sure. There are others that you can find out for yourself as you read and study the Bible and helpful commentaries.[1]

Old Testament reality	Link to Christ
Events	
Creation	Jesus is the Word of God through whom all things were created.
Exodus	Jesus is the one who defeats all oppressing powers and liberates people from slavery.
Gift of land	Jesus is our inheritance and grants "rest" from enemies.
Anointing of King David	Jesus is the anointed messianic King, son of David.
Return from exile	Jesus brings forgiveness, restoration to God, and a new covenant.
Persons	
Adam	Jesus is the perfect image of God.
Noah	Jesus rescues from judgment.
Abraham	Jesus lived in perfect faith and obedience.
Melchizedek/Aaron	Jesus is the perfect High Priest.
Moses	Jesus is the liberator of his people and the mediator of the new covenant.

---

1. I have given a much fuller explanation of typology—that is, seeing these patterns of correspondence between Jesus and the Old Testament—in *Knowing Jesus through the Old Testament.*

Old Testament reality	Link to Christ
Joshua	Jesus (the Greek form of Joshua) is the Saviour and leader of his people.
David and Solomon	Jesus is God's anointed King.
Esther	Jesus is the one who saved his people, at the risk/cost of his own life.
Institutions	
Passover	Jesus is the sacrificial lamb whose blood protects from death.
Temple, priesthood, sacrifices	Jesus is the "place" through whom we have perfect atonement, forgiveness, and access into God's presence.
Jubilee	Jesus brings release and restoration for those enslaved.

As always, we need to be careful how we use such similarities when preaching. Here are some things to keep in mind.

- If you are teaching on an Old Testament text and you observe that there is some analogy or comparison with Christ—particularly if one of the New Testament writers *quotes* from your Old Testament text and makes a comparison—then of course at some point in the lesson or sermon you will want to tell people about that and explain it. It is always good to show people how the Bible connects together in that way, and how Christ "holds it all together." *But* remember that your main job is to explain and apply the Old Testament text itself in its own context and teach the message God wants people to hear from *that* text. By all means, make the link with Christ, but don't just "jump to Jesus" immediately and ignore what the Old Testament author was saying.

- Remember that, when a New Testament writer quotes an Old Testament text, it is for a specific purpose or to illustrate a particular point that he (the New Testament writer) wants to make. That does not mean that when *you* preach from that same Old Testament text you are limited to how the New Testament used it for that particular point. For example: the voice from heaven at the baptism of Jesus echoes three Old Testament texts—Isaiah 42:1; Psalm 2:7; and Genesis 22:2. But if you are preaching from one of those texts (in the whole chapter they come in), you cannot simply say, "This is about the baptism of Jesus." No, you must ask what the whole chapter meant in its original Old Testament context and preach *that* message. In the course of your sermon you can make the link to Christ as appropriate, but your sermon is about the Old Testament text, not just about Jesus. Here's another example: both the writer to the Hebrews and James make use of Rahab as an *illustration* of faith demonstrated in action (Heb 11:31; Jas 2:25–26). But if you are preaching on the whole story of Joshua 2 and 6 there will be a lot more to think and preach about than only the faith of Rahab (even though she is certainly a key character of the story).

- A similarity in *one* respect does not mean similarity in *all* respects. The Old Testament characters who prefigured Christ in some way (as above) were also sinners like us and some of them did pretty terrible things in their lives. At that point, of course, there is no similarity with Christ.

- Stick to the *broad* sense of similarity that the New Testament itself teaches and don't be tempted to run off into guessing at all kinds of other similarities in the minor details of an Old Testament text. For example, the tabernacle was primarily the place of God's presence in the midst of his people and the place where sacrifice took place to atone for the sins and uncleanness of the people. In both these respects the New Testament sees Christ as its fulfilment. Christ now is "God in our midst," and Christ provides atonement and cleansing for sin and access to God. But some people have gone on to read all kinds of significance into the coloured threads and precious stones used in constructing the tabernacle—all very imaginative, but distracting, and not supported within the Bible itself.

Example

I was preaching once on **Judges 3:7 – 11**, the little story of Othniel, at the beginning of a series on the book of Judges. I wanted to show that Othniel sets a pattern for the other judges in the book. But I also wanted to explain why judges like him are included in Hebrews 11 as models of faith in action (in spite of the fact that some of them, like Samson, did some very strange things). Simply,

- Othniel was God's choice (God raised him up).
- He had God's Spirit working through him.
- He was the agent of God's salvation—he put things right for Israel and delivered them from their enemies.
- And he brought God's peace (or "rest").

So in these respects, Othniel is a model for the kind of leader God called and used at that time when they acted in faith and obedience. But the whole book of Judges paints a very gloomy picture of human sin and evil that just keeps going on and on and getting worse. Even the greatest of the judges could not prevent that happening in the long term. The book points beyond itself to the great wickedness of fallen humanity and ultimately points to God's great solution in the One who came to put things right for good.

So I briefly pointed out how Othniel, for all his obscurity, is a tiny model of Christ in those same respects. For Christ was chosen and raised up by God as his anointed Messiah. Christ was filled with the Holy Spirit of God. Christ came to save and deliver his people, not just in the land of Canaan but in the whole world. And Christ made peace—peace with God and one another. I tried to follow the example of Hebrews 11, which concludes not by telling us to concentrate on those great heroes of faith in the Old Testament but rather to "fix our eyes on Jesus" (Heb 12:1 – 2). So, in the sermon as a whole, I mainly preached on the story itself against the background of its context in Judges 2 especially. I did not preach that Judges 3 is "all *about* Jesus." But I built a link between that text and Christ by observing a similarity between the work of judges like him and the ultimate work of Christ.

MAKING LINKS WITH CHRIST THROUGH CONTRASTS

And now for something completely different! Sometimes we can make a link from the Old Testament to Christ (or the New Testament in general) by seeing not a similarity but a clear difference or contrast. Some of these contrasts are vast and obvious, and we know them as essential elements in the gospel itself. You just can't miss these ones, for example:

- Adam and Eve disobeyed and brought us death. Christ, the last Adam, obeyed and brought us life.

- The Old Testament shows sin in all its dimensions. Christ brings salvation in all its dimensions.

- The covenant with Israel was made through Moses at Mount Sinai, sealed with the sacrificial blood of animals, and called for obedience to the law. The new covenant was made through Christ, sealed with the blood of his self-sacrifice, and calls for the obedience of faith through the Holy Spirit.

- In the Old Testament nobody could go into the presence of God in the holiest place in the temple except the high priest once a year on the Day of Atonement. Dramatically, at the moment of Christ's death, the curtain in the temple was torn in two from top to bottom, for Christ's own sacrifice has opened the way for us to enter into God's presence.

- In the Old Testament God redeemed one nation, Israel, and other nations were not included yet in the people of God. In Christ, God extends redemption to all nations, and Gentiles are included in God's family.

- The Old Testament story takes place primarily in one land, promised and given to one people. Christ sends his disciples to take the good news to the ends of the earth and to all peoples (as the Old Testament itself promised).

So if we are preaching an Old Testament text in which we read about some sin or failure (there are plenty!), we can point to the salvation that Christ alone brings. If we are teaching on a text in which we see restrictions or limitations that we know were lifted or abolished by Christ, we can point that out. If our text focuses on something that affected only Israel in their land, we can draw attention to the longer biblical story that opens out to all nations and the whole earth.

However, as before, we need to be careful in how we handle apparent contrasts and differences. We should not simply paint a dark and negative view of the Old Testament in order to make the gospel shine brightly. That is a wrong kind of contrast.

Here are some things that do make a significant difference.

History Makes a Difference

The main reason for the difference and contrast between the Old and the New Testaments is the historical movement of the great story of God's redeeming work. From the earlier to the later parts of the story, things move on and change. So what was accepted by God at one stage was no longer the right way to behave later on. But this does not mean there is a *contradiction* between Old and New. Rather there is development and progress as God reveals more about himself and continues to act, save, judge, and teach in many different ways across many generations.

There are very substantial changes and contrasts between what I am now as an adult and what I was as a child. There are things that were right and good in those early years which would not be so now. There are things I could not do then that I can do now, and things that I was sometimes allowed to do then that would be out of place now. But that does not mean that my adulthood is a *contradiction* of my childhood or somehow cancels it out as of no importance at all. Those early years were an important time of learning and growth, an essential *preparation* for who I became as an adult. They are part of the single long story of my whole life (so far).

That's why it is so important to help people see that the Bible as a whole is one continuous story (like a lifetime, only many times longer!). We need to remember those symbols in Chapter 2. Of course there are differences between what we read in Stage 3 and where we are now in Stage 5. But that is precisely because they are *stages*. God is the living God of history, and he did not do everything all at the same time or reveal everything all at once.

Christ Makes the Difference

In between Stage 3 and Stage 5, of course, stands Stage 4 — the gospel stories about Jesus Christ. And *that* is what makes all the difference. All that God promised in the Old Testament has been, or will be, fulfilled through Christ. Many things that were connected in some way to the original form of those promises in the Old Testament have changed because Christ has come. It is Christ who has made the difference. It is Christ who has caused the contrast between the Old and the New Testaments.

That means that when we observe something in the Old Testament that we now know has changed, or when the Old Testament commands something that we no longer practise, or when we notice a strong contrast between what the Israelites were commanded or allowed to do and how we as Christians behave — we should ask the vital question: "What is it about *Christ* (who he was and what he did) that has made this difference or caused this contrast?"

We should not just shrug our shoulders and say, "Oh well, all that stuff is way back in the Old Testament, and the Old Testament just doesn't apply to us any more, so forget it." No, we look for the *biblical and theological reasons* for the change. Let's look at some examples, starting with one that should be obvious and familiar.

Example: Sacrifice

Do we as Christians take a lamb along to the place of worship, find a priest who will help us sacrifice the animal after confessing our sins over its head, and then pour the life-blood on an altar? No, of course not. Yet the Old Testament Israelites did that for centuries. There are laws commanding it in the Old Testament which we do not obey. What has made the difference? We know the answer because the New Testament spells this contrast out very clearly in many places and especially in Hebrews. Jesus himself made the ultimate sacrifice of himself, bearing our sins in his own body on the cross. His blood has made perfect atonement for the sins of the whole world. And through Christ we have access into the presence of God without the need for a sacrificing priest, altar, or temple. Indeed Christ himself *is* that temple, the dwelling place of God with us. So the stark *contrast* between what the Old Testament Israelites were *commanded* to do and what we are *forbidden* to do is explained because of *what Christ did*. So if we are preaching about those Old Testament sacrifices, we will have to show how they prepared the way for the sacrifice of Christ and help us to understand its meaning.

Example: Food

Then what about food? Do we as Christians take great care to avoid all the foods deemed unclean in Leviticus (especially pork), and make sure we never mix milk and meat products? Most of us never even bother to think about those "clean/unclean" distinctions in the Old Testament law any more.[2] But why not? Many people, if asked, would probably say, "Because they are in the Old Testament." But that's not a good enough answer. The command "Do not commit adultery" also comes in the Old Testament, but we wouldn't say that that means it doesn't apply any more. No, we need to ask, "What difference has *Christ* made to the food laws, to produce such a contrast between then and now?"

To answer that question, we have to ask another: "What was the point of the clean/unclean distinction in the first place?" The answer is given in **Leviticus 20:25–26**. It was symbolic. It was a constant reminder to Israel that God had made a distinction between them as his own covenant people and all the rest of the nations—at that point in history. Every time they cooked a meal they were reminded that they were called to be different from the nations around them. In the Old Testament era the distinction between Jews and Gentiles was fundamental to God's purpose since he was bringing salvation to the whole world *through* Israel.

But Christ, the Messiah of Israel, brought salvation for *all* the world, fulfilling God's promise to Abraham. Therefore, *in Christ* that distinction between Jews and Gentiles has been abolished. In Christ, God has made us both together into one new humanity, as Paul explains (Gal 3; Eph 2–3). So, since the distinction between Jews and Gentiles in the Old Testament era has been abolished in Christ, the law that symbolized that distinction is similarly abolished. This is what God had to teach Peter in his vision to prepare him to be willing to go to the home of Gentile Cornelius and preach the gospel to his household also (Acts 10).

---

2. Jewish people who have come to accept and believe in Jesus as Messiah, Lord, and Saviour (Messianic Jews) usually do in fact choose to follow the food laws in the Old Testament on the grounds that it is part of their Jewish cultural heritage, and they choose to live as Jews while worshipping Jesus. But for most Messianic Jews their observance of the food laws is a matter of freely chosen cultural identification with their own people, not one of obligation *under* the law.

Example: Violence, vengeance, and cursing

This is harder, for sure. One of the biggest contrasts most of us feel between the Old and New Testaments is the way there is violence, vengeance, and cursing in the Old, whereas these things are forbidden in the New. That is true, but we need to be careful again not to dismiss the Old Testament outright.[3]

First of all, we need to remember that Stage 3 of the Bible story involved the land and nation of Israel who, though they were God's covenant people, were still very sinful themselves and lived in the midst of a fallen world of nations in which conflict and wars were as common then as they are today. God did not save the world from up in heaven. He got involved in the real world, and the real world is a nasty place. The Old Testament does not polish up the story but tells it as it was.

And what difference has Christ made? Christ won the ultimate battle against sin and evil by absorbing and defeating it at the cross. And the people of God in Christ are no longer a single nation cultivating and defending a single land but a multinational community without territorial borders. The church crosses all boundaries and we are called by the Prince of Peace to be peacemakers and agents of reconciliation in the world through Christ—not to warfare and conquest.

Second, we should remember that the Israelites believed that God was a God of justice. God repeatedly says that he will put down the wicked oppressors and rescue and help the poor and needy. The Israelites had experienced God doing this for them in the exodus and many events after that. So we need to put the prayers about vengeance and the cursing of enemies into that context. They were appealing to God to do what God said he *would* do to the wicked—only do it soon, please.

And what difference did Christ make? He took the ultimate curse of God upon himself, suffering in our place the full weight of God's just judgment. So although he calls us still to hunger and thirst for justice and for God's will to be done on earth as it is in heaven, our way must now be the way of the cross, the way of suffering and forgiving love. We are to bless, and not curse; to renounce vengeance and overcome evil with good; to forgive as God in Christ has forgiven us.

---

3. I have wrestled with this problem more fully in my book *The God I Don't Understand: Reflections on Tough Questions of Faith* (Grand Rapids, MI: Zondervan, 2009). We will also think about this issue a bit more in chapter 14 in relation to the cursing psalms.

So, we must teach the Old Testament in a way that properly shows where the gospel of Christ and the way of Christ have made a difference and caused contrasts like the ones noted above. But we should not do it in a way that denounces or denigrates the Old Testament itself. Rather, we should show how, in the great flow of the Bible story, Christ has made the difference — and we now live in response to all that he accomplished and taught at Stage 4.

MAKING LINKS WITH CHRIST THROUGH THE RESPONSE THE TEXT CALLS FOR

"We live in response," I just said. Yes, and so did the Old Testament Israelites. The life of God's people (in Old or New Testament eras) is always lived in response to what God has done and what God has said. That is why our preaching of God's word from any part of the Bible should be aimed at people's hearts and wills — seeking a response. So when we study any passage of Scripture in order to preach it, we should be asking, "What response did this text call for at the time? What did the writer or speaker of these words expect his readers or hearers to do? What was the *aim* of this text when it was written and then read among God's people?" And then later we will go on to ask, "What response do I want to seek from my hearers as I *preach* this text in today's world — a response that in some way matches the aim of the text itself?" It is not enough to simply explain the text. It is not enough even to make a link of some kind to Christ. There has to be a "So what?" moment. God's word calls for response, and part of our task in preaching and teaching is to make that unavoidably clear.

When I'm preaching from the Old Testament, I often find that the kind of response the text calls for is one that can connect very well with Christian believers. This is hardly surprising since, after all, the Old Testament story is part of our story. We belong to the same people of Abraham, through Christ. We worship the same living God. We are called to the same mission — to serve God in the world, to bear witness among the nations, and to live and walk in the way of the Lord. So when the Old Testament Scriptures spoke to the Israelites words of encouragement, blessing, promise, and hope, or words of command and exhortation, or words of rebuke, challenge, and judgment — we can "listen in," knowing that the same God speaks to us in the same ways.

But of course, I always need to remember that I am *not* preaching to Old Testament Israelites, even if the text I'm preaching from was first spoken or written to them. I am preaching to people who know the Lord Jesus Christ (assuming this is a sermon to Christians—and even if it is not, I would be calling people evangelistically to respond in faith to Christ). I am preaching from words written in Stage 3 to people who live in Stage 5, and I must not ignore Stage 4. I need to call people to respond to God, as the Old Testament did; but I must do it in relation to what God has done through Christ. What does that mean? Here is an example.

Example

I love preaching **Exodus 19:1–6**. God was speaking to the Israelites after he had brought them out of Egypt to Mount Sinai. He tells them what he wants them to be for him in the world—a priestly and a holy people in the midst of the nations. And he tells them how they can be such a people—through keeping God's covenant and obeying him. Now all of those points can be applied to Christians. In fact Peter does exactly that in 1 Peter 2:9–12. So we can explore, in preaching, what it meant for Israel to be "holy" (perhaps referring to Lev 19) and to obey God's law, and how that was supposed to shape their life as a society to be a witness to the nations. They would be "priestly" in bringing the knowledge of God to the nations (just as Israel's priests were to teach God's law to the rest of the people). And they would be "priestly" in being the means by which God would draw the nations to himself (just as Israel's priests brought people back into fellowship with God through their sacrifices). And then we can apply these thoughts to how Christians are supposed to live such distinctive ("holy") lives among the nations that God becomes known to the world and the world is brought to God (1 Pet 2:12). All that is very missional, very responsive, very practical, very preachable.

But here's the key moment. What did God actually say *first of all* to the Israelites in Exodus 19:4? He pointed to *his own initiative of saving grace* in redeeming the Israelites out of slavery in Egypt. "You have seen what I have done," God says. And indeed they had. It was only three months earlier that they had been slaves—suffering oppression, exploitation, and state-sponsored genocide. But now they were free. God had saved them. *And it is on that foundation* that God calls for their response. Obedience to God's law was to be motivated by experience of God's saving grace.

Where does that point us? It points us directly to Christ and to that "departure [*exodus*], which he was … to bring to fulfilment in Jerusalem" (as Luke says in his account of Jesus in conversation with Moses and Elijah at his transfiguration, Luke 9:31). And so I make the link between the Old Testament exodus and Christ as our Redeemer and use it to talk about the response that the text calls for—holiness and obedience to God. We too are called to be holy and to live in a way that pleases and honours God (notice how Peter uses Exod 19:3–6 in 1 Pet 2:9–12). But, like Israel, we must put all our obedience in the context of God's redeeming grace, and for Christians, that sends us to Christ. It's as if God were to point to the cross of Christ and say, "You have seen what I have done. Now then, how will you live in response to what I have done for you?" Our response then becomes Christ-centred and gospel-motivated.

Of course, there are many other responses that biblical texts call for than just obedience. In the Old Testament we find that God speaks through the stories, the laws, the prophets, the psalms, the wise men and women. And all kinds of responses are expected: trust, perseverance, courage, hope, joy, grief, repentance, wise living, or some specific act of obedience. And usually we will find that there are echoes of those very same responses called for in the preaching of Jesus in the Gospels and in the rest of the New Testament. We can make those links, and keep them anchored in Christ and motivated by the grace of the gospel itself.

MAKING LINKS WITH CHRIST THROUGH THE GOSPEL OF GRACE

I come to this point last not because it's the least important, but rather because it's the most important. This is the foundation of all that has been said above. Faithful biblical teaching should, and will, produce a response, as we've just been saying. And people's response should, through the presence and work of the Holy Spirit, reflect the response that the biblical text itself was seeking to produce. We want people to think, feel, and act in ways that are in line with what God says in his word in whatever passage we are opening up for them in our preaching.

But responding to God's word can (and should) create a crisis. It is the crisis of "How can I?"

- How can I live in the way God wants?
- How can I repent when I know I don't want to?
- How can I trust God and his promises and step out in faith?

- How can I praise and thank God when life is so tough and I feel so abandoned?

- How can I be faithful to God in the world, surrounded by all the gods and idols of the people around me?

- How can I bear witness to God when I'm just plain scared?

- How can I seek justice and peace in the world when evil is so powerful and I feel so small and weak?

- How can I live with this suffering when God seems so far away?

- How can I be a person of integrity and truth living in a world that forces people into corruption in order just to survive?

- How can I believe in the sovereignty of God in my contemporary world when so much seems out of line with his will?

- How can I find satisfaction in life and work when it all ends in death anyway?

All of these are questions that people in the Old Testament wrestled with too. And all of them arose out of the response that the word of God challenged them to make, in one way or another. Several times the Old Testament recognizes that the most honest answer to many of those questions is simply, "I just can't." That's exactly the response that we hear from Moses, Gideon, and Jeremiah when God called them to serve him. And it's what Joshua told the people of Israel when they enthusiastically said that they *would* serve the LORD God only. With no tact or flattery whatsoever, Joshua bluntly told them, "You are not able to serve the LORD" (Josh 24:19). Similarly, both God and Moses warned the Israelites that they would fail to do all that God wanted, and they would end up under his judgment (Deut 29:22–28; 31:20–21, 24–29).

So the hard fact is that the word of God, on the one hand, drives us to see the response we *ought* to make, but on the other hand, also tells us ruthlessly that we will *fail* to make that response well, or fully, or even at all.

And if our preaching is being faithful to God's word, especially in preaching and teaching the Old Testament, it ought to produce that *double* effect.

- Our preaching should hold up before people very clearly what God expects, what God longs for, what God is seeking from us as his people. This is the way God *wants* us to live. These are God's standards. And we should give people every possible encouragement to respond positively. We appeal on God's behalf, calling people to love him and obey him with all their heart and soul.

- And yet, and yet ... Deep down we know our own weakness and failure only too well, and even if our hearts respond with a willing "Amen!" to what the Bible tells us, we know that our wills and our actions will not always follow. We know that we fail, "through weakness, through negligence and through our own deliberate fault" (as the Anglican prayer of confession puts it). And our preaching needs to acknowledge that fact.

What does the preacher do then?

Well, you can always shout louder, and many preachers do! You can just go on hammering people with what they should and shouldn't do. You can load them with guilt and try to build up their courage. You can exhort, hassle, warn, and threaten. But none of those things will solve the problem of "I just can't." Because that kind of preaching is really just legalism or moralism. It is just preaching all the rules and duties, all the things that Christians are supposed to do and not to do. Or it is just telling people all the time to try harder, do better, do more, love more, care more, give more (especially).

No, when our preaching holds out the response that God wants but also shows how far short we all fall from that (including the preacher), that is when we *must* preach Christ. Faithful preaching of the Bible (and especially of the Old Testament) should produce *a Christ-shaped vacuum*—a sense of the desperate need for the grace and power of God that comes only from the gospel. For that reason, preaching from the Old Testament should be gospel-centred preaching—*not* because it is always evangelistic but because it always leads us to see that the gospel of the saving grace of God through Jesus Christ is the very heartbeat, centre, point, and purpose of the whole Bible from beginning to end. This is what the whole Bible story is ultimately *for*.

This does not mean that once we have made the link with Christ and the grace of the gospel, we then just let people off the hook of the response they need to make to the word of God. Far from it. It is the grace of the gospel that then *generates* the right response — of faith, repentance, or obedience — in practice. That is why Paul said that his whole life's work was aimed at producing "the obedience of faith ... among all the nations" (Rom 1:5 ESV). He wanted to bring people to faith in Christ first, through the gospel and the preaching of the Scriptures (the Old Testament, remember). But then *he wanted those who had come to faith to live it out* through the power of the Spirit living within them, in transformed lives that were the proof and the fruit of gospel faith.

QUESTIONS AND EXERCISES

1. If you have notes of sermons that you have preached or studies you have taught in the past on Old Testament texts, get them out and read them again. Did you make a link with Christ in any of the ways mentioned above? Did you link the text in some way with the gospel of grace? If not, what revisions might you want to make if you were to preach or teach any of them again?

2. Look at the chart in section 3. Select Bible texts that would illustrate each of the boxes: the Old Testament texts in the left-hand column and the New Testament texts in the right-hand one.

3. Prepare a sermon or study, or a series of sermons or studies, on any of the following texts:

   - Deuteronomy 6:1–9
   - Deuteronomy 30:11–20
   - 1 Samuel 3
   - Isaiah 52:7–10
   - Hosea 6:1–16

   Your aim is to understand, explain, and apply the text itself. But consider also how you might make a link between the text and Christ in any of the ways mentioned in this chapter.

PART 2

HOW CAN WE PREACH AND TEACH FROM THE OLD TESTAMENT?

CHAPTER 6

God's Story and
Our Stories

E verybody loves a good story. Telling stories is part of human
life from a very early age. Children love hearing stories long
before they are able to read them for themselves. Stories
are interesting and exciting—and we remember them long after
we've forgotten other things. Many preachers know this very
well and spend most of their sermons telling stories. The only
trouble is that often the stories preachers tell are their own (or
plucked out of some book of "sermon illustrations"), when the
Bible itself—the book God has given us—is one big story in itself
and full of smaller stories inside. Many congregations survive on
a thin diet of "the preacher's stories" and never enjoy the wonderful banquet of Bible stories—except perhaps when they were
children, and then it was only the safe and sanitized few stories
that were "suitable."

THE STORY GOD HAS GIVEN US

In the Bible God has told us one *single big story* that spans the
whole of space and time. That single big story is broken up into
several *mega-stories* that take up whole chunks of history. And each
of those mega-stories is constructed out of many *small stories*—the
ones we usually have in mind when we talk about "Bible stories."
Let's think for a moment about all three levels of story in the
Bible, for it will be important later. Check out Appendix 1 for the
more detailed content.

The Single Big Story of the Bible

This can be told very quickly. Look again at the six symbols in chapter 2. They show us the whole Bible on the back of an envelope.

1. God created the world and all that is in it, including the human race, made in God's image.

2. We rebelled against God and threw the world into chaos and evil.

3. God promised Abraham that he would reverse that and bring blessing and salvation to the world through his people, Old Testament Israel, even though they themselves sinned and failed.

4. God kept his promise through his Son, Jesus Christ, who dealt with sin and evil through his death and resurrection.

5. Ever since then, those who are Jesus' followers have been reaching out, in the power of the Holy Spirit, to bring the good news of salvation to peoples all over the world.

6. Jesus Christ will return, and after final judgment and the destruction of all that is evil, God will live forever with his redeemed people from all nations in the new creation.

Sometimes this is called the biblical *metanarrative*. This means that it is the narrative that stands above all the other stories in the Bible and includes them within itself. It is the overarching sweep of the Bible's whole message. And you can see that it has a beginning (creation) and an ending (new creation, which is really a new beginning). And you can also see that right at its centre, as the key to the whole story, is the Lord Jesus Christ and what God has done through him.

This great biblical metanarrative, or single big story, answers the fundamental questions that all human beings ask:

- What is this world we live in?

- Who are we, and what does it mean to be human?

- What has gone wrong with everything, and why are we in the mess we are in?

- What is the solution to all the "wrongness" in the world and ourselves?

- Where will it all end, and is there any hope for the future?

Of course, the answers the Bible gives to those questions by telling its single big story are the essence of our Christian faith. Our Christian "worldview," and all our Christian doctrine and theology, really flow from the Bible's great big story. All the key elements of what we believe as Christians are drawn from this grand universal narrative. Think of all the major Christian doctrines and you will see how they can all be found along this great story line: the doctrines of God, creation, humanity, sin, salvation, Christology, the doctrine of the Holy Spirit, ecclesiology, mission, eschatology. These are not abstract philosophical beliefs. They summarize the meaning of all the great moments in the biblical story. We need to have a connected understanding of our faith, a consistent worldview. And for that we need to grasp the Bible story as a whole—a single big story.

The Mega-Stories within the Bible

These are the blocks of narrative that describe major phases within the overarching whole Bible story. We can see several large narrative blocks in the Old Testament. For example:

- There is the span from God's promise to Abraham through to the establishment of the kingdom of David.

- Then there is the span from Solomon to the exile.

- Then comes the span from the return from exile to the coming of Christ.

These happen to be the three large divisions that Matthew sees when he comments on his genealogy of Jesus (Matt 1:1–17).

And then, within those mega-blocks, there are large narrative sections that "hang together," such as the life of Abraham, or the exodus and wilderness period, or the settlement in the land and period of the judges, or the period from the birth of Jesus to the arrival of Paul in Rome (spanning Luke's two volumes—his gospel and the book of Acts), and so on. Sometimes a whole book is devoted to a single great period of the Bible's history—such as Joshua or Acts.

We need to know the broad outlines of these mega-stories within the Bible. Often they carry a message on a large scale, which they emphasize through all the smaller stories. For example:

- The predominant message of the mega-story from Abraham through to David is that God keeps his promises in spite of many obstacles along the way. God is faithful. We need to keep that message in mind when we read any of the smaller stories within that big one.

- The predominant message from Solomon to the exile is that God is patient with the sinful generations of Israel over many centuries. In all that time they get worse and worse in rejecting God and God's commands—but in the end God acts in justified judgment. Israel's own sin results in Israel's near destruction. God is just.

When we grasp the broad message of these mega-stories, it helps us read the small stories from the right perspective in their context.

The Small Stories

There are hundreds of episodes that happen within those larger narratives. Each one is a story in itself, but each one is linked with the others in making up the larger whole. There can be many small stories within a narrative (a mega-story). This may be hard to translate in some languages, but in English we could distinguish the three levels like this (from smaller to larger):

- *Stories:* the smaller, individual stories. Each of these describes some event that involves one or a few major characters and a short span of time.

- *Narratives:* the larger narrative blocks (mega-stories), made up of many smaller stories, describing a significant distinct period over a longer span of time.

- *The metanarrative:* the grand overarching shape of the whole Bible, providing its essential message and truth.

It is important to think of all three levels when we come to preach or teach from Bible stories. Usually, of course, you would be preaching from one of the smaller Bible stories. But you need to see your one story (your sermon or lesson text) in the context of the longer narrative that it is part of (which might be the whole book of the Bible it is in). You should not just treat one story in isolation and pull a few moral lessons from it. If you do nothing more than make a few points from a single story and do not see it in its wider context, you might actually miss the whole point of the story. You have not thought about the reason why the biblical author included that story at that point in his wider narrative. You might even be in danger of distorting what the author wanted to say by focusing on *incidental* things in the story and not interpreting it in the light of its *whole context.* I'll explain more about this below. But for now, here's the key point:

Don't read a Bible story without thinking of the wider narrative it is part of and its place within the whole Bible big story. Really, this is no different from what you already know about all Bible interpretation: *Read every text in its context.* All we are doing here is expanding that from thinking about a verse, or short passage, to Bible stories. Do the same thing. Read in context.

A WORLD OF STORIES

So the Bible itself is a story and contains many stories. But, of course, it is not the only book in the world that does so. Stories are found everywhere, in all cultures—some of them written down, but many of them remembered and told orally. Stories are a very important part of human life. Let's think about what stories do and how they work. That will help us appreciate all the more why God chose to make his book, the Bible, one big story full of many stories. And that, in turn, will help us realize how important it is to include the Bible stories in our preaching and teaching plans. I hope, at least, that it will inspire you to use the Bible stories in your preaching and teaching and not just your own or other people's stories!

What Do Stories Do?

Here are five things that stories in general do in human society. When we've thought about these five points, we will see that each of them also applies to the function of stories within the Bible.

1. *Through stories we tell each other who we are.* In the course of my work, I get introduced to many different audiences, in churches, colleges, and public meetings. The person who introduces me always asks me something about "my story." So, depending on the time available, I talk about what has happened in my life at key points. That's who I am. Of course, as a human person made in God's image I am more than just my life story. But it's the telling of that story (even a tiny bit of it) that helps people know me — even if they've never met me before. And of course, those who know me best are those who have shared some or most of that story with me — family and long-term friends. Stories are essential to personal identity. That's why God gave us the wonderful gift of memory. How often friends and family say, "Do you remember when …?" — and tell a shared story again. That's also why it is such a deep personal tragedy when someone loses their memory through dementia or injury. It is as if they have lost their identity, lost what made them who they are — their story. For all of us, life itself is a story.

2. *Through stories we hold our communities together.* People who have been bound together by a common experience will tell stories that keep that memory alive. The stories say, "This is who we are because this is what happened to us." These stories may be very ancient or very recent. It doesn't really matter — these are the shared stories that everybody knows. I grew up in Northern Ireland. The Protestant community there tells again and again the stories of the victories of King William III over the Catholic forces of James II in 1689–90, celebrating them annually in colourful and noisy parades. They have done it for over three hundred years. The stories are part of their identity.

   Communities that have shared a tragedy will tell their own stories of that time and bond together around that common experience. It may be a natural disaster, a time of economic decline and loss, or war-time devastation. The stories shape the cultural memory of the community. And if you have a part in that story—a story of your own that connects to the community story—then you belong. People know what you are talking about when you tell your story.

3. *Through stories we express and pass on moral values.* What stories do parents tell their children in your country? Of course, many children's stories are just for amusement and entertainment. But often stories pack a message. They provide examples of behaviour that will produce good results and behaviour that will end in tears or worse. Stories about animals are popular. Some animals are good and heroic. Some are deceitful, wily, and come to a nasty end. Some are naughty but become good in the end. But through hearing those stories repeatedly, children learn about life and about what kind of behaviour is good to imitate and what to avoid. Stories are the way societies pass on their values over many generations.

4. *Through stories we cope with the present and hope for a better future.* The most powerful stories in any culture are those that help to give some meaning to why things are the way they are in the present—particularly when the present is painful (as was the experience of slavery, for example). At the same time, some stories (like songs) can keep alive the hope of a better future. Stories can imagine a new reality. Stories can create a new world that we can look forward to.

5. *Through stories we can expose and challenge things that are wrong.* In countries where there is freedom of speech in the press and media, one of the most powerful ways to challenge corruption and wrongdoing in society is by telling personal stories. A newspaper or a TV documentary will tell the story of an individual who has suffered injustice at the hands of "the system." The story will get retold in other media and be talked about widely. It may "go viral" on the Internet. The story may be shocking. It may contradict people's assumptions about the authorities. The story, with its human interest, will be more powerful than any number

of enquiries, reports, and speeches by politicians. We remember that story far longer than the political debate.[4]

All of the above points are true about what stories can do in human culture in general. You could probably add other points as you think about the stories that are common or currently in the news in your country. But what I want to stress right here is that *the stories in the Bible have the same sorts of functions and power.* The following five points show how the Bible does all the things mentioned in the five points above.

1. How do we know who Abraham was, or David, Hannah and Elisha, or even Jesus? Through their stories. Their identity and character are revealed in the Bible stories about them—few or many.

2. What held the people of Israel together over thousands of years? It was the constant retelling of their core stories from their Scriptures. Christians too are defined as a community (even in their many different cultures) by the central gospel story of Jesus of Nazareth and what happened to him in his birth, life, death, and resurrection. That story, and the stories within that story, tell us who we are as the community of Christ-followers.

3. How did Israel know what their God YHWH was like and how they could live in a way that would please him? By telling the stories of God in action—particularly in the story of the exodus and all that followed it. If YHWH was the God who acted in love, compassion, justice, as well as in rejection of lies and evil, then so should his people. The stories of the Old Testament were a massive project in the moral education of a whole culture. The message was: "This is who we are and this is how we behave, because this is our story."

4. And when Israel was under the hammer, how did they sustain hope? By retelling the stories of God redeeming them in the past out of Egypt and then knowing that God could

---

4. The single photo and then the family story of little three-year-old Aylan Kurdi, drowned off the coast of Turkey, changed the whole debate in the media and politics in Europe about the refugee crisis from the Middle East.

do the same again in the future—and by painting word pictures of what that future would look like, in God's time.

5.When King David needed to be challenged over his adultery with Bathsheba and murder of Uriah, what did the prophet Nathan do? He told David a story—which David probably thought was a judicial case—and let David judge himself. The story trapped David into self-condemnation. And if we still need any convincing about the power of stories, just think of the parables of Jesus. So many of them are surprising and shocking—and exposed wrong thinking and attitudes. And we remember them far better than if Jesus had started making political speeches.

So, when we preach Bible stories, they are not "*just Bible stories*"—handy little pieces of local interest, like a tourist attraction, from which we can point out a few superficial lessons. They are powerful tools in the hands of God who gave them to us. Stories do a lot of work in our hearts and minds. God knows that. So let's preach and teach the stories God has given us and let them do the work God intends.

What Makes Stories Work?

Can we pick out what it is about stories that makes them work in those ways? If we can do that, it will help us when we come to handle the stories of the Old Testament. If we know how stories in general do their work, we can "work with them" when preaching or teaching from Bible stories. Here are some ways in which stories are active and dynamic, showing why they work so well. The points below are marks of *good* stories—by which I do not mean stories about good people but stories that are well constructed and that stand the test of time. Such stories last for generations. In that sense, the reason why the Bible stories are so well known among cultures that have been impacted by the Christian faith is not only because they are in the Bible, but also because they are such powerfully "good" stories—stories that are very memorable and that go on "doing their work" in our minds and hearts again and again.

The following points are true of stories in general. In the next chapter we shall see some examples from Old Testament stories.

A Good Story Engages Our *Interest and Imagination*

Every preacher knows this instinctively. If the congregation seems a bit unresponsive to your sermon—maybe looking a bit bored—if you start to tell a story, even before you get past the first line or two, you can see the interest rising. People want to hear what happened, and then what happened next, and then how it finished. Maybe that's why some preachers do little else but tell stories—it's the only way they know to keep their listeners interested since they have so little else to say. I've proved this in classrooms too. When I've been teaching for a while, sometimes I stop abruptly and say, "You know, something very strange happened while I was on my journey here today." Immediately people look up and take an interest. They want to know what happened. They want to hear the story. I usually then disappoint them by saying, "Actually, nothing happened. But I notice how interested you all became when you *thought* I was going to tell you a story. That shows how powerful stories are in engaging attention. That's why God gave us so many stories in the Bible. God knows how to get our attention."

Why does a good story keep us interested? Because it engages our imagination. And imagination is one of the greatest gifts God has given to human beings. We have the amazing ability to create in our minds imaginary alternative realities that are utterly different from where we actually are at any moment. Right now, in my mind, I can be somewhere else. I can imagine myself in some other part of the world and what I might be doing there. Here I am, swimming in the sea off the coast of Africa. Or I can imagine being in some situation in the historical past and what it was like back then. Here I am beside Jeremiah in besieged Jerusalem. I can imagine some imaginary future, and what that will be like—whether something bad or good. I can imagine conversations I never had or never will have with people I know well or never knew at all. I can imagine great dreams for the future—not just for myself but even for my country or the human race. That kind of imagination gets called "vision."

Good stories make us live "inside" them, in our imagination. We see, hear, and experience in our imagination what the storyteller describes. And so we are desperate to know what happens next and how things will turn out. We enter into the world of the story—even if it is fiction (like the parables of Jesus)—and imagine ourselves there.

A Good Story Has an Intriguing *Plot*

The plot is what drives any story forward. It is the events that happen, in some kind of sequence. The sequence may not be straightforward ("this happened, and then this happened next"). A good storyteller may take you backwards and forwards in time. But ultimately, the plot must have a beginning point. Then it will take you through one or more complications, problems, and challenges, describing the ways the people in the story tried to solve those problems. Eventually the plot will bring you to a conclusion—whether in a good way or not.

By "intriguing," I mean that a good plot will have things that keep the reader or listener wondering and curious. There will be *surprises* ("Wow! How on earth did that happen?"). There will be *suspense* ("How can she ever escape from this danger or threat?"). There will be *shocks*, sudden and unexpected arrivals, joyful moments, sudden tragedy, things turned upside down, and so on. There may be times when you (the reader or listener) know something that the characters in the story do not know, so you watch in suspense until they discover it. There may be times when the opposite is true, and you only find out much later something that somebody in the story knew all along.

However the writer or storyteller does it, they must keep you "following the plot." And one of the clever things, even about very long stories, is that you can remember the plot and summarize it very briefly.

A Good Story Has Strong *Characters*

By "strong" I don't mean that the main character in a good story has to be a superhero. I mean that, even if the person is weak, physically or in other ways, their character is drawn strongly. Good stories usually have one main character, a few other "supporting" characters, and any number of other people who might play a part in the story but are not given any "colour" or character in themselves.

As we read or listen to a story, we identify with the main characters—either positively or negatively, or sometimes both at different times. Some of the people in a story may be very good, others very evil. But often a good story will show that life is often more ambiguous than that. Real people are not just good guys and bad guys, heroes and villains. And good stories can show good people making wrong choices or bad mistakes, and bad people turning around and doing something noble in the end.

Characters in a story produce "human interest." We find ourselves responding to their thoughts, motives, and actions (whether we know them to be historically real people or completely fictional). We assess and judge them. Maybe we admire or despise them. We think, "Would I have done that?" We puzzle over the dilemmas and challenges that the characters in the story face, and take an interest in how they overcome them (or don't), and why. We want to know how it all turns out for them in the end.

A Good Story Leaves *Gaps* for Our Curiosity

Why was that character in that place at that time? The storyteller may not tell us and leave us to guess. What happened between this event and that later one, and was one the cause of the other? The storyteller might not tell us and may let us fill it in for ourselves. Did that character know the truth at that point in the story? We are not told. We are left wondering and guessing: What was going on in the mind of the main character when they did that terrible/wonderful thing?

A good story does not tell you everything but leaves gaps for your own imagination to fill. Not only does that make you engage with the story in the act of wondering "What? Why? How?" but it also makes the story more memorable. It affects you more when you've had to do some of the work yourself. A really good story is "interactive"—between the storyteller or writer and the reader or listener.

A Good Story Makes the Reader or Listener the *Judge*

Some stories end by telling us what we should think about what happened in the story—explaining its meaning for us. Jesus did that with his story about the sower and the four kinds of soil. But that is rare. The best-told stories leave us to judge for ourselves on the basis of all we have read or heard. That's why some of Jesus' parables ended with "Whoever has ears to hear, let him hear"—that is, "Think about what I've just told you and make your own mind up."

So good stories not only interest and entertain us, but they also challenge us to make a response of some kind. The story may raise all kinds of moral issues as the characters in the story work their way through the plot. We, the readers, are called to evaluate their choices, actions, and motives. And the story may well challenge our own values and assumptions and make us see things differently.

Before we move on in the next chapter to think how all this applies to the stories in the Old Testament, take a moment to think about the stories that are well known in your country or culture—perhaps some of the books that have been written, or movies that everybody has seen, or the great religious epics, perhaps, or tales of glorious ancestors. Why are they so enduring? Why do they get included in people's education? Can you see if any of the above points are true about them, in the way they work in the minds, hearts, and values of people in your culture?

What Makes Stories "True"?

There is one other point we need to mention before moving to the Bible. You might be thinking at this moment, "Yes, OK. This is all very interesting about stories in general. But the Bible is not just 'stories'—it is history. It is the *true* story of God and Israel in the Old Testament, and of Jesus and the church in the New Testament." And of course you are right, and I agree with you completely.

But there is no contradiction between affirming that the Bible gives us *reliable historical truth* (what happened; what God did in history) and observing that it gives us that historical truth in the form of *very well-crafted stories that are memorable and powerful.* In other words, when I say that we need to understand and appreciate the *form* of the historical texts in the Old Testament, and how they work as stories (which we do need to do in order to preach and teach them well), I am *not* saying that they are "made-up stories" with no historical facts. There is no reason why they cannot be *both* based on historical facts *and* told in a skilful way that engages our imagination and interest in all the ways mentioned above (and below, when we come to the Old Testament stories). Personally, I am convinced that they are both.

But there is one more point to make here. When we are talking about the "truth of the Bible," it means much more than just historical facts. Let's think of an Old Testament story for a moment. What about David and Goliath? What is "the truth" of that story? Well, at one level of course we would want to say that it truly records an event that happened in the history of Israel and the life of David. So we might say, "I believe that this is a true story. This is what actually happened." Fine. I agree.

But is that all you would preach from the text? Of course not! You know very well that the writer of the story wants to tell us much more than a mere historical fact: "Goliath was a very big man, but the boy David killed him, and the Philistines ran away. Hurrah!" That's the truth. But the truth of the story goes much further. What truth does it tell about *God?* What truth does it tell about *God and Israel?* What truth does it tell about *God and David?* Indeed, the writer has given us a clue to that deeper truth of the story in what David said to Goliath before he shot his stone: "This day the LORD will deliver you into my hands ... and *the whole world will know that there is a God in Israel*" (1 Sam 17:46; my italics). When you preach the truth of the story, you will be looking for what it *meant* (for Israel), and what it *means* (for us)—not just the fact that it happened.

So when we are dealing with Old Testament historical narratives, we can see that *part* of the truth in them is the historical facts they record—but that is not the *whole* of their truth. We need to look deeper and ask questions about why the narrator included the story and told it in that way. What truth is embedded in the story that goes beyond the facts alone?

QUESTIONS AND EXERCISES

1. Discuss one or two of the most famous stories that are commonly told within your country or culture. In what ways can you see that the points made in this chapter apply to them?

2. What do those stories *do* in the minds of people (from childhood) in your culture?

3. What stories are told in your country or culture that help to hold people together?

4. Can you think of stories that are common in your culture that express what your culture admires as good and beneficial or bad and harmful?

5. In preparation for the next chapter, pick any well-known Bible story and begin to think how the points made in section (b) above ("What Makes Stories Work?") apply to that story.

CHAPTER 7

Five Questions to Ask When Preaching and Teaching Old Testament Stories

Let's now turn back to the Bible again. Let's imagine you've been planning your preaching or teaching (I hope you do!) and you think it is time to spend some time in the Old Testament. And you decide to go through one of the historical books for a few weeks. So perhaps you choose a selection of the stories in that book. What steps do you need to take in preparing to preach or teach from each story? Here are five steps that I find helpful:

- When and where?
- What and how?
- Who?
- Why?
- So what?

Let's use the story of **David and Goliath** as a working model to illustrate the questions as we go along. You'll need to have 1 Samuel 17 open in front of you.

WHEN AND WHERE? THE SETTING

Every story has a setting. This may be totally imaginary in the case of myths and legends. But historical narratives are set in a particular time and place, and that background is important in understanding the story and its meaning. We should try to answer the question at three levels.

The Immediate Setting of the Story Itself

Usually this will be in the form of some short description of local detail. We need to know the basic circumstances. In our working model, the narrator gives us the immediate setting in 1 Samuel 17:1–3. There is a war. The Philistines have invaded and attacked the Israelites during the reign of Saul. Battle lines have been drawn up, with the two armies on opposite hills and a valley between. We know from earlier stories that the Philistines were very fierce enemies. So this is a very threatening situation. That's the immediate setting for what follows in the story.

The Wider Setting within One of the Bible's "Mega-Stories"

Every Old Testament story in the historical books comes within a wider narrative. In our working model, the killing of Goliath is one incident in the life of David. And the life of David is part of a broader narrative of the beginning of monarchy in Israel, starting with Saul. So this one *story* is part of the longer *narrative* of how David rose from humble beginnings to become king over all the tribes of Israel. We therefore need to read this story of David and Goliath, not just as an isolated "hero" story (small boy floors big giant! Hurrah!). The world has many stories like that, and if that is the only message you preach from the story ("No matter how big the problem or how small you feel, you can win in the end"), you are seriously under-using the Bible. When we put it in its own setting we see it as part of *God's plan and purpose* for David and then for Israel, and eventually, of course, for the whole world through the Son of David.

The Whole-Bible Setting

When and where does this story take place within the great sweep of the Bible's single big story? It happens in the Old

Testament, that is, before Christ. That makes a difference. It is not telling us how Christians should deal with their "enemies." It happens after Israel has come out of Egypt and settled in the land (so some of God's promises have already been fulfilled). But they have not yet gained the whole of the land, including the city of Jerusalem (so there are promises still to be fulfilled). Similarly, with any story in the Old Testament, think about where it fits in the whole long story.

Checklist

☐ What comes before this story?

☐ What comes after it?

☐ How is the meaning of this story affected by its own immediate surrounding context?

☐ Is it before or after God's promise to Abraham?

☐ Is it before or after the covenant and law given at Mount Sinai through Moses?

☐ Is it before or after Israel settled in the land of Canaan?

☐ Is it before or after the division of the kingdoms after Solomon?

☐ Is it before or after the exile?

Knowing where and when it happened will affect how we understand what happens in the story itself, what the characters in the story do or do not know already, and how they act and react.

Can you see that it really is important that you read your whole Bible again and again and become very familiar with the whole story? You need to know where the stories fit in the whole-Bible big story.

WHAT AND HOW? THE PLOT

Every story has a plot. Something has to *happen*. And something has to *make things happen* in such a way that things actually change from one situation to another. So we need to ask, "*What* happens in this story, and *how* does one thing lead to another?"

If I say or write, "Yesterday I sat in my favourite chair at home," that may be true, but it is not a story just by itself. Nothing happens! But if I say, "Yesterday, I was sitting in my favourite chair at home when suddenly there was a loud banging on my door. When I opened it, a man with torn clothes and blood on his face shouted, 'Come quickly, we need help!'"—then I have begun a story. A peaceful situation has been interrupted. A problem has arisen. There is a challenge, and it could lead to all kinds of complications and dangers—who knows? Immediately you want to know: Who was the man at the door? Why did he have blood on his face? Did I run out to help? What happened next? And so on. A plot has begun.

Of course, every story has a unique plot of its own. But most plots have the following parts in common:

1. An *opening situation*

2. A *problem* (a conflict, complication, or danger)

3. A *process of trying to overcome that problem* (sometimes leading to other problems along the way)—this will usually be the longest part of the story

4. A *climax*, when the problem reaches its worst, but then at last comes...

5. The *resolution*, when the problem is finally dealt with and overcome

6. A *closing situation*[1]

Now look at how the writer of 1 Samuel has "plotted" the story of David and Goliath:

1. *Verses 1–3: The opening situation* (same as the "setting" above). As readers, we expect the next part of the story to describe a battle between the two armies. But...

---

1. If you think about it, the Bible as a single big story follows this broad plot line. We begin with (1) God's good creation. Then comes (2) the fall, and all that sin brings into life on earth. Then comes (3) God's promise to Abraham and the long story of Old Testament Israel until (4) God himself comes in the person of his Son, Jesus Christ, and achieves his climactic victory over evil in the cross and resurrection. This leads to (5) the long period of "already—but not yet" as God's mission through the church brings the resolution that was accomplished by Christ to the ends of the earth. And finally (6) we reach the closing scene—the new creation—which of course is not just the ending of the Bible's long story, but the beginning of a new story that we will not know till we are in it.

2. *Verses 4–11: The problem.* Goliath! This guy is a giant of a man, with armour that makes him more like a tank. If nobody can fight and kill him, it will be back into slavery for the Israelites.

3. *Verses 12–40: The process of trying to overcome the problem.* At this point we see how clever the storyteller is. He weaves into this plot bits of the plot of another story—that of David and his brothers. He describes the conflict between the older brothers—big brave soldiers, but just as scared as the rest—and the kid brother who should be back home with the sheep, not pestering the grown-ups with impudent questions. Will the brothers force David to go home? But David gets taken to Saul. He makes his ridiculous offer to fight Goliath—with God's help. But then another obstacle arises: David can't cope with Saul's armour. So he's going to the fight unarmed—well, except for a sling and stones. Meanwhile, while this part of the plot is being prolonged, the giant is out there swaggering and shouting the whole time!

4. *Verses 41–47: The climax.* Goliath can't believe his eyes! He mocks and threatens David. But David's reply points out what the whole story is about: Goliath is challenging not just the army of Israel, but the God of Israel (as David had already said in v. 26). So the fight belongs to God, and so will its result.

5. *Verses 48–54: The resolution.* David stuns Goliath with his perfectly aimed shot and then kills him. The Israelites chase the Philistines all the way back to where they came from.

6. *Verses 55–58: The closing situation.* Saul is impressed with David's exploit and enquires whose son he is. That is a bit surprising since David had already been a musician in his court (16:14–23). But then, Saul was suffering from some kind of mental/spiritual illness and may not have paid much attention to the family identity of this village guitar-player. Or perhaps he had heard the suspicious story about what had happened at the home of Jesse (16:1–13) and now had even more reason to be wary of David. This lad was a giant slayer, not just a guitar player!

And that closing situation, of course, leads on to the start of a new plot—Saul's persecution of David. That's often the way with Old Testament stories: the resolution of one plot leads to the start of another.

Checklist

So when you work on a Bible story in order to preach or teach it, you need to ask these same questions:

- ☐ *What* happens in the plot of the story?

- ☐ *How* has the storyteller woven it all together so that it reaches a satisfying conclusion?

- ☐ What is the *sequence* of scenes in the story?

- ☐ Can you observe at least some, if not all, of the six *elements of a plot* listed above?

Don't focus on just one small part of the story or one small detail in the descriptions. It is very easy to get obsessed about side issues that puzzle *us* in a story but are not what the Old Testament narrator wants to focus on. Grasp the whole plot and observe how it has been structured. It really helps to write out a summary of the plot of the story—scene by scene, marking out the transitions and making use of the outline above. Only then are you in a position to think about what the story *means*. Only then can you teach it faithfully.

Look out also for these other features of a good plot:

- ☐ *Suspense*. A storyteller wants to keep you "hooked" and wanting to know what happens next. But sometimes you are kept waiting! Look at verse 11. It ends with the Israelites "dismayed and terrified." How on earth can they deal with Goliath? We want to know—fast! But the writer starts telling us about David and his family. Then we hear that weeks are going by (v. 16). Then we have the story of the packed lunches David is to take to his brothers. How is that going to solve the Goliath problem? And so it goes on, from one scene to another, before we get to the climax.

- ☐ *Surprise*. Many biblical stories contain sudden turns, surprises, and shocks. The surprise in this one, of course, is the whole point of the story—an unarmed young sheep watcher slays a monster whose armour is too heavy for him to carry all by himself. But it is in the surprise that we see God at work.

☐ *Humour.* Bible writers know how to raise a smile. David's interaction with his older brothers and other soldiers is surely meant to be a bit comic. Imagine it as a scene in a movie. But the humour only underlines how serious the situation was, and how impossible everybody thought it was to fight Goliath, and how ridiculous (or arrogant) David's offer must have seemed.

WHO? THE CHARACTERS

Every story is about somebody. Usually there will be one central character—the person who plays the leading role in the whole story. Sometimes there may be more than one, and sometimes the focus of a longer story may shift from one person to another. But a key question you must ask is: "*Who is the central character in this story?*" This will be the person about whom we know the most in the story. They are "three-dimensional" characters—or, as we might say, "life-like." In our working model, this is clearly David.

Then, in addition to the one central character, there will usually be one or more secondary characters who either oppose or support the central character in overcoming the problem that is driving the plot. We may be told some details about these characters, but they are more "two-dimensional." They assist or obstruct the plot as it goes along, but they are not the centre of attention at every point of the story. In our working model, I would put Goliath (obviously) in this category and probably also Saul. They are not quite central, but they are essential to the whole plot as it unfolds. And we learn something about their character, usually from what they say.

And sometimes there may be any number of other people in a story. These are mentioned with very little detail. They may be named (like Jesse, Eliab, Abner), or they may just be there as contributors to the story (the Israelite army, Goliath's shield-carrier, the soldier who answered David's question). They are "one-dimensional"—that is, they are part of the story but with no real "character" of their own as far as the story is concerned.

Checklist

Again, as you prepare your sermon, it helps to write down your answers to the "Who?" question.

☐ Who is the main character?

☐ Who are the secondary characters?

☐ What other people are part of the story? (Look carefully. Sometimes a person who seems very insignificant may actually play a very important role at some point in the story. Bible stories are good at surprising us like that.)

Now comes the interesting part. *How does the writer portray the major characters in the story—meaning mainly the central character and the second-level supporting characters?*

They were human beings like ourselves, so we instinctively identify with them. We are curious to know whether their *actions* (what they do in the story) are good or bad. And that depends partly on *why* they do them, so we are interested also in their *motives.* How can the storyteller let us know the answers to those questions? Well, sometimes he may tell us directly. We are familiar with how many of the kings of Israel and Judah are introduced with the line, "He did evil in the sight of the LORD." That's clear enough. But in many of the stories the storyteller is not so direct as that.

However, the storyteller can depict the characters by what they *say.* So pay close attention to any *dialogue* or any *speeches* that are part of the story.

Checklist

☐ Is there, for example, any contradiction between what a character says and what you know from what the narrator has already told you?

☐ Is there conflict between one character and another in the story? Which one can you trust?

☐ What does a character's speech tell you about what is going on inside their mind?

☐ How does a speech by a character in the story tell you what the narrator wants you to understand as the meaning of the story?

And even more interesting ...! We tend to like simple stories in which one character is clearly the "good guy" and another character is clearly "the bad guy." And indeed there are some stories like that (David and Goliath is pretty close to that simplicity). But the Bible is often much more realistic and true to life. For life is complex and people are ambiguous. Good people can make mistakes. Bad people can turn around and change. So when you are preparing to preach or teach from Bible stories, don't be afraid of complexity.

This is most easily seen when you look at a sequence of stories in the lives of some major Bible characters. For example, Abraham trusts and obeys God, sure. But he can slip into deception and lies (twice). And his treatment of Hagar and Ishmael is pretty abysmal. Or think of David. So much promise. So many wonderful stories in his early life. But he could be ruthless too. And ambitious. And could he control his sexual appetites? Apparently not. And then, when he fell into terrible sin, even though he experienced God's forgiveness, he could no longer control his own family.

So when you come to preach or teach on Old Testament stories, do not think that you have to tell your listeners in simplistic terms, "Be like this character," or "Don't be like that one." There may be some truth in that, but almost certainly at least some aspect of every character's behaviour will raise questions. They were only human like us. The Bible is honest about people — even the great heroes. So when you preach about them, *be as honest as the Bible itself is.*

And that leads to a final point about characters. *Who is the central character in the whole-Bible story?* Clearly it is *God.* The whole Bible tells the story of how God, the Creator of the world, has acted in human history to save the world from the consequences of sin and evil. God is the one who drives the whole story forward, through the promises of the Old Testament, the climax in Christ in the New Testament, to its ultimate destination in the new creation — his dwelling place with us forever. That means, then, that even when God is not prominent in a particular Bible story,[2] he is still there as the one who is involved (and in charge) of the story as a whole. Every particular story will have its human characters,

---

2. Or even when God is not mentioned at all — as in the book of Esther. But while God is not mentioned in Esther, any reader who knows the rest of the Old Testament can spot the "fingerprints of God" all over the story.

but behind and beyond what the story tells us about them stands God. Every story is ultimately about God in *some* aspect (however small) of how the purpose and plan of God is being worked out.

Think of the Bible as God's "biography" (at least in relation to the history of the world). A biography is about one particular person—the main character, the subject of the whole book. But that person's biography may include lots of stories that involve other people, stories from every phase of the life of the "hero." However, even when we are reading a particular story within a biography that involves other characters, we know it is there to tell us something about the *main* subject. It will shed light on some aspect of his or her character. Or it may explain why they acted in a certain way. Or it may show us the results of what they did—expected or unexpected, happy or tragic. When we've read the whole biography, we will have read many, many small stories. But the main result of reading a biography—indeed, the whole point of writing one in the first place—is that we come to know the person who is the focus and centre of the whole biography, no matter how many other people feature in the book. That's how it is with the Bible. It is full of many human characters, but the *central* character—the one that the whole book is about—is God himself.

Checklist

So when we read and preach *any* Old Testament story, we must ask what it tells us about God.

☐ How is God involved in this event or series of events?

☐ Where does this story fit into what God has been doing so far in Israel?

☐ How does this event affect what God does later in Israel's history?

☐ What do I learn from this story about the character and purposes of God?

☐ How should I respond to God in the light of what this story reveals about him?

WHY? THE NARRATOR

Every story needs a storyteller—whether it is being told orally or in writing. We can use the term "the narrator" here to mean the person who has given us the Bible story we are reading and teaching. Very often, we never even think of the narrator and just take the story for granted. But *somebody* had to write it down and then collect and edit it into the larger blocks we have in the historical books of the Old Testament. Mostly we don't know who those writers and editors were—by name. So why should we care about them at all? Here are two good reasons why we should think about the narrator—both of which are important for when we try to understand a Bible story in order to preach and teach it.

The Narrator Chose to Tell This Story; So We Ought to Ask, Why?

The people who wrote the books in our Bible had to be *selective*. Remember John's wonderful gospel? At the end John points out that there were many things that Jesus said and did—so many that all the books in the world couldn't contain them (John 21:25)! So John had *selected* the stories he chose to include in his account. And he tells us why he'd chosen those ones—"that you may believe that Jesus is the Messiah, the Son of God, and that by believing you may have life in his name" (John 20:31). Well, that's very clear. But unfortunately most other Bible narrators do not *directly* explain why they selected the stories they have included. But that should not stop us from asking the question, for there may be different reasons and plenty of clues to help us see what those reasons might be.

What that means is this: when we read a Bible story, we should not only ask the questions listed above about the story itself—the setting (when? where?), the plot (what? how?), and the characters (who?). We also need to ask, *Why is this story in the Bible at all?* For what reason (or reasons—there may be several) has the narrator chosen to tell us *this* story when there must have been many more that he has chosen to leave out?

Think about it. The history of Israel in the Old Testament (not to mention the history even before Abraham) covers more than a thousand years. Every year would have been full of all kinds of events—thousands and thousands of possible stories. But the

Bible is not just a massive collection of annals and anecdotes. It is not just a mixed bag of sweets (even though, sadly, some churches preach and teach it like that). The narrators and editors of the Bible books have carefully selected their material, and we owe it to them to respect that selection and think about their reasons.

And remember, behind those human narrators and editors stands God himself, who has given us his word through their work. So what *they chose* to include is what *God wanted* to be included. Surely that is important, then, for our preaching and teaching. The reason we choose to *preach* this story ought to reflect in some way the reason why the narrator chose to *write* it and why God chose to have it *included* in the Bible.

I can think of four broad kinds of reasons why stories are selected for inclusion in the Bible.

Some Stories Record Foundational Historical Events on Which Our Faith Is Based

These are unique events, in the sense that they are seen as major acts of God within the history of salvation. They are the "skeleton" of the whole Bible narrative—the spine and bones to which all the other stories are attached. Thinking only of the central part of the story, slung in between the beginning (creation and fall) and the end (new creation), I would include in this category:

- God's promise to Abraham
- The exodus
- The Sinai covenant
- The gift of the land of Canaan
- God's promise to David
- The exile and return from exile
- The birth, life, death, resurrection, and ascension of Jesus of Nazareth
- The outpouring of the Spirit at Pentecost
- The second coming of Christ

Why are these stories included and told? Because they are crucial moments in God's great plan of salvation for the world. So we should preach and teach them, not to pull out lessons to apply to how we should live but rather to point to the saving love and grace of God. These were what the Old Testament calls "the mighty acts of God."

Some Stories Illustrate the Kinds of Experiences That Faith and Obedience May Involve

Many of the single stories and longer narratives in the Old Testament show what it means to hear God's promise and respond to it. Some of them describe what it means to experience God's salvation in all kinds of situations. So, at one level, they point to the trust and obedience of the human characters. But more importantly, they point to the faithfulness of God. God can work through even the most difficult or dangerous circumstances (think of Joseph). And often God works in surprising ways. God can bring redemption, victory, life, blessing—even when life seems full of danger, defeat, death, and curse.

Some Stories Illustrate the Suffering and Cost That Faith and Obedience May Demand

Many stories are not "nice." The Bible is very honest and realistic. Even good people, who are seeking to be faithful and obedient to God, suffer bad things. Sometimes God rescues them (Jeremiah). Sometimes he does not (the prophet Uriah—in the same chapter, Jer 26). Hebrews 11 gives us a catalogue illustrating *both* experiences—those who received blessing and salvation through faith, and others who were commended for their faith but suffered without being delivered in their own lifetime (look carefully at Heb 11:35–40).

Some Stories Illustrate the Consequences of Sin and Rebellion

Some of the nastiest stories in the Old Testament have to do with the way God's judgment falls on those who persist in disobedience and rebellion or on societies that have become utterly corrupt and degraded (Sodom and Gomorrah, the Canaanites, Israel and Judah). But even in such dark narratives there are moments of God's redeeming hand at work. Lot and his family are rescued. Rahab is saved. The remnant of Israel survives in exile and eventually returns to the land. Again, we need to preach these stories, not just to expose the sin of human beings but also to teach the character of the God of righteousness and grace.

So, going back to our working model of the story of David and Goliath, ask the question, "Why?" Why do you think the editor of 1 Samuel included this story?

Here's a hint. Look carefully at the *main speeches of David* in the story, in verses 26, 32, 34–37, 45–47.

- How does David see the challenge of Goliath?

- How does David expect to win the fight?

- What does David expect people will come to know when he kills Goliath?

- Who is Goliath's real enemy?

- What is the narrator saying to the reader through the answers to all these questions?

In short, I think the narrator has told this story to show that, at least in his early days, David was a man who knew and trusted God and understood that God would defend his own name and reputation for the sake of God's own people. David would have to go through a lot more testing (in the coming chapters), but the narrator is showing us the quality of this young man who was going to be God's anointed king and how his life would bring glory to God and his people (until he fell into sin and spoiled it all) because he trusted in the living God.

The Narrator Chose to Tell the Story This Way; So We Ought to Ask, How?

In the example immediately above, the narrator used the *speeches* of the characters not merely to give the story a bit of life and colour (and humour, v. 29) but also to show what the story is really all about and how it speaks about the God of Israel. That is just one example. It is always a good idea to look carefully at the speeches and dialogue that the narrator includes in the story. Often that gives us clues to the narrator's own perspective and intention.

Every story has a series of *scenes* as the focus changes from one moment to the next or from one person and then another. Who controls how these scenes are presented? The narrator, of course.

Try to think of the story like a movie. What you see in a movie depends on the camera angle. And behind the camera(s) stands the director. He decides how much to show you, when to focus close up on someone's face or pull away to a panoramic shot. He decides when to move from one scene to another, whether to "flash back" to something that happened much earlier. The whole thing is filmed from his *point of view*. And that is the same for Bible stories. We read and "see" the whole story from the angles that the narrator chooses for us. We see the story from his point of view.

Checklist

So as you read and prepare to preach or teach a Bible story, think about *how* the narrator has told the story.

☐ Has the narrator built *suspense and surprise* into the story? Can you build them into your sermon?

☐ What does the narrator *emphasize*, and how does he do it? Look for *repetition* of words or phrases; they usually mean that the narrator really wants you to notice something. Make sure your audience notices it too.

☐ How does the narrator *pace* the story? Does he cover a lot of time in a few verses but then pause to cover a short period in a very long and intensive narrative? Stories can move fast or slowly. Think of how both techniques happen in the stories of Joseph or Moses.

☐ Does the narrator leave *gaps* for you to fill in by your own imagination (e.g., in 2 Sam 11: Why did David not go out with his army to fight when springtime came? Did Bathsheba have any choice whether to consent to David's advances or not? Did Uriah know what had happened between David and Bathsheba? Did Joab know? The narrator simply doesn't tell us the answers to these questions). Let your audience think about possible answers rather than insist on your own guess being the right one.

☐ Does the narrator build in great *contrasts* between one story and another?

☐ Does the narrator tell the story in a way that *echoes other stories* in the Bible? For example, there are elements in the stories of Joshua and Elijah that echo those of Moses. There are ways that Noah and Abraham are "second Adams" (Jesus, of course, is "the last Adam").

SO WHAT? THE READER

Every story needs a listener or reader. And that's you as you prepare to preach or teach a Bible story, and it's your audience when you are preaching or teaching it to them. The story calls for some response—directly or, more often, indirectly.

The best example of a direct response to a story is actually a story within a story (2 Sam 12). David has taken Bathsheba and arranged for the death of her husband Uriah. Problem solved, he thinks. But not in God's sight. So God sends the prophet Nathan to confront David with his sin. But how does Nathan do that? *He tells a story* about how a rich man with more sheep than he could count stole a poor man's only lamb and cooked it for dinner. Almost certainly David thinks he is hearing an actual case, and he explodes with anger and gives his verdict. He *responds* to the story with a clear moral and legal judgment. Then Nathan says, "You are that man!" Brilliant! By getting David to judge *the story*, Nathan has made David judge *himself.*

Well, not every Bible story, or every sermon or lesson, will produce *that* effect! But it should produce *some* effect. In fact, one of the ways the biblical narrators do their job so well is that they almost *compel* the reader to respond in some way—to exercise their moral thinking and assess what happened in the story.

- Which moments or actions in the story were good and which were bad?

- What was right or wrong in the attitudes and actions of the characters?

- For what reasons have you judged what was good and bad, right and wrong, in the story?

- What was pleasing or displeasing to God?

- How and why did things turn out the way they did?

- What should we learn?

- In the light of this story, how should we ourselves think, speak, and act now, in our own lives?

And here's where we need to remember something that I explained in chapter 2. We are reading and preaching the stories of the Bible *from within the story of the Bible as a whole.*

Remember those six great stages of the Bible drama? We live in Stage 5. But all that happened in Stage 3 (the period of Old Testament Israel) is *part of our story*. In other words, this single big story and these many smaller stories *involve* us. They are part of the way God brought salvation to us. And they are part of the way God will bring redemption to his whole creation. And we, in our turn, are part of that story too, for God has called us to participate in his mission. We continue the story as followers of Christ in the power of the Spirit. So all that has gone before in the biblical story of God at work in the world at that time needs to connect to the life we now live in this world for God in our own day. That is, we must *respond* to the story that God chose to tell us in the Bible — in all its multiple stories.

Checklist

I think this means that we should not just ask about the *application* of a Bible story, but also about its *implications*. What do I mean by that?

We tend to read a story from the Bible and then simply ask, "How does that apply to me?" Then we pull out a few nice principles — some good advice that we could have taken from any story, whether in the Bible or not. Or we may feel that the story doesn't really apply to us at all — in which case, why is it in the Bible, and why bother reading or preaching from it?

Instead, we need to ask:

☐ How am I implicated in this story? I belong to this people, as a child of Abraham through Christ. God is still the same God, and God has saved me and grafted me into this people. God was at work back in the time of this story, and God is still at work today. So in what way should I now respond to my God, having read this story of "my" people?

☐ Where do I fit into God's *whole story* in the light of *this particular* Bible story?

☐ How does this story help me in my commitment to be a follower of Jesus and obey his command to make disciples of all nations?

☐ How does this story challenge me to participate faithfully and effectively in God's big story in my generation?

☐ What does this story teach me about the God who has saved me and made part of his people to share in his mission?

QUESTIONS AND EXERCISES

1. If you have preached or taught on a number of Old Testament stories before and still have notes of your sermons or lessons, take a look at those notes again. Are there any ways in which you would now preach the story differently in the light of what we have studied in this chapter?

2. Read the story of Abraham and Isaac in Genesis 22:1–19 carefully. Work through it, on your own or as a group, and ask the five main questions of each section of this chapter. Share your thoughts, if working as a group, and consider what difference your observations would make to how you would preach or teach it.

CHAPTER 8

Seven Dangers to Avoid When Preaching and Teaching Old Testament Stories

The last thing I want to do is discourage you from "having a go" at preaching and teaching the wonderful stories of the Old Testament! But no matter how enthusiastic you are, there are a few things to be careful about. Most of them follow on from what we've already said. I hope the following points will not come across as merely negative. The intention—which must be true for all of us all the time in our preaching and teaching—is to try to do the job better and avoid whatever is unhelpful.

DON'T TURN THE STORY INTO A FEW MORAL PRINCIPLES

This is the danger of *moralizing* the Bible's stories. That means that I draw a few simple moral ideas from the story and teach them to people. For example, I might say that in the story of David and Goliath, "A small person with few resources overcomes a great obstacle because he has faith in God. So don't be afraid of big problems. Trust God." Well, that is true, of course. But it is surely not the only thing, or even the most important thing, that the story is telling us.

Moralizing in that way usually ignores the historical setting of the story within the Old Testament. It doesn't think about the reason the narrator has included the story. It pays no attention to how this particular story fits into the wider story of the development of God's relationship with Israel and the fulfilment of God's promise. It fails to connect the story to God's fulfilment of his promise in Christ. And it reinforces the misunderstanding that the *only* reason the Bible stories are there is to teach us to imitate the "good guys" in the Bible and not do what the "bad guys" do. Of course there *are* many lessons we can learn from the Bible stories, and that is one part of their purpose. But we should not *reduce* the colour and rich variety of the Bible's stories to simplistic moral principles.

Also, if we keep moralizing the Bible stories in that way so that all we ever tell people is "Do this" or "Don't do that," we can be in danger of undermining the overall message of the Bible, which has to do with the amazing good news of the saving and sovereign grace of God. We'll come back to this point at the end.

DON'T TURN THE STORY INTO A FEW SPIRITUAL TRUTHS

This is the danger of *spiritualizing* the Bible's stories. Usually this practice involves jumping straight from the story to make some connection with Jesus and our relationship with him. So, for example, I might say that "David had faith in God. That teaches us to put our faith in Jesus if we want to be saved. Jesus is strong enough to overcome our biggest enemy, which is sin and Satan." Again, that is true. But to preach only that is to ignore the bulk of the story itself and to pay no attention to its earthy setting in the history of Israel. It makes all the Old Testament stories into nothing more than mini-pictures that illustrate a New Testament spiritual truth. And once you understand that spiritual truth, you don't really need the Old Testament story any more. This kind of preaching pays no attention to the *real* things that happened to *real* people in *real* history and what God's involvement in those realities tells us.

Sometimes people take an Old Testament story and even say that it is "about Jesus" — as if he were there in the story. We have already seen, in chapter 4, why we ought not to do that, even though there may be valid ways to make a connection with Jesus at some point in our sermon (as we saw in chapter 5).

You can spiritualize the exodus story. "In the exodus, God delivered the Israelites from slavery to Egypt. That is a picture of God delivering us from sin through the cross of Christ." Well, undoubtedly the New Testament does indeed use the exodus as a way of explaining the great liberating power of the cross. But if you *only* preach that message from the exodus, you are ignoring the fact that God delivered real people out of real political oppression, economic exploitation, and state-sponsored genocide. The story teaches us (just as it taught the Israelites) that God cares about those things. The God of the Bible is passionate about justice and compassion for the poor and oppressed. That is a major part of the truth of the exodus story, and it should not be lost or overlooked by spiritualizing the whole narrative into a picture of salvation from sin (only).

You can spiritualize the story of Joshua and the land of Canaan. "God gave Israel the land of Canaan as their inheritance. That is a picture of the great inheritance we have in Jesus Christ, or it is a picture of 'heaven' when we 'cross the Jordan' and arrive in the 'promised land.'" And yes, again, it is true that the New Testament does see such meaning in the land of Israel in the Old Testament. But if you *only* preach that message from the stories of the promised land, you ignore all that the Old Testament says about the real, earthy, land of Israel. It was the proof of God's faithfulness to his promise. It was also a huge economic responsibility for the real farmers and families of Israel. God told Israel that he expected them to live on that land with economic justice and compassion. There are so many laws and stories about life in the land of Israel which have a lot to teach us about how God expects us to live on God's earth. They do not just point spiritually to Jesus or to "heaven."

DON'T LOOK FOR FANCIFUL HIDDEN MEANINGS IN THE STORY

This is the danger of *allegorizing* the Bible's stories. An allegory is a story that is intentionally written in such a way that all the characters and details of the story have some spiritual or moral significance. The best-known example in the Christian world is John Bunyan's famous book, *The Pilgrim's Progress.* All the people, places, and events in the story were invented by Bunyan to describe different aspects of the Christian life. Readers know that when Bunyan describes the Slough of Despond, Doubting Castle, or Vanity Fair, he is really talking about depression, lack of faith, and worldliness, respectively. But when we read stories in the Old Testament, they are talking about what they are talking about—not something else. They do not come with secret codes and hidden meanings.[1]

Back to David and Goliath. David took five stones from a stream. If we ask why (and I'm not even sure we should bother asking why), probably it was because that is where you find rounded stones, and he took five to be well prepared. The narrator just tells us what happened, with no comment. And yet so many preachers start guessing about what those stones, or the stream, or David's sling "represent." They don't "represent" anything—they are just themselves, just facts in the story, a shepherd boy's standard equipment. Have you heard preachers telling you that the five stones stand for:

- Five things about David: courage, confidence, preparation, faith, victory (or whatever other ones you want to list)?
- The five books of Moses?
- The five loaves of Jesus' miracle?
- The five ministries of the church—apostles, prophets, evangelists, pastors, teachers?
- The five wounds of Christ?

Other allegorical interpretations say:

- The stones were taken from a stream of water, which represents the Holy Spirit, so they were "anointed."

---

1. People did know about allegorical stories, or fables, in Old Testament times, and they could use them effectively. Jotham's fable in Judges 9 is a story about trees. But everybody knew he was talking about Abimelek and his ambition to be king. His words had symbolic meanings, and people knew how to interpret them. But the historical narratives of the Old Testament are not symbolic in that way. They may point towards Christ in various ways, but they are not full of hidden meanings. They simply tell us what happened and why.

- David is Jesus. Goliath is the devil. The stones are us ("living stones"). The stream is the Holy Spirit. The sling is prayer.[2]

The trouble with preaching like that is that it can all sound very clever and very spiritual, and it may even make spiritual points that are true in themselves (we *do* need to resist the devil in the power of the Holy Spirit and with prayer), but such fancy ideas are not what the narrator was trying to say by telling the story.

That kind of fanciful allegorizing can have some seriously bad effects. It can distract attention from the story as a whole and the purpose of the narrator in telling the story by focusing on minor details and treating them as symbolic of things that have nothing to do with the story itself. It pays no attention at all to the setting of the story within its context in the history of Israel and the great sweep of God's plan in the whole Bible. It can lead a congregation to think, "I cannot read and understand Bible stories for myself. They all have hidden meanings, and I need the pastor to tell me what they are." It replaces the simple authority and power of the inspired Bible text itself with the clever guesswork of the preacher. People forget the Bible text and remember "what the pastor told us it meant."

I am not denying that some stories may have several *levels of significance*, especially when we see them in the light of other parts of the Bible. In chapter 5 we took note of various ways in which we can see significant pointers to Christ in Old Testament narratives. There are links and connections within the whole Bible narrative. The New Testament writers sometimes saw more in an Old Testament text than its immediate meaning when they read it in the light of Christ. But that does not mean that the original story was "just an allegory," or a picture of something completely different from the historical events it was talking about.

---

2. I have found all these "interpretations" (and even more) on websites offering sermons on Bible stories. The "explanation" that he took five stones because Goliath had four other giant brothers (2 Sam 21), and David needed the stones to kill all of them, is not allegorical but purely speculative. We know nothing about what David knew about Goliath or the rest of the Philistines. The fact is, *the narrator simply does not tell us* why David took five stones, presumably because he thought it was either obvious or insignificant. Anything we say to explain it is pure guesswork and frankly a waste of time.

Example

In **Joshua 8**, after the defeat of Ai, Joshua killed the king of Ai and hung his body on a pole. What is going on here? Well, first of all we ought to connect this with the statement in Deuteronomy 21:22–23 that anyone hung on a pole after being found guilty of great sin was under God's curse. So Joshua's action was a visible demonstration that the defeat and destruction of the Canaanites was an act of God's judgment on their wickedness and not just random violence (as God had explained in Deut 9:4–6). We place the story in its preceding Old Testament context, which helps to explain the meaning of what was going on.

But then, second, we may rightly remember that Paul points out how *Jesus* also was "hung on a pole" in the crucifixion (Gal 3:13). But that was not for his own sin and wickedness. No, Jesus bore the curse and God's judgment *in our place*. So, in preaching that story, we could mention this connection with Christ and the cross. Because Jesus died for us, we do not need to stand under God's judgment as the Canaanites did. The story of God's victory over the Canaanites is part of the same story that ultimately leads to God's victory over evil at the cross. It is part of the Bible's whole story of salvation.

However, what we should *not* do is treat Joshua 8 (or that part of it) as merely an allegory that is "really" all about Jesus. We should not say, "The pole *represents* the cross"; or "The king hanging on the pole *represents* King Jesus hanging on the cross." That is allegorizing the story and turning small details into the main idea. Those details don't "represent" anything. They are simply facts in the story. But other parts of the Bible give them extra significance.

DON'T FLATTEN THE STORY INTO DOCTRINAL SERMON POINTS

This is the danger of *generalizing* the Bible's stories. Some preachers love stories and tell lots of them in their sermons — unfortunately, mainly their own stories, not the Bible's stories. But other preachers *don't like* stories and hardly ever use them (which is strange, since Jesus clearly used them powerfully and often in his preaching and teaching). These preachers are passionate about Christian *doctrine*. They believe in *teaching* their people the great doctrinal truths of the Christian faith. And that is wonderful. I wish more preachers had that passion. But the danger is that this can lead them either to ignore more than half the Bible (which is in narrative form, not obviously doctrinal). Or, when they do happen to preach from a Bible story, their passion for doctrine makes them *ignore the story itself* and turn it into a few doctrinal headings.

They might handle our model story in this way:

> Preacher: "Well, I'm sure we all know the story of David and Goliath, so let's not waste time going through it. Here are the three doctrines we must learn from it.
>
> "First, *God's sovereignty.* God had chosen David. He was God's elect future king. [Then might come a lengthy teaching on the doctrine of election.]
>
> "Second, *God's power.* David trusted in the power of God, which was greater than all the size and strength of Goliath. [Then might come a lengthy teaching on what the rest of the Bible says about God's omnipotence.]
>
> "And, third, *God's salvation.* God saved David and the Israelites from the Philistines. But we know that God's salvation is only through Christ." [Then might come a lengthy teaching on the doctrine of salvation, substitutionary atonement, etc.]

Don't misunderstand me. All those are true and important biblical doctrines. And we could say that it is certainly better to see what the passage teaches us about *God*, and not just draw general moral lessons for ourselves. That is, doctrinal preaching is certainly better than moralizing preaching, since it keeps God at the centre.

But something has gotten lost, hasn't it? What has happened to the story—with all its interest, suspense, surprise, plot, characters, dialogue, drama, and excitement? We have lost the hard edges and specific flavour of *this unique story* as the narrator told it. We could preach about the sovereignty, power and salvation of God from almost anywhere in the Bible, so what was the point of doing it from *this* story if we don't let the story do its own work in people's imaginations, hearts, and minds?

Here's a thought. God could have given us the whole Bible as a book full of doctrines all nicely arranged by topic. And indeed God *has* given us some books in the Bible that are predominantly teaching us what we need to know and believe—books full of teaching, such as some of the letters in the New Testament. But instead, God has chosen to give us the Bible as a book in which more than half consists of stories. If God thought that was important, we should not just ignore them or transform them all into doctrines when we preach them.

Actually, as we saw in chapter 2, all the great doctrines of our Christian faith are based on the single big story of the Bible as a whole. And in many ways the smaller narratives of the Bible reinforce and illustrate the flow of doctrinal teaching that is embedded in that story. What we believe (as Israelites or Christians) is founded on what God has done. That is what makes the big difference between Christian doctrine drawn from the Bible and philosophical religious speculation drawn from human clever thoughts.

Have you ever wondered why the Israelites believed what they did?

Suppose you heard an Israelite singing **Psalm 33.**

> The word of the LORD is right and true;
>   he is faithful in all he does.
> The LORD loves righteousness and justice;
>   the earth is full of his unfailing love.
>   *(Ps 33:4–5)*

Imagine you go up to them and say, "Excuse me, but *how do you know all that*? How do you know that God is truthful and faithful? How do you know about God's justice and God's love?" (Those are all great doctrines, by the way.)

I think the Israelite psalm singer would answer, "How much time have you got? Sit down here and let me tell you our story—a whole bunch of stories, in fact."

And then he would tell you the stories of God's promise to Abraham and how God kept it. That's how he knows God is *faithful.* He would tell you about God destroying the arrogant injustice of the Egyptians and saving his people. That's how he knows God is *just.* He would tell you about God's loving care and provision for his people in the wilderness. That's how he knows God is *loving.* And so on and on. At some point he would get up and say, "So that's our story. That's how I know what God is like and that's why I believe what I do. Can I get back to my singing now, please?"

In short, *Israel learned their doctrines from their stories.* And that is why it was so important to keep telling those stories again and again, from generation to generation (Deut 6).

So, by all means work hard to make sure your audience understands the core doctrines of the Christian faith. But don't ignore the Bible's stories in doing so. They are your best allies. They harness our learning to our imagination—and that's powerful. Let the stories do their own work—the work God put them in the Bible to do. Preach and teach them![3]

DON'T GET BOGGED DOWN
IN DIFFICULTIES AND DETAILS

This is the danger of *complicating* the Bible's stories. Of course, many of the stories in the Old Testament do raise questions in our minds. This happens especially if there are miraculous elements (which is not nearly so common as people think). We want to know how the sea parted when the Israelites crossed over, or how and why the walls of Jericho fell down, or what the plagues of Egypt really were, or where Elijah actually "went," and so on. But if the Bible does not take time to explain these things to satisfy our curiosity, then we should not waste time in the pulpit offering all the possible explanations we have heard or read. Tell the story and leave such details to God's power and wisdom.

Then also, of course, the Old Testament stories happened in the world of the ancient Near East, and we now know a lot about that part of the world in ancient times through archaeological discovery. Sometimes it is helpful to tell our audience information that will help them understand the Bible story better or put it into its historical and cultural context. But a sermon or Bible study is not the place for you to show off all the knowledge you may have gotten from reading books. You should include in your preaching or teaching only enough information that *genuinely* helps people understand the text better. Otherwise you will be tedious and boring, and people will lose interest in the story itself—which is tragic.

As we considered above, many of the stories in the Old Testament have descriptive details (like David's five stones or the particular fruits that Abigail loaded on donkeys to take to David). Don't be tempted to try to explain every detail in the story as if they were all important at the same level. In particular, don't get

---

3. Dale Ralph Davis talks about how the Bible stories are "doctrinal bones clothed in narrative flesh" in *The Word Became Fresh: How to Preach from Old Testament Narrative Texts* (Fearn: Christian Focus, 2006), 127.

bogged down trying to figure out numbers, dates, and details like that. Taking *the story as a whole*, what has the narrator emphasized? What really matters in the way the narrator has presented the characters and woven the plot together? What things really "fill the camera" as the scenes move along? Then concentrate on those major things in your sermon.

Sometimes Bible stories are embarrassing, nasty, or shocking. We may be tempted to explain them away or to show why it was not really as bad as it seemed. Don't do that. God tells it as it really is in this world. People are sinners and can do things that are desperately wicked and depraved. The marvel of the Bible is that God continues to work with and through even fallen, sinful people. And in the end God accomplishes his purpose—in spite of all the problems we caused.

DON'T CREATE WRONG EXPECTATIONS

This is the danger of wrongly *personalizing* the Bible's stories. By that I mean reading an Old Testament story as if it were all about me (or preaching it as if it were all about the listener in the pew). Now this is where we need a careful balance. On the one hand, yes, of course, I ought to be asking, "What does this story mean for me? How should I respond? What are the personal implications of this story in my life/our lives?" But on the other hand, the danger lies in thinking that whatever God did in the story for the hero of the story, God is bound to do for me (or you). It's *as if I were that person in the story*, and I can just claim the whole story for myself. I treat the story as a promise to me personally.

Do you know the old gospel song, "It is no secret what God can do; what he's done for others, he'll do for you"?[4] Well, if we're talking about God forgiving our sins and giving us eternal life through faith in Jesus Christ, that is true. But if we think it means that God will *necessarily* do for us whatever he did for people in the Bible stories, we are wrongly personalizing the text. We are reading into it implied promises that are not there.

So I could preach the story of God protecting Elijah and feeding him by the ravens in a way that implies that God will do exactly the same for us (perhaps without the ravens). Or because God kept

---

4. Chorus of "The chimes of time ring out the news," by Stuart Hamblen. It was a gospel song from the 1950s.

Daniel safe in the lions' den that God will always keep us safe from any danger. And yet we know that, even within the Bible itself, God did not always prevent faithful people from being attacked or killed (Heb 11 makes the point forcibly). We should certainly be *encouraged* by stories of God's provision and protection, and we can certainly *pray* for God to do the same for us. But we cannot simply assume that every story is a personal promise that God will always do exactly that for us.

Once, in a preaching class at a college where I was teaching, a student preached a sermon from Jeremiah on how God promised to bring the exiles of Judah back from Babylon to their own land. He told us that his imaginary congregation were Christian refugees from an African country in his own country. He preached the Bible text as a *promise* from God that *they* (the African refugees) would definitely and soon be able to return home.

But we cannot turn stories about what God *did* do — stories that do indeed demonstrate what God *can* do — into blank-cheque promises about what God *will* do, or *must* do for you, me, and everyone. Why not? Because the Bible itself does not do that. In fact, it gives us examples that disprove that kind of wrong expectation.

- God saved Joseph from prison, but the baker lost his head (Gen 40).

- God rescued Moses from death in the Nile, but many other baby boys must have been drowned there.

- God protected Jeremiah from being killed by a mob, but the prophet Uriah was killed by King Jehoiakim (Jer 26).

- God blessed Abraham with increasing wealth, but Jeremiah suffered loneliness, hatred, and physical beatings and imprisonment — *because* he trusted and obeyed God faithfully.

- Peter was rescued from prison by an angel, but James was executed by the sword (Acts 12).

- Jesus healed many people, but God did not take away Paul's "thorn in the flesh" — which was probably a physical ailment. And on one occasion Paul had to leave a colleague (Trophimus) behind because he was sick (2 Tim 4:20). I'm sure Paul prayed for him, but God did not immediately heal him.

Daniel's three friends had the right perspective on this. When Nebuchadnezzar threatened them with the burning fiery furnace, they gave their classic reply: "If we are thrown into the blazing furnace, the God we serve is able to deliver us from it ... *But even if he does not*, we want you to know, Your Majesty, that we will not serve your gods or worship the image of gold you have set up" (Dan 3:17 – 18; my italics). They knew (from the many stories of their people) that the God of Israel was perfectly able to save them. But they also knew that God was not bound to do so. So they trusted in God's sovereignty, but they left room for God's freedom. Their point was that, no matter what their living God did or didn't do, they would not serve any other god.

So we can certainly do what the psalmists do. That is, we should certainly use the great Old Testament stories of God's saving power as an *encouragement* to our faith and prayer ("our God is able"). And of course we can be completely assured of God's perfect salvation in and through Christ ("whoever calls on the name of the LORD will be saved"). But we should not use those Old Testament stories to *promise* people that they will always be kept safe and never face suffering, hunger, disease, persecution, or death. Don't raise false expectations.

Here's another way we can raise false expectations — and it may seem surprising. It's by being selective in the stories you choose to preach and teach — if you only pick all the "good" ones.

Here you are, planning your preaching again, and you decide to preach on a series of Bible characters from the Old Testament. So you pick one encouraging story from each of the lives of, let's say, Abraham, Jacob, Joseph, Moses, Joshua, David, and maybe Elijah. And you want to show, as your overall theme, that faith in God overcomes difficulties. So you preach your way through those great stories. I'm sure it will be very encouraging to your people.

But it might also have this more hidden effect. The stories selected all seem to say that *so long as you trust God, everything will turn out fine*. So people in your congregation may be tempted to think:

- *Either:* "Now I'm a Christian and trusting God, life will be a road of rich blessings and victories."

- *Or:* "Nothing is going right for me. Life is a mess and I am suffering great hardship and pain. So either I do not have the faith that all those people in the Bible had, or maybe God doesn't love me for some reason."

Neither of those is true or right, but it could be the effect of preaching only the "good" stories.

A better strategy would be to preach through the whole series of stories that make up *one* person's whole life—such as Abraham, Jacob, Joseph, or David. Then it becomes very clear that they faced all kinds of problems, caused by both their own failure and sin as well as the hatred or lies of others: deception, jealousy, dysfunctional families, sexual immorality, violence, disobedience, depression—it's all in there. Sometimes things went badly wrong for them. And yet God kept on working through such people in spite of such things. *That gives a greater sense of reality.* Your preaching will be more "true to life" and more balanced and faithful to all the Bible teaches. That's the kind of balance that Hebrews 11 includes. Yes, many people did great things and won great victories by faith. But others, *who were also commended for their faith,* suffered loss, hunger, homelessness, violence, and death (Heb 11:35–40).

DON'T SUBVERT THE GOSPEL

This may seem very surprising. How could you possibly undermine the gospel by preaching Bible stories? Well, quite easily, in fact. I actually think it happens all the time in the way Bible stories are told to children, and sometimes it's no better in the pulpit or adult small groups.

I read a report once that said that if you ask children in a good church where the Bible is being taught, "Why did Jesus die on the cross?" they will answer, "So we can have our sins forgiven." But if you ask them, "How do we get to heaven?" many will answer, "By being good." That is the message they have picked up—even if it was not what was being explicitly taught. "You have to be good." "Why?" "So you can go to heaven. Only good boys and girls go to heaven." And that "message" is subtly reinforced by story after story from the Bible in which the children hear that God loves and cares for the good person in the story, and the bad people get punished. So the message they hear is, "You need to be good so God will love you and do nice things for you—and especially so that you can go to heaven."

Now I hope you can see that that is the very opposite of the gospel. It is the denial of the gospel of God's grace. The message of the Bible is *not* that you have to be good and only then will God love you and give you his blessings. The amazing, counter-cultural, unexpected, good news of the Bible is that God loves us in spite of our sin and rebellion; that God has acted to bring us salvation and blessing; that God's grace comes first, and our obedience and "being good" is a *response* to grace—never, ever, the means of earning or deserving grace.

That gospel truth is as much part of the Old Testament as of the New. God takes the initiative. God calls Abraham and makes a promise to him—and Abraham responds in faith and obedience, and then God blesses him. God has compassion on the Israelites in slavery in Egypt and acts to deliver them. Only after that does God ask them to obey him and keep the covenant. We will think more about the significance of that order of events in the next chapter.

We need to remember that the stories of Israelites in the Old Testament are stories of people who *already knew about and had experienced the redeeming power of God's love and grace*—first. It was only *after* God had redeemed them out of Egypt and brought them into the land of Canaan that God told them to obey him and gave them the promise that if they obeyed him, then they would *continue* to enjoy his blessings. But if they disobeyed and went after other gods and fell into all kinds of social and spiritual evils—then they would suffer God's anger and judgment.

The order is:

1. God acted to save and bless the people and give them the great gifts he had promised.

2. God then called for the people's love, worship, and obedience in response to his covenant.

3. God promised to continue to bless those who responded to his grace in covenant obedience.

4. But if people turned away from their saving God, they would inevitably suffer the consequences of their own sin and evil.

The problem is this: when we preach some Old Testament stories, we often leave out the first two points and concentrate only on points 3 and 4. Of course, the first two points might not be included as part of the particular story we are preaching. But that is precisely why it is so important to see each small story as part of the longer story. *All* the small stories about Israelites in the land *presuppose* the previous history of salvation and the covenant—which is essentially the Old Testament gospel story of God's saving grace. That is to say, all the stories that illustrate points 3 and 4 are based on the facts of points 1 and 2.

If we forget that, we very easily turn Old Testament stories into little pictures of "blessing as reward for obedience" or the opposite. We preach that if our people will be obedient (often focusing on rules that we ourselves think are important—the essence of legalism), then God will bless them in all kinds of ways. Then we illustrate that idea from any Old Testament story that seems to prove it—*ignoring the original story of God's saving grace*. In that way we subvert the heart of the gospel of grace and substitute for it a kind of "God loves the good people" message. The effect is either to feed people's pride and legalism (I am being blessed because I am being very good) or to drive them to despair because they never feel good enough.

Always remember: in the Old Testament as much as in the New, obedience to God was never a way of *earning* God's blessing but rather the proper way to *respond* to God's salvation and the only way to *enjoy* the continued blessing of God that flowed from God's grace.

QUESTIONS AND EXERCISES

1. Discuss whether any (or all!) of the above dangers apply to the kind of preaching and teaching you hear on Old Testament stories. Which do you think happens most often, and what problems does it cause?

2. As before, if you still have notes of sermons or lessons you have preached or taught in the past on Old Testament stories, read them again and see if there are any ways you would now want to revise or change how you presented them to avoid some of the dangers we have considered in this chapter.

SAMPLE OUTLINE

Note: This is an outline of a sermon or lesson on **Genesis 22:1–19**. You may have worked on it yourself, as suggested at the end of chapter 7. Because the story involved a long walk, I decided to "walk through" the story several times:

- First of all, to help the audience live in the story by bringing it to life, follow the narrator closely and observe how well he sustains the suspense and surprise and leaves us wondering sometimes about what Abraham and Isaac were thinking. This was the longest part of the sermon/lesson.

- Second, I walked through the story, more briefly, with Old Testament Israelites who would have heard it often to show how Abraham became a model for them of obedience under testing. How does this story fit within the wider Old Testament story?

- Third, I linked the story to the New Testament, where it is used as a picture of God the Father and God the Son cooperating in the willing sacrifice of the cross for our salvation.

- Fourth, I showed how the New Testament uses the story to encourage us in our walk of faith and obedience.

Walking with Abraham through Testing
Genesis 22:1 – 19

Heartbeat: Abraham and Isaac together model *both* what God has done for us, *and* how we are called to respond to God in faith and obedience.

Walking with Abraham and Isaac

V. 1 "After these things" (ESV) What things? = ch. 21: the joy of the birth of Isaac and then the tragedy of sending Hagar and Ishmael away. Abraham was left with only Isaac.

"God tested Abraham." So we (the readers) know it's "only a test": Abraham didn't. For him it was a terrifying reality.

"Abraham!" "Here I am" — repeated three times, vv. 1, 7, 11 — punctuating the story.

V. 2 "Your son, your only son, whom you love — Isaac": emphatic build-up of phrases.

"Sacrifice him!" The shock and surprise! Had God forgotten his promise?

The suspense of the story. Did Isaac know what was intended? Did the young men know? The narrator is skilful in engaging our imagination in the tension of the story.

Vv. 5–8 What do Abraham's words mean? A kind of desperate prayer? Faith that God could raise Isaac from death? Ironic — "God will provide a lamb" = my son!

Vv. 9–10 Isaac's willingness. He was not a child but a youth. He could easily have run away if he'd wanted. His father was 100 years old.

Vv. 11–14 The voice and the substitute.

Vv. 15–18 God's promise reconfirmed — faith and obedience. This is the climax of the Abraham narratives since chapter 12. God has tested Abraham's faith, and now God builds Abraham's obedience into his ongoing promise, which is now confirmed by an oath.

Walking with Israel

Three words in the story come again and again in the story of Old Testament Israel:

- Testing (v. 1)
- Fear (v. 12)
- Obedience (v. 18)

See how they are used in Exodus 20:20; Deuteronomy 8:2, 10:12 — examples of God testing Israel to see if they would be obedient.

But where Abraham was faithful and obedient, Israel sadly often failed.

Abraham as a model Israelite — in faith and obedience.

Walking with the Father and the Son

Echoes of this story in the New Testament:

- Jesus' baptism—"My Son, whom I love"—probably echoes Genesis 22:2 as well as Psalm 2:7
- John 3:16: God as the Father who gave his only Son
- Romans 8:31–32: God did not spare his only Son but gave him up.

However, as God walked that road with Abraham and Isaac in Genesis, he knew that one day he would walk in the same land with his own Son—and at the end of that day, there would be no substitute for God's Son. Rather, he would become the substitute for us, the lamb of God who takes away the sin of the world. And as Isaac willingly submitted to his father, so the sacrifice of Christ was both the will of God the Father and the willing self-giving of God the Son—acting together for our salvation (Gal 1:4).

Walking in the way of Abraham

The New Testament uses this story to encourage both faith and obedience—and trust in God's provision in times of testing.

- Hebrews 11:17–19—proof of Abraham's faith
- James 2:21–23—proof of Abraham's obedience
- 1 Corinthians 10:13—testing comes with provision

CHAPTER 9

Understanding
Old Testament Law

I t's always good to know what you are talking about before you open your mouth. So before we start talking about *Old Testament law*, let's be clear what we mean by that phrase. When Jesus (and Jewish people before him and ever since) spoke about "the Law, the Prophets and the Psalms [or Writings]" (e.g. in Luke 24:44), they were referring to the three great sections of what we now call the Old Testament, in its Hebrew form.

- *The Law* meant the first five books of the Bible — the Pentateuch — from Genesis to Deuteronomy. That is the foundation block of the rest of the Bible.

- *The Prophets* were divided into "the former prophets" (namely the historical books from Joshua to 2 Kings) and "the latter prophets" (namely Isaiah, Jeremiah, Ezekiel, and the Book of the Twelve: Hosea–Malachi).

- *The Writings* included everything else (Psalms, Job, Proverbs, 1 and 2 Chronicles, Ezra–Nehemiah, and five little books — Ruth, Esther, Lamentations, Ecclesiastes, and the Song of Solomon).

So in that canonical sense, "The Law" is used to translate the Hebrew word *torah* and refers to the whole Pentateuch. But it is not a very good translation because the word *torah* does not mean "law" in our modern sense of "legislation." Rather *torah* means "guidance" or "instruction." And of course, the Torah includes extensive narratives, like the books of Genesis, half of Exodus and Numbers, as well as laws (and also some songs and poems).

But when we talk about "Old Testament law," we usually mean those parts within the Torah which actually do look more like laws in our sense of the word—commandments, legal cases, judges and witnesses, detailed instructions, legal penalties, and so on. That kind of material is mostly found in the second half of Exodus (especially Exod 20–23), Leviticus, and Deuteronomy (especially Deut 12–26).

From here on, in these two chapters, 9 and 10, we are thinking and talking mostly about Old Testament law in that second sense. So when I speak of "the law," "Old Testament law," or "the law of Moses," I usually mean those parts of the Torah which are full of commandments and instructions. Of course it is important to take those actual laws in the context of the narrative of the whole Torah. But our main focus is on those sections of laws *within* the books. How should we understand, and then preach and teach from, those great passages in which there are so many detailed commandments and instructions?

In this chapter I want to help us think rightly about the law—to understand why it is there in the Bible, how it fits into that great Bible story, and what it meant for Israelites in the Old Testament times. Then, in chapter 10 we will ask how we can find the relevance of Old Testament law for Christians today. How can we preach and teach it in a way that makes that relevance clear while at the same time being careful to remember the gospel of God's grace in Christ and that we walk by the Spirit and are not, in Paul's sense, "under the law"?

OLD TESTAMENT LAW WAS PRAISED AS THE GIFT OF GOD

This is where I want you to sit up and listen and think a bit differently from usual. It may feel uncomfortable at first. It usually does when I teach this part—but trust me. I want us to be faithful to the Bible—the whole Bible, not just some bits of it. Ready? OK.

Where do you go if somebody asks you what Christians are supposed to think about Old Testament law? Very likely you would turn to the Apostle Paul and those places in Galatians and Romans where he says some fairly negative things about the law. It exposes our sin. It shows we are all guilty before God. It leads to death. It is powerless to make us right with God. It functioned like a guardian to keep Israel in check — until Christ came. But now, through faith in Christ, we are no longer under the law of Moses. Thank God, and breathe a sigh of relief!

Now I want you to be quite sure that I accept and believe all that Paul says in the New Testament! And a little later we will come back to that. But what I want to do right now is point out two things.

First, Paul was engaged in a serious conflict with people who were giving so much importance to the Old Testament law that they were in danger of minimizing or misunderstanding what had happened through the coming of the Messiah, Jesus. For them, keeping the law of Moses was a vital badge of belonging to the one nation that was in covenant relationship with God — the Jews. If anybody else wanted to be part of that covenant people, they had to keep the whole law of Moses (get circumcised, keep the Sabbath, eat only ritually clean food, etc.). That was the only way to truly belong among the righteous people whom God would accept on the last day. They were making the law a condition of salvation, the way to be right with God.

But Paul says that their whole understanding of the law was wrong. *The law was never meant to be the means of salvation.* Salvation had always been, and still is, a matter of faith in the promises of God, which we now place in Christ. So Paul was arguing with people who had *distorted* the law into something it was not intended to be. We do need to listen to that argument in order to understand some of Paul's letters. But it is not the best place to start thinking about the law itself *in its Old Testament context.* And that leads to my second point.

Second, then, what happens if instead of starting our thinking about Old Testament law with the Apostle Paul, we start with those to whom it was actually given — the Israelites of the Old Testament? Let's ask some of the psalmists what the law means to them. Here's what they say:

> The law of the LORD is perfect,
>   refreshing the soul.
> The statutes of the LORD are trustworthy,
>   making wise the simple.
> The precepts of the LORD are right,
>   giving joy to the heart.

> The commands of the LORD are radiant,
>   giving light to the eyes.
> The fear of the LORD is pure,
>   enduring forever.
> The decrees of the LORD are firm,
>   and all of them are righteous.
> They are more precious than gold,
>   than much pure gold;
> they are sweeter than honey,
>   than honey from the honeycomb.
>   *(Ps 19:7–10)*

> I will walk about in freedom,
>   for I have sought out your precepts...
> for I delight in your commands,
>   because I love them...
> Oh, how I love your law!...
> Because I love your commands
>   more than gold, more than pure gold...
> All your words are true;
>   all your righteous laws are eternal.
>   *(Ps 119:45, 47, 97, 127, 160)*

What do you hear in those songs of praise? Not a terrible burden of legalism. Not moans and groans about how hard it all is. Not anxiety and guilt. Rather, we hear *thanksgiving* for a wonderful gift of God. We hear *appreciation* for something that is a blessing and a very practical help for living. We hear them *valuing* God's law as something precious (more than gold) and sweet (more than honey).

> Devout Israelites delighted in the law as a gift of God's grace and token of God's love, given to them for their own good (Dt. 4:1, 40; 6:1–3, 24, etc.). They saw it as a blessing in itself, and the means of enjoying God's continued blessing (Dt. 28:1–14). They recalled that the revelation of the law to Israel was a unique privilege, granted to no other nation (Dt. 4:32–34; Ps. 147:19–20). They urged one another to obey it, not in order to get saved, but because God had already saved them (Dt. 6:20–25). They delighted in it as the road to life (Lv. 18:5; Dt. 30:15–20), and as the river of fruitfulness (Ps. 1:1–3).[1]

---

1. Christopher J. H. Wright, *Old Testament Ethics for the People of God* (Downers Grove, IL: IVP Academic, 2004), 282.

I think this is the right place to start if we want to think about (and teach) the Old Testament law within its proper biblical context. We will, of course, need to come to Paul and understand what he means when he says that we, as Christians, do not live "under the law." That's where we are now—within Stage 5 of the great Bible story. But, as with any part of the Old Testament, we need to move back in our minds to Stage 3 and study these texts in their own context first of all. When we do that we will find a much more positive picture—initially, at least.

And coming back to Paul for just a moment: remember where we began in chapter 1. It is Paul who tells us that "All Scripture is God-breathed and is useful for teaching, rebuking, correcting and training in righteousness, so that the servant of God may be thoroughly equipped for every good work" (2 Tim 3:16–17). Well, the law was the very first foundational part of the Scripture that Paul was talking about. So he would have included the law in that sentence. Even if other people were using the law wrongly and putting it in the place where only Christ should be, Paul tells us clearly that the law itself is "God-breathed [inspired by God] and ... useful." There is no point in boldly declaring "*all* Scripture is inspired by God and is useful" unless we also write above every chapter in an Old Testament book, including the law, "*This* Scripture is inspired by God and is useful."

So let's step back into the Old Testament and try to stand or sit alongside the Israelites and see the law from their point of view within the great story of God's dealings with them.

OLD TESTAMENT LAW WAS GIVEN TO PEOPLE WHO HAD EXPERIENCED THE GRACE OF GOD

Once we go back to that big single story of the Bible, we see again just how vitally important it is for understanding any part of the Bible. *The law comes within a story.* It was given to people who had already experienced God at work. Before we even reach the legal texts of the Torah, we have had a book and a half of preceding narrative (all of Genesis and half of Exodus). So we have already read the story of creation, the fall, the call of Abraham and God's promise to him, and God's redemption of Israel out of Egypt, and the making of the covenant between God and Israel at Mount Sinai. That is, we have already moved through Stages 1 and 2 and the beginning of Stage 3 before we even get to the law. This great narrative and all its significance is the context of the law. We need to keep that story very clearly in mind whenever we read or preach from any part of the law itself. Never preach the law of the Old Testament without the story of the Old Testament that goes before it.

The law was given by *this God*—the God who created the whole earth and all nations, the God who made a covenant with Abraham that included a promise of blessing for all nations. And the law was given to *these people*—the people God had just delivered out of slavery as an act of compassion and justice, the people who now stood in covenant relationship with God. God's redeeming grace was already in action. So when we teach Old Testament law to people, we need to make sure they know the God who gave it and the story that surrounds it. He is the God of grace and it is the story of grace.

Checklist

We must, therefore, always preach Old Testament law on the foundation of God's saving grace. Anything else will lead people to legalism, despair, or pride. We should not preach the law without the gospel. But remember, the gospel begins with Abraham (as Paul affirmed in Gal 3:6–8). That is to say, God gave his law to people who already knew about God's covenant promise of blessing and had already experienced God's mighty redemption. So here are some questions to ask when you are studying a passage of Old Testament law with a view to preaching or teaching from it.

☐ Does this particular law include any reference back to God's redemption of Israel from Egypt—or does it occur in a group of laws or a chapter which includes such a reference? For example, Leviticus 19 is full of very practical laws, but it constantly refers to God by his covenant name the Lord/YHWH, and finishes with a reminder of Egypt.

☐ The whole list of Ten Commandments begins with the fact of God's redeeming Israel before the first commandment is listed. What does this say about the whole of the rest of the law?

☐ Can you help your listeners see the shape of the books where the laws are found? For example, the laws in Exodus (including the Ten Commandments) come *after* the story of redemption in the first half of the book. Likewise, the book of Deuteronomy, which was a renewal of God's covenant with Israel just before they crossed the Jordan into the land of Canaan, begins with chapters that tell the story of how God redeemed Israel out of Egypt, revealed himself to them at Sinai, and led them through the wilderness (chs. 1–4)—*before* coming to the Ten Commandments and other laws. And again, at the end of the main section of laws, the history of redemption is celebrated all over (ch. 26).

Here are three wonderful passages from within the Torah itself that make this point very clear. I love preaching from them!

Examples

a) Exodus 19:1–6: The law was given to people whom God had already redeemed

God has brought his people to Mount Sinai. Now it is time to tell them what it all means and what he wants from them. But the very first thing God does is to point back to the past. "You yourselves have seen what I did ..." (v. 4). And indeed they had. It was a very recent memory. As verse 1 says, it was only three months since they were being whipped and killed as slaves in Egypt. Now they are free. And God says, "I did that. I brought you out from that terrible oppression." The exodus was an act of God's saving grace, motivated by his compassion for their suffering and his faithfulness to his promise to Abraham (Exod 2:23–25).

Only after God has reminded them of that story of redemption does he then go on, "Now if you obey me fully and keep my covenant ..." Grace comes first. Obedience comes second, as the proper response to grace. Grace comes *before* the law. Even the structure of the book of Exodus would show us that. There are eighteen chapters of salvation (nearly half the book) before we get a single chapter of law, starting with the Ten Commandments.

I am stressing this point because many people still have a very mistaken idea about the difference between the Old and New Testaments. They think that the difference is that in the Old Testament you got saved by obeying the law, whereas in the New Testament you get saved only by grace through faith. But that is a terrible distortion of the Scripture. They are correct, of course, in what they say about salvation in the New Testament. But grace was just as much the basis for salvation in the Old as well. God saved his people out of his own love and faithfulness and *then* made a covenant with them that included keeping his law. That view of the Old Testament (salvation by keeping the law) is very similar to the false teaching that Paul was combating. It is not what the Old Testament itself teaches.

Even the Ten Commandments, which seem to be setting out the primary principles of the whole law, begin with a reminder of saving grace: "I am the LORD your God, who brought out of Egypt, out of the land of slavery" (Exod 20:2). They were given to people whom God had already redeemed.

In England there are many ancient churches that have the Ten Commandments written up on the wall (along with the Lord's Prayer and the Creed). But unfortunately they nearly always start with the first commandment and leave out God's opening statement. That is posting law without "gospel." It is telling people what they must do without first telling them what God has done.

b) Deuteronomy 6:20 – 25: Gratitude was a motivation for obeying the law

Read these verses. They put us in the heart of an Israelite home in which the family is seeking to live in covenant obedience to God. And then the son asks his father what is the meaning, or the point, of all the instructions they are observing. "Why do we do all these things, Dad?" Now when children ask "Why?" parents sometimes answer, "Because I tell you to!" So the father could have gone straight to verse 24, "The LORD *commanded* us to obey." Wouldn't that be enough? "God said it. Just do it! Stop asking questions, boy."

But no, when the son asked about the meaning of the law, the father was to tell him the story. What story? The story of salvation, the story of Israel's redemption out of slavery in Egypt and the gift of the land of Canaan. Look how the father has to tell all of verses 21 – 23 before coming back to God's commandments in verse 24. The very meaning of the law is found in the "gospel" — the good news of God's saving righteousness. "Son, look at all that God has done for us. Now then, that is why we obey him."

Obedience, therefore, is a matter of our right response to what God has done. That is what the phrase "that will be our righteousness" means in verse 25. The father is not talking about some kind of righteousness that could be earned or deserved by obedience ("works righteousness," as it gets called). No, the father is not telling his son how to "get right with God." What he means is: God has proved *his* righteousness by doing what was right — putting down the oppressor and liberating the oppressed. That is God's righteousness in action. Now, *our* righteousness will be seen in living rightly in the way God wants. Our obedience to God is not how we *earn* righteousness but how we respond in the only right way to God's saving righteousness for us.

c) Deuteronomy 15:11 – 18:
Release of slaves after six years

After six years of service, it was the statutory right of a Hebrew slave to be given their freedom unless they chose to remain with the household they were in (see Exod 21:1 – 11). But Deuteronomy tells the owner to provide a generous redundancy package — to mirror God's gracious generosity to them in the past: "And when you release them, do not send them away empty-handed. Supply them liberally from your flock, your threshing-floor and your winepress. Give to them as the LORD your God has blessed you. Remember that you were slaves in Egypt and the LORD your God redeemed you. That is why I give you this command today" (Deut 15:13 – 15).

It couldn't be clearer, could it? God's redemption was the foundation and motivation for obeying God's command. Generosity to the needy was commanded (not just suggested). It was a *law* for Israel. But that law of generosity was rooted in the generous grace of God toward Israel. Read the whole of Deuteronomy 15:11 – 18 — it is filled with the language of generosity in response to God's blessing.

There are many other places where this principle (redemption as the basis of a law; obedience as a response to saving grace) can be seen. The Israelites were to remember what God had done for them in bringing them out of Egypt and then let that affect the way they behaved toward others — especially those who were weak and vulnerable in their society (as they had been in Egypt). They should care for foreigners in their midst because they had experienced God's care for them when they were foreigners in Egypt. So foreigners were to be treated on equal terms under the law as native-born Israelites (Exod 23:9; Lev 19:33 – 36).

Imagine that we could transpose Exodus 19:4 into the New Testament. It would be as if God, instead of pointing back to the exodus, were to point to the cross of Christ and say, "You have seen what I have done. Now then, will you live in obedience to my Son as your Saviour and Lord because of what he has done for you?" In fact, that is more or less what the New Testament actually does do. For although we are not "under the law" any more, there are certainly major *commandments* in the New Testament for us to obey.

Jesus said (and repeated it three times), "A new *command* I give you: love one another." But then he immediately went on, "*As I have loved you*, so you must love one another" (John 13:34; 15:12, 17; my italics). His love comes first. Indeed, as John later wrote, "We love *because* he first loved us … since God so loved us, we also ought to love one another" (1 John 4:19, 11; my italics). Grace first, then obedience. It's the same principle—whether in the Old or the New Testament. Even the Apostle Paul, who insists that we no longer live under the law of the Old Testament, had plenty of instructions and commands for Christians to obey. Here's one: "Forgive one another." That's not a polite suggestion that we might like to consider occasionally. It is a straight command, not an option. But once again, notice how Paul provides motivation based on grace. "Be kind and compassionate to one another, forgiving each other, *just as in Christ God forgave you*" (Eph 4:32; my italics; compare Col 3:13 and Rom 15:7).

OLD TESTAMENT LAW WAS GIVEN TO SHAPE GOD'S PEOPLE FOR THE MISSION OF GOD

So far in this chapter we have been standing with Israel at Mount Sinai looking *backward* to the past. At the time when God gave his law to Israel he had *already* acted by making his covenant promise to them through Abraham and then redeeming them out of slavery in Egypt. The law was given on the foundation of past grace—God's grace experienced in their history. As they remembered that history of God's salvation, they would be motivated to obey God's law.

But we can also look at the law from the other direction. What was God's purpose for Israel looking *forward*? This seems an important question to ask, and yet many people ignore it. People often ask, "Why is the law of Moses there in the Bible? What is the point of it?"—and then they try to answer that in terms of Christian theology, where it seems to raise all kinds of problems and arguments. But suppose, instead of asking "*Why the law?*" we first of all ask the question, "*Why Israel?*" After all, whatever purpose was in the mind of God when he gave the law to Israel at Mount Sinai must have been in line with the purpose God had for Israel as a people from the start.

Now we know very well what God's purpose for Israel was—ever since God made his promise to Abraham. God's long-term purpose was to bring blessing to all nations on earth through Abraham's descendants (Gen 12:1–3). Against the dismal background of Genesis 3–11—Stage 2 of the Bible's great story—in a world of people and nations scattered in sin and judgment, God announces that he plans to bring *blessing* into the world. And God says that he will do that through the people descended from Abraham and that ultimately all nations on earth will find blessing through Abraham's people—meaning Old Testament Israel, of course.

That is what I mean by "the mission of God." That is the great goal of all God's work within history. And that is the reason why the people of Israel in the Old Testament were called into existence, created, chosen, redeemed, and brought into covenant relationship with God. All of that was *not for their own sake only* but ultimately so that they could be the means by which God would bless people from all nations. That is why the Apostle Paul calls Genesis 12:3 "the gospel in advance" (Gal 3:8). It was indeed very "good news" that, in spite of human sin, God still planned to bless the nations. We know now, as Paul explains, that God has kept that promise in and through Christ, "the seed of Abraham." But until Christ came, God's mission proceeded through Old Testament Israel.

But what has this got to do with Old Testament *law*? Well, think of it like this. If you wanted to accomplish a purpose *through someone else*, what kind of person would you want them to be? You'd want them to think like you and act like you and do what you would want. You'd need them to be accountable to you and act with integrity in your name. Otherwise, how could they achieve *your* purpose if they just ran off and did their own thing in their own way and forgot all about what you asked them to do?

So here is God, with this great plan and purpose to bring the knowledge of God, the blessing of God, and eventually the salvation of God, to all nations on earth. *What kind of people* would God need to have for that purpose? God would need a people who would act in *God's* ways, who would show the world what *God* is like by living by God's standards and priorities. A holy people, in other words—holy as God is holy. So God enters into a covenant relationship with Israel, in which he says:

- I have chosen, called, and redeemed you [*election and redemption*].
- So we belong to each other: you will be my people; I will be your God [*covenant*].
- Now, here is the way I want you to live [*law*].
- I give you this law to help you live in ways that will both please me and be best for you, and will also show my character to the nations.
- Follow my laws, for my sake, for your own sake, and for the world's sake.

So, a major part of the purpose of the law in the Old Testament was to *shape* Israel for their participation in the mission of God. They were to be different from the nations in order to be a light to the nations.

Examples

Here are some texts that express this point. Again, I love preaching and teaching from them!

a) Genesis 18:18–21: Keeping the way of the LORD

This story comes from hundreds of years before the law was given, of course, but it shows clearly *why* the law was given later. You might find it helpful to read the whole of chapter 18, and just note where it is leading in chapter 19.

God has been enjoying a meal with Abraham and Sarah in the company of two angels. The three visitors are on their way down to Sodom and Gomorrah to bring judgment on them (which comes in ch. 19). But on their way they stop to renew God's promise to Abraham and Sarah that they will have a son of their own—very soon. Then, as they leave, God has a little conversation with himself—about Abraham and his purpose for him.

> Abraham will surely become a great and powerful nation, and all nations on earth will be blessed through him. For I have chosen him, so that he will direct his children and his household after him to keep the way of the LORD by doing what is right and just, so that the LORD will bring about for Abraham what he has promised him.
>
> (Gen 18:18–19)

Verse 18 is a clear echo of 12:1–3, and we can see how important that "bottom line" is. God is thinking not only of Abraham but of his universal purpose for the world through the nation yet to be born.

But then look carefully at verse 19. In one single sentence God binds together three things:

- *God's choice of Abraham:* "I have chosen him" *[election]*

- *God's requirement:* "he will direct his children and his household after him to keep the way of the LORD by doing what is right and just" *[ethics]*

- *God's ultimate purpose:* "the LORD will bring about for Abraham what he has promised him—i.e., blessing for all nations, v. 18 *[mission]*

And in between each of these there is an expression of intention—"*so that.*" God is telling us *the reason why he chose Abraham* (so that he will be the starting point of a community that will be different from the world of Sodom by walking in a different way—the ways of justice and righteousness). And then God tells us *why he wants Abraham's community to be different* (so that God can keep his promise of blessing for the nations).

Now that middle part of the verse uses two very important phrases. "The way of the LORD" and "doing what is right and just" are among the most prominent concepts in the law (and indeed in the whole Old Testament). The law had not been given yet, but already God is pointing to the purpose it would have later. The law would help to shape the people of Abraham to live in the way God wanted—the way God taught Abraham. God's purpose for Israel included this *ethical* agenda to *live* as the people of God. And for that purpose God gave them his law. It was part of the mission of God and of Israel.

So when we preach and teach from the Old Testament law, we need to remember this part of its function—to shape God's people to be the agents of God's mission to the nations. God's people were called to live in the way God instructed them because God wanted them to be "fit for purpose"—to be part of the fulfilment of his mission for all nations.[2]

---

2. As I said, I love preaching from this text. I have put an outline of my sermon at the end of the chapter.

b) Exodus 19:5–6: Israel was to be a priesthood in the midst of the nations

We come back again to this key text from Exodus 19. Remember that above we saw how God first of all points to his *past grace*—"You have seen what I have done" (v. 4). Then God calls Israel to obey him—pointing forward, of course, to the law that he is just about to give at Mount Sinai. And God says what will happen *if* they obey his law:

> Now if you obey me fully and keep my covenant, then out of all nations you will be my treasured possession. Although the whole earth is mine, you will be for me a kingdom of priests and a holy nation.
>
> (Exod 19:5–6)

Notice, first, that God does *not* say, "If you obey my law, I will save you and you can be my people." He had already saved them from Egypt; they already were his people. Also, God does *not* say, "If you obey me, I will bless you with all kinds of good things."[3] The text does not promise what Israel will *get*, but rather tells them what they will *be*. They will *be something* for God in the midst of "the whole earth" and "all nations." That is the wider context that God points out (maybe he had a better view of the whole earth and all nations from the top of Mount Sinai).

In the context of "the whole earth" and "all nations," Israel as a nation was to be God's priesthood. In order to understand what that means, we need to know what was the role and function of priests in Old Testament Israel. Priests in Israel stood between God and the people. They were middlemen, mediators, operating in both directions. On the one hand, they were to teach God's law to the people (Lev 10:11; Deut 33:10). That is, through the priests God would be known to the people. On the other hand, the priests were to bring the people's sacrifices to God and make atonement at the altar so that people could come back into worshipping fellowship in God's presence. That is, through the priests people would be brought back into relationship with God.

So now, says God to Israel as a whole community, you will be for me to the nations of the world what your priests are for you. Through you I will teach the nations my ways and make myself known to them. And through you I will ultimately draw the nations to myself in redemption and

---

3. I often set this text, Exodus 19:1–6, for groups to work on for a sermon outline in Langham Preaching seminars. And frequently the group comes up with this idea: "obey God and you will get richly blessed." That may be true (though not in the way the Prosperity Gospel proclaims). But it is simply not what this text says.

covenant. Both of these were fully accomplished, of course, only by Jesus, the Messiah of Israel—the perfect Mediator and High Priest. But just as priests represented God to the people and represented the people to God, so Israel were meant to do that for the nations.

But that priestly role could only happen as Israel were also a *holy* people and lived in obedience to the covenant law. Holiness meant being distinctive, reflecting the character of God in everyday ordinary social life (Lev 19). In other words, the law had the function of shaping Israel to be that representative people, making the character and requirements of God known to the nations. That's a missional function. The law itself was a revelation of God. But so also are those who live it out in loving, grace-filled obedience.[4]

c) Deuteronomy 4:5 – 8: Israel was to be a visible model to the nations

The book of Deuteronomy is full of motivation. That is, it wants to *encourage* people to keep God's law, and offers all kinds of reasons why they should do so. We've already seen one of the strongest: remembering the exodus and God's great act of salvation. Another common one is that obedience to God's law would give Israel a good and secure life in the land. Here in Deuteronomy 4:5 – 8 we have an unusual motivation.

Moses urges Israel to follow God's law carefully—*so that the nations will notice.*

Observe them carefully, for this will show your wisdom and understanding to the nations, who will hear about all these decrees and say, "Surely this great nation is a wise and understanding people." What other nation is so great as to have their gods near them the way the LORD our God is near us whenever we pray to him? And what other nation is so great as to have such righteous decrees and laws as this body of laws I am setting before you today?

(Deut 4:6 – 8)

Israel should not think only of itself, for God does not think only of Israel. If Israel would live in the way God sets out for them in his law (with its comprehensive system of social, economic, political, judicial, and family life), they would be a *very different kind of society* from the nations around. They would arouse curiosity. Questions would be asked. And those questions would be about the God they worshipped and the justice of their laws. God's people should be an advertisement for their God.

---

4. I have placed a sample outline for this text also at the end of the chapter.

This principle—that when we obey God the world around will take notice—is not confined to the Old Testament. The same dynamic is there in the New Testament. When we live in the way God wants, as disciples of Jesus and in obedience to him—we get noticed. It may not be comfortable. It may cause us trouble. But at the very least, our lives ought to raise questions about the God we worship and why we live as we do (the same as for Israel in Deuteronomy). In other words, our obedience is also missional—it is part of the way we fulfil God's mission through his people to the world. Disciples of Jesus are to be distinctive—as much as salt and light are from corruption and darkness. And when we do live like that, people will see and ultimately come to glorify God (Matt 5:14–16; 1 Pet 2:12). We are to live in a way that brings others to the knowledge of God.

So then, when we preach or teach from Old Testament law the first thing we must do is remind Christians of the grace of God to which they must respond (looking back to the story of our salvation). But then also we must remind them of their responsibility: to live distinctively as God's people in the midst of the people who surround them (looking forward to God's ultimate mission of blessing the nations). Those whom God has redeemed are to live for God's glory in the world. That was part of the purpose of the law in the Old Testament. God's people are created for his praise and honour, so that the nations may know who the living God is: that was the mandate of Israel, and it remains ours in Christ.

OLD TESTAMENT LAW REFLECTED THE CHARACTER OF GOD

Here's another reason why we should feel encouraged to preach and teach from the law of the Old Testament: it reflected the character of God himself. As I mentioned above, one of the commonest expressions for obeying the law is "to walk in the ways of the LORD." But what does that mean? Well, one sense of the phrase is to follow along, going where the person in front leads. "Oh, let me see thy footmarks, and in them plant my own," as we sing.[5]

---

5. John E. Bode, "O Jesus, I Have Promised," 1868.

Example

At one point in the book of Deuteronomy, Moses offers a summary of the whole law. He gets it all down to five basic requirements. Here's what he says:

> And now, Israel, what does the LORD your God ask of you but to *fear* the LORD your God, to *walk* in obedience to him [literally, to walk in all his ways], to *love* him, to *serve* the LORD your God with all your heart and with all your soul, and to *observe* the LORD's commands and decrees that I am giving you today for your own good?
>
> (Deut 10:12 – 13; my italics)

That's all God wants: that we should fear God, walk in his ways, love him, serve him, and obey him.

Now supposing some keen young Israelite shoots up a hand and asks, "OK, we'll try to do all that, but tell us please, Moses, what does it *mean* to 'walk in the ways of the LORD'?"

Moses had his answer ready. Here's what God is like:

> For the LORD your God is God of gods and Lord of lords, the great God, mighty and awesome, who shows no partiality and accepts no bribes. He defends the cause of the fatherless and the widow, and loves the foreigner residing among you, giving them food and clothing.
>
> (Deut 10:17 – 18)

He is the great God who owns and rules the universe with full authority and power. And he is the God of absolute integrity—he cannot be corrupted or bribed like so many human judges. But when this great God gets into action, where will you find him? Where you least expect—among the poor and needy, the family-less, the homeless, the landless. Those are the ones God cares for and provides for. That is God's way. So, "if you are going to walk in the ways of the LORD God, then," Moses continues without pausing for breath, "*you* are to love those who are foreigners, for you yourselves were foreigners in Egypt" (v. 19; my italics).

In other words, Israel was to reflect the integrity, justice, compassion, and love of God in their own dealings with others. They were to imitate those aspects of the character of God. That's what it means to "walk in his ways."

This strong motivation in Old Testament law can also be seen in the way Leviticus 19 punctuates its demands for Israel's ethical life—on the farm, in the family, in the court, in the neighbourhood, in business, in ethnic relations—with the simple statement, "I am the LORD; I am holy, so you must be holy."

Imitation of God is a strong theme in Old Testament law, but it does not stop there. It is the same basic principle that undergirds the teaching of Jesus about our behaviour. We are to model what we do on what we know about who God is and what God does (Matt 5:45–48; Luke 6:27–36).

Checklist

The question we need to ask before preaching any passage of the Bible is not first of all (or only) "What does this mean to *me*? What does this tell *me* to do?" With some of the laws that were given to ancient Israel in their society and culture the answer to those questions may be, "Very little, or nothing at all—directly." Remember, the law was written *for you* (that is, for you to learn from, as Paul says), but it was not written *to you*. It was given *to Israel* centuries before Christ. Rather we start by asking:

- ☐ What does this law show of the character of God?

- ☐ How does this law illustrate God's values and priorities?

- ☐ What does the surrounding context of this law say about the things God cares about?

- ☐ If that is what God is like, if that is what God values, if that was the way God wanted things to be in Old Testament Israel—then what would God want in today's world that would embody the same principles in some way?

Sometimes the answers to those questions may be difficult to find. Or they may be very puzzling as we struggle to understand why on earth God gave some of the laws he did. And we will need to balance any answers we suggest with what we know about God from the rest of the Bible. In the next chapter we will explore all this a bit further.

OLD TESTAMENT LAW EXPECTED THE JUDGMENT OF GOD

I wonder if you have come across the "Plan A—Plan B" theory of the Old Testament? It is quite common, and goes like this:

God wanted to save the world through Israel. So he made a covenant with them and gave them his law so they could be saved. That was Plan A. Unfortunately, the Israel plan was a disaster since Israel failed so badly to keep God's law. So God realized that people couldn't

*get saved by keeping his law. So he abandoned that idea and came up
with Plan B. He sent Jesus instead so that we can be saved by Christ's
obedience and sacrificial death in our place.*

Well, it may be a common view, but I'm afraid it is quite
wrong.[6] Israel's failure did not take God by surprise. Now, first
of all, we do see that God called Israel to know him, love him,
worship him, and obey him. Of course. That is what God wanted
from Israel because it is what God has wanted from all people since
he created the human race. But God knew that the Israelites were
human beings — sinners like the rest of the human race. God knew
that they would fail. *And God told them so well in advance.* Far
from being a surprise, Israel's failure was fully anticipated by God.

At the end of Deuteronomy there are some very important
chapters — Deuteronomy 29–32. See if you can find time to read
them right through all at once — now would be good! But here is
a very brief outline before you start. God says something like this:

- Israel, I have saved you from slavery and made you my
  covenant people.

- I have now given you my law to help you live in the way
  that will be good for you and bring you blessing. And
  you have made your covenant commitment to love and
  obey me.

- *However*, I know very well that you will *not* keep this law.
  You have shown how rebellious and sinful you are even
  while Moses is with you. As the generations go by after his
  death, you will become even worse.

- So, you *will* bring down upon yourselves all the threats and
  warnings that I have built into this covenant. Because you
  will persistently break my covenant you will experience the
  curses of the covenant, not its blessing.

---

6. One part of the "Plan A theory" is very wrong — and you should
spot it immediately. God did not give Israel his law so that they could be
saved by keeping it. We saw above that God had already acted to save them
and make them his people. He gave them his law not so they could earn
salvation but for them to *respond* with love and gratitude to the salvation
God had already given them.

- My judgment will fall, through your enemies, and you will be driven out of this land and scattered among foreign nations.

- *However*, I want you to know now, even before all this happens, that judgment does not have to be my final word or your final condition. There can be hope beyond judgment. I am still the God of grace, love, and forgiveness. I will *enable* you to seek me with all your heart and soul, to love me and obey me. So turn back to me. Choose life, not death!

So you see, the law itself (in Deuteronomy) anticipates the future failure of Israel. Indeed, those chapters of Deuteronomy not only give us a clear theology of sin, judgment, repentance, grace, and restoration; they also give us the history of Israel in advance. For that is the route that Israel did in fact travel through the whole of Stage 3 of the great Bible story.

And meanwhile, within the law God provided a means for the regular cleansing and atonement for sin—in the sacrificial system in Leviticus. That did not in itself "solve the problem" (as the book of Hebrews clearly points out). And later the prophets strongly accused the Israelites of imagining that so long as they kept the sacrifices going in the temple, they could carry on in their rebellion and disobedience and avoid God's judgment. But God was not fooled. And God's judgment did fall—in the terrible experience of exile in Babylon.

So when we turn back to the Apostle Paul, we are not surprised (any more than God was) that the law in itself could not make sinners and rebels good and perfect. But the fault was not in the law but in the people. That's why Paul talks about the law being "powerless ... because it was weakened by the flesh"—meaning our sinful human nature (Rom 8:3). That's why the Israelites found that the law brought them death. It exposed their sin. And it brought them under God's curse and judgment. But here's the key point: *this was not a new discovery by Paul. The law itself had said as much!* The law called for Israel's faithfulness, but the law also expected Israel's failure. It was realistic. But then the law had also pointed beyond judgment to *future hope* in the saving and restoring grace of God. It pointed, in other words, ultimately to the Lord Jesus Christ—as Paul saw so clearly.

So then, when we preach and teach Old Testament law we should also do those same two things. First of all, when we show people what God wants, holding up the ideals and standards that are contained in the law God gave to Israel, we ought to be realistic. We are just as much sinners as the Israelites were, and we simply don't live this way. We fail, just as they did. We need to recognize our desperate inability and unwillingness to live in God's way. The sad story of Israel is our story too. But then, second, we can lead people from recognizing their failure back to the promises and grace of God. For that too is there in the law. When you know you have sinned, where do you go? Back to the God of grace. That is what Israel had to learn, and it is still the gospel truth for us.

Please pause now to read the whole of **Deuteronomy 30.** It is utterly realistic about the fact that Israel would fail and would inevitably suffer God's judgment. God *knows* that will happen. But it is also wonderfully open about the power of God to overcome even that—no matter how far away the people might go in their sin and rebellion. God promises that he will give them a heart to love him (v. 6) so that they can again turn to him and obey him with all their heart and soul (vv. 2 and 10). God is not imprisoned by human sin. There is an open future and an open choice before the people. So the chapter ends with a powerful evangelistic appeal to turn back to God and choose life, not death (vv. 19–20).

In our preaching and teaching, we can certainly connect the point of the whole chapter (Deut 30), including its concluding appeal, to the gospel. For both the law and the gospel are agreed on three essential biblical truths (which make good outline headings!):

- *Failure is a fact.* All have sinned—whether Jew or Gentile—and failure and sin are facts of life, facts of history, facts illustrated again and again in the Bible. Even disciples of Jesus know this. Ask Simon Peter.

- *Failure is foreseen.* God knows this about us! He was not surprised by Israel's failure. Jesus was not surprised (though deeply grieved) by Peter's failure. In fact, he warned him about it in advance. The whole story of the Bible shows God, in full awareness of our sinfulness, failure and rebellion, taking action to overcome it and reach out to us and bring us back.

- *Failure can be forgiven.* The saving grace of God is affirmed in the Torah. The psalmists knew it and depended on it (e.g., Pss 25, 32, 51, 130). And of course it is there for us ultimately in the cross of Christ.

This is the message we can preach and teach from Old Testament law. That is why the Apostle Paul would have certainly included the law in what he says about the Scriptures as a whole. The Old Testament Scriptures are not only "useful," they are also "able to make you wise for salvation through faith in Christ Jesus" (2 Tim 3:15). And then, when we have put our faith in Christ, God comes to live within us through the Holy Spirit (as he also promised in other parts of the Old Testament — e.g., Jer 31:33; Ezek 36:26–27), enabling us to live by the Spirit — not by trying to keep all the Old Testament law — in a way that actually satisfies the whole point and purpose of the law (Rom 8:4).

QUESTIONS AND EXERCISES

1. Do you agree that we should approach Old Testament law first of all in terms of how the Old Testament Israelites saw it — e.g., in Pss 1, 19, 119 — rather than only in the way Paul talks about it in his controversy with "Judaizers"? How helpful has it been to approach it from this angle first?

2. If the law was viewed positively in the Old Testament, what is the reason why Paul speaks negatively about it? What is the context of Paul's argument?

3. What would you now say to someone who still believes that in the Old Testament times salvation was by keeping the law, whereas only in the New Testament does it become a matter of grace? How would you explain that grace and salvation came *before* the law? What texts would you use in your explanation?

4. Prepare a sermon or lesson on Deuteronomy 6:20–25.

SAMPLE OUTLINES

Read these outlines alongside the fuller discussion of the texts in section 3 above.

Announcing God's Mission Agenda
Genesis 18:19–21

Sodom and Gomorrah As a Picture of Our World

Verse 21 describes an "outcry" against the cities. That shows there was oppression and suffering there. Same word as the Israelites "crying out" during their oppression in Egypt. See also the violence and perversion in chapter 19; but also the social sins of violence, arrogance, and affluence described in Isaiah 1:9–10, 16–23; and Ezekiel 16:49–50, where Jerusalem and Judah are compared with Sodom. This is still the world we live in.

Abraham and the Promise of God's Mission

God renews his promise to Abraham and Sarah. 18:18 is a direct echo of 12:3. This is God's mission, God's agenda, God's vision—blessing for all the nations. Even on his way to judgment, God remembers his plan of salvation.

The Way of the LORD As a Programme for God's People

V. 19. (See the summary above.) God "reminds himself" of his purpose in choosing Abraham: that he should be the "founder" of a people who would walk in the way of the LORD rather than in the way of Sodom. Our way of life (doing what is right and just) is a vital link between our calling and our mission.

Who Are We, and What Are We Here For?
Exodus 19:1–6

Past Grace: God's Salvation

V. 4. God points to his own initiative of saving grace: "you your-selves have seen what I did." Grace comes before law—in the story and in the structure of the book of Exodus. Who we are and what we do for God is always a response to what God has done for us.

Future Grace: God's Mission

V. 5b. "All nations ... whole earth." This is the language of the Abrahamic covenant. Israel would have a special relationship with God, but God's eye is on the whole world. Important balance of the particular (what God had done for Israel) and the universal (his purpose for all nations).

Present Grace: God's People Living in God's Way

Vv. 5a and 6. Israel's mission was to be God's priesthood in the midst of the nations. Just as their priests stood between God and the rest of the people (teaching God's law and offering the sacrifices), so Israel as a whole would be the people who would bring God to the nations, and bring the nations to God. In one sense, fulfilled in Christ. But we still have that "priestly" role in the world—Romans 15:16; 1 Peter 2:9–12. We are the living representatives of the living God.

CHAPTER 10

Preaching and Teaching from Old Testament Law

I hope that last chapter was a help in "getting into" the Old Testament law and understanding what it's doing in the Bible. In this chapter we will try to see what we can "get out of" the Old Testament law for preaching and teaching today. Paul says that, like all Scripture, it is "useful for teaching, rebuking, correcting and training in righteousness" (2 Tim 3:16). The question is, How?

Paul also tells us that we are not now living "under the law" because we have put our faith in Christ and are living by the Spirit. So if we are not supposed simply to do all that the law of Moses tells us, what use is it to us at all? Are there some parts we should still obey while ignoring all the rest? Or should we be trying to find something "useful for teaching," and so on, in all of it?[1]

To help us answer such questions, first I will show that although the law was given to Israel, God intended it to be *a model* at a much wider level for other people. So when we use the law to help us think how we should live in today's world in our own nations, we are doing what God wanted in the first place. Second, I will show how Old Testament law tried to *benefit people*. It was not there to spoil everybody's fun, but to make life better for all. And that is something that applies to all nations and cultures. So we have

---

1. If you want a fuller discussion of Old Testament law, you might find helpful chapter 9, "Law and the Legal System," in my book *Old Testament Ethics for the People of God* (Leicester: IVP, 2004). I cover such things as the different kinds of law in Israel (criminal, civil, family, ritual, and compassionate), the administration of justice, and the scale of values in Old Testament law.

something to learn for our own benefit. Third, we need to discern *the values and priorities* that are there in the law—including in those parts that we find difficult, such as some of the very severe laws that imposed the death penalty. And finally, I will suggest a way of *building a bridge* from the world that we see in the law of ancient Israel to the world we live in today.

THE LAW OF ISRAEL WAS MEANT TO BE A MODEL FOR THE NATIONS

Let's go back to the beginning of the Bible story.

Stage 1: God created the heavens and the earth and then created human beings in God's own image, to live on the earth. We could portray this as a triangle, with three points all in relation to each other, as shown. This is the triangle of creation. Each of the three lines represents a relationship that works in both directions. So, the earth was created by God and belongs to God ("The earth is the LORD's," Ps 24:1). Human beings are created to love and serve God and one another and to use and care for the earth. The earth, as part of God's creation, gives glory to God and is a blessing to human beings who live on it.

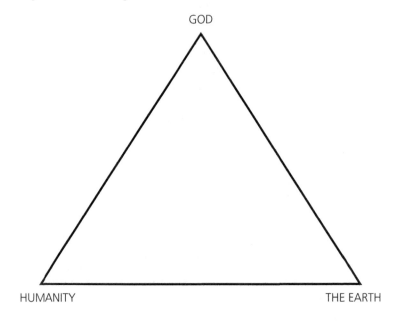

GOD

HUMANITY   THE EARTH

But, sadly, every one of those lines and relationships has been broken, twisted, and spoiled by the effects of the fall (**Stage 2** of the Bible story). Human beings are fallen and sinful. We distrusted God's goodness and rejected his authority. As a result, God brought a curse on the earth in its relation to us, and the earth is "frustrated" (as Paul says in Rom 8) in its purpose of glorifying God. And human beings live in alienation from each other, in all the hatred, injustice, and violence that arise between people, families, tribes, and nations.

Nevertheless, although the triangle is distorted and fractured because of sin and evil, it is still there. God is there, the earth is there, and we are still here as fallen human beings living on earth but alienated from God. In a sense, all of us are somewhere on that bottom line of the triangle, in every era and generation of history.

So what did God do about the problem?

That's where **Stage 3** begins, as we've seen already. God called Abraham and made great promises to him.

- God promised Abraham he would become a great nation under God's blessing and protection.

- God promised to give Abraham's descendants a land to live in.

- God promised that all nations on earth would find blessing through Abraham.

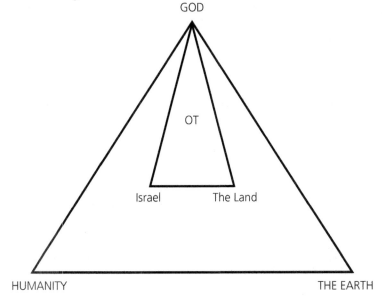

Can you see the sequence? *One* nation, *one* land; then *all* nations in *all* the earth. We could picture this as another triangle within the outer one (see diagram). When God launches the great biblical story of redemption (portrayed in the inner triangle), it starts with one man who becomes one nation (Israel) to whom God gives one particular land (the land of Canaan). But what God was doing in that one nation was intended to bring blessing and salvation to all nations of humanity. And the land of Israel becomes a microcosm of God's will for life on earth in a wider economic sense. And the combination of a redeemed people living in the promised land also becomes a foretaste of the redeemed humanity from every tribe, language, and nation living in the new creation — the new heavens and new earth that we see portrayed in Revelation 21 – 22.

This inner redemption triangle of the Old Testament — of God, Israel, and the land — becomes a model, or paradigm,[2] of God's wider intention for the rest of the nations in all the earth (the outer creation triangle). Israel was meant to be "a light to the nations" in their covenantal relationship to God in worship and in the quality of their society (remember Deut 4:6 – 8) — in economic, political, social, familial, and personal spheres.

This means that Old Testament law, as part of that inner triangle of God's redemptive work in Israel, was *intended* to have relevance to other cultural and historical contexts in the creation triangle — for any nation on earth, including our own. So, as shown in the next diagram, what took place within that inner triangle of God, Israel, and the land — including the gift of the law of Moses — can be drawn out, as it were, and considered in relation to our own context. That's where we will find it "useful," as Paul said.

---

2. A paradigm is an example, model, or case that is very specific in its own details but which then serves as a pattern for thinking about issues, problems, or situations that may be very different but where the same principles apply. There are paradigms in science. That is when scientists use a particular solution that they know by experiment and proof as a way of looking at and solving other problems. There are paradigms in language. If you are learning a foreign language, you will learn certain pattern verbs and nouns, etc., which will then apply to many other words of the same sort in many different sentences. There are paradigms in law. Judges use the judgments delivered in specific cases of the past as "precedents" from which they derive principles for deciding other cases before them.

So when we preach and teach Old Testament law, we are not trying to enforce it literalistically—that is to say, thinking that we can ask people to do exactly what it says in the text, just as it stands. None of us now lives in ancient Israel. The law of Moses was given to *them then*, not to *us now*. We do not live "in" that inner triangle. We live on the "bottom line" of the outer triangle—living in one of the nations on God's earth. What we need to do is to look for what God taught and required within that inner triangle (Old Testament Israel), and then ask how that still addresses and challenges the context in which we live in the outer triangle—wherever that may be. Old Testament law, by telling us what God required of *that* society at *that* time, can still challenge the church and society on issues of social ethics and justice in *these* times. We stand, as it were, among the observing nations of Deuteronomy 4:6–8, asking questions not only about the kind of God Israel worshipped and the kind of society they were meant to be, but also how the answers to those questions can help us in engaging our own contexts in our preaching and teaching within the community of faith.

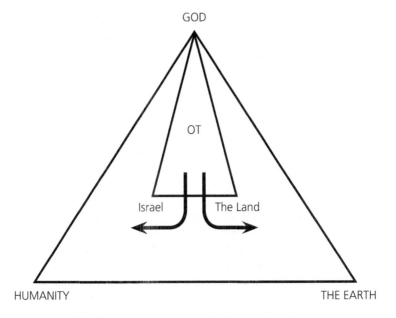

THE LAW WAS GIVEN FOR HUMAN BENEFIT

What did Jesus mean when he said, "The Sabbath was made for man, not man for the Sabbath" (Mark 2:27)? He meant that the Sabbath law was supposed to be for human benefit. Jesus got angry because the leaders of his day had turned something good and beneficial into a burden that people had to submit to. It was as if the law was the master and humans were serving it, whereas, said Jesus, God's idea was the other way round. He gave the law to serve human needs and help people live in better ways. Taking weekly rest was one example of that. It was a strict law, but it was intended for people's own good. Weekly rest is good for you!

When Jesus said that about the Sabbath, he could have been speaking about the whole law. God gave his law to Israel not to keep himself happy or to take pleasure in finding fault with Israel's failures but *for their own good*. Deuteronomy says this again and again (e.g., Deut 4:40; 5:29; 6:24; 10:13). And as we saw in the last chapter, Israelites who truly loved and worshipped God realized full well that by obeying God's law they were in the best place. Keeping God's law (living in God's way) was the way to a life that was wise, healthy, satisfying, and productive — a blessing, in fact. The whole book of Psalms begins with a joyful celebration of the blessing that comes from seeking to live in God's way (read Pss 1 and 19). Basically, obedience to God is good for you. And when you think about it, since God made us in the first place, the best way to make life work is to "follow the Maker's instructions." God knows what will contribute most to human flourishing. That's what he wanted for Israel — only they were so often too blind to see it and went their own way, into the terrible mess of sin and suffering that we see in the rest of the Old Testament.

Examples

The following are some examples of situations where Old Testament law shows its concern for people's benefit and needs. These are situations where there is a clash between a stronger person's *rights and claims* and another weaker person's *needs*. In such situations we find that Israel's law gives a higher priority to the person who is vulnerable and needy. Sometimes this legal priority happens even when somebody else has legitimate claims. It seems that God is saying: "Don't look only at the legal rights and wrongs of the case. Pay attention to where the greatest need is. Think who is most vulnerable or suffering most and care for them as a priority." This is not "blind justice," but justice with eyes very much open—eyes that *see* people in need. And yet at the same time, Old Testament law warned Israelite judges against *favouritism*—distorting justice out of misplaced pity for a poorer person (Exod 23:3, balanced with 23:6). Take a moment to read each of the biblical texts below.

a) The need of a refugee slave as against the claims of their owner (Deut 23:15–16)

This is a very counter-cultural law. In all other societies where slavery has operated (ancient and modern), the legal rights and claims of the slaveowner have always come first. For a slave, running away is an offence, often punished by death, and anybody who takes in a runaway slave is committing a serious offence. Your legal duty would be to send the slave back or hand them over to the authorities.

But what does Israel's law say? First of all, it *prohibits* Israelites from sending the slave back to his or her owner. That in itself is amazing and unexpected. But then it also *commands* them to allow the slave to live safely in any place of his or her own choosing in the community. They were to give priority to the human need of the weaker party (the slave) over the legal claims of the stronger party (the owner).

Clearly this very humane law would undermine slavery altogether if most slaves simply chose to run away. The fact that the law sees this as an exceptional situation implies that slavery in Old Testament Israel was not normally harsh and cruel in the way that we tend to think of slavery (Roman galley slaves or black African slaves). So if a slave in Israel *did* run away, it would be assumed that the owner was in fact treating him or her very badly (contrary to the laws of slave protection in Exod 21:20–21, 26–27). In that case, says Israel's law, you must put the slave's needs first. People matter more than claims. A cruel slaveowner might think that they had property rights on their side. But they did not have God's law on their side. God's law was to protect *people in need*, not to protect the property rights of violent or abusive masters.

b) The need of a female prisoner as against the power of a soldier (Deut 21:10–14)

Here is another law which at first reading may make us wrinkle our noses. We would like to say that there should not be wars, and there should not be prisoners, and women should not be captured as prisoners of war. Well, that would all be true in an ideal world. But God deals with *reality in a fallen world*. And part of the strategy of Old Testament law is to cope with nasty realities and then try to soften the worst effects for those caught up in them.

In this case, the law permitted the victorious soldier after a battle to take a woman from among the captives. But what is he allowed to do? Well, we know that one of the most horrible aspects of warfare in all ages has been, and still is, the appalling suffering of women at the hands of soldiers—raping, enslaving, or killing them. Sometimes systematic rape of women is used as a deliberate tool of war to humiliate the enemy. This law of Israel rules that out right from the start.

First of all, the soldier may take only *one* of the captive women as his fully legal *wife* with all the responsibilities such a status put on him and the rights it gave her. Rape and slavery are ruled out. Second, even having made her his wife, he is to give her one full month of adjustment after her traumatic experience before he may exercise the normal sexual right of a husband. That is, he is to allow her a time of mourning before he even has sex with her at all. And then, third, if after all that he regrets his decision, he is not to profit from his mistake by selling her as a slave and dishonour her in that way. No, he has made her his wife, so he must divorce her properly and let her go free.

War is horrible. Women suffer greatly when soldiers win battles. But it seems that this law is trying to put the needs of the weak and vulnerable person (she is a woman, a foreigner, and a captive) above the customary rights of the powerful person (he is a man, a soldier, a victor, and a husband).

c) The need of a debtor as against the legal claims of a creditor (Deut 24:6, 10–13)

One of the ways the Old Testament tried to help the poor was by encouraging others to lend freely and without charging interest. It was a righteous thing to do and pleasing to God (Pss 37:26; 112:5; Prov 19:17). We are talking here about borrowing because of poverty and need—not borrowing as an investment in a commercial deal. This would typically be the case of an Israelite farmer who needed to borrow some seed-corn to sow a crop for next year or something relatively simple like that. It is not talking about banking credit and debt in a commercial economy.

In all societies, lending and borrowing need to be properly controlled. Usually those who lend require some kind of security for their loan. The borrower will give something to the creditor as a pledge, or collateral, to make sure they pay off their debt. That again is the simple economic reality, and Israelite law accepted it.

However, yet again, Old Testament law puts itself on the side of the weaker party (the poor person who has to take a loan) by requiring the creditor to respect the needs of the debtor and not deal with them harshly. First of all, the poor person still needs to be able to make their own bread and feed themselves and their family. So the creditor must not deprive them of the means to do that (the grinding stone that every household had for making flour). Second, the poor man needs shelter and warmth at night. So the creditor must not take basic clothing as security, or if they do, they must return it by nightfall (so why take it in the first place, if the person is so poor that all they can offer you is the coat on their back?). And third, even the need of the poor for the dignity and privacy of their own home is to be respected. The creditor must not barge into the debtor's home and take whatever they want. No, they must stay outside and allow the debtor to choose freely whatever they want to offer in pledge.

We know that in many societies the way money lenders deal with their debtors can be very harsh indeed. All the power, and sometimes most of the law too, is on the side of the creditor. But here in Israel, God looks at it the other way round, from the angle of the needy person who has to borrow in order to survive. That person's needs must be given priority and protection — over against the legal rights and claims of the wealthier lender.

d) The need of the landless as against the legal rights of the landowner (Deut 24:19–22)

Imagine that you are a farmer in Israel working your piece of land. You might think: "This is my land. I have done all the hard work of clearing it, ploughing, sowing, and harvesting. Surely I am entitled to 100 percent of the produce of what my own hard work and investment have produced! Every last grain, grape, and olive belongs to me. Everybody else can look after themselves and stay off my land!"

But God counteracts such an attitude with this law of gleaning. Actually, God himself is the ultimate landlord (Lev 25:23). And as landlord, God reserves the right to insist that *all* Israelites in the land should "eat and be satisfied" — even if they are poor or without land and family of their own. So God gave such people freedom to glean in the fields at harvest time and insisted that the harvesters make sure that there were plenty of gleanings left to be gathered. This law concerning gleaning in the fields, olive groves, and vineyards is also found in Leviticus 19:9–10. The story of Ruth and Boaz is a good illustration of an Israelite farmer carefully obeying this law (Ruth 2).

So once again, human need is put first. Care for the needy must take priority over the personal benefits of land ownership. And that is especially true if people are hungry (Deut 23:24–25).

Now let's go back to Jesus. Since the law itself contained these and other examples of putting human needs first, we can understand why Jesus became angry when the Pharisees and legal experts turned the law into a *burden* instead of a *benefit* to the needy (e.g., Mark 7:9–13; Matt 23:23). Many of the parables of Jesus teach mercy and compassion even when strict justice or popular expectations would go in a different direction (e.g., Matt 20:1–16). In this Jesus reflects the inner spirit and thrust of the law itself.

So then, we should preach and teach Old Testament law in a way that shows it was intended for human benefit. We should highlight the law's own priorities for the weak and needy and ask our people to think about what these could mean in today's society—not least within the church itself. There is plenty of material in the law that shows the heart of God for the needs of human beings, especially the vulnerable, those who are socially, economically, ethnically, or sexually disadvantaged in our fallen world. We can preach and teach those texts powerfully. They are indeed "useful for teaching, rebuking, correcting and training in righteousness." But (to repeat) remember to connect them to the character and saving grace of God. Otherwise we may just stir up legalistic guilt or sentimental idealism.

THE SCALE OF VALUES IN OLD TESTAMENT LAW

There are more than 600 individual laws in the law of Moses (so I'm told—I've never counted them for myself). But they are not all "just the same." There are *different kinds* of laws. Some laws deal with serious criminal offences; some deal with civil disputes between citizens; some deal with family matters, like marriage, divorce, and the upbringing of children; some regulate the sacrificial and ritual arrangements of Israel's religious practice; some simply urge the Israelites to be compassionate and caring. And there are *different values and priorities* within the law. Some are more central and important than others. People did ask the question, What really matters? What is the most important thing in God's law?

As we saw above, *Moses* answered that question with five things: to fear the LORD, walk in his ways, love him, serve him, and obey him (Deut 10:12–13). *Micah* reduced it still further to three: to do justice, love mercy, and walk humbly with God (Mic 6:8). And then finally Jesus reduced it to two, when someone asked him that very question: to love the LORD your God with all your heart and soul and strength (Deut 6:4–5) and to love your neighbour as yourself (Lev 19:18).

When Jesus gave that reply, the teacher of the law who asked the question made an interesting response. " 'Well said, teacher,' the man replied. 'You are right in saying that God is one and there is no other but him [Deut 6:4]. To love him with all your heart, with all your understanding and with all your strength, and to love your neighbour as yourself *is more important than all burnt offerings and sacrifices*' " (Mark 12:32–33; my italics).

Jesus immediately commended him for his answer. But it was not a sudden flash of some new idea. That teacher was simply echoing the way the Old Testament Scriptures also said that some things are far more important than others—even within God's law. Think, for example, of the words of Samuel to Saul: "To obey is better than sacrifice" (1 Sam 15:22); or the words of God to Israel through Hosea: "I desire mercy, not sacrifice, and acknowledgment of God rather than burnt offerings" (Hos 6:6); or of the voice of Proverbs: "To do what is right and just is more acceptable to the LORD than sacrifice" (Prov 21:3).

So when we are reading passages of Old Testament law with a view to preaching and teaching from them, we ought to be asking, What are the most important laws here? What values and principles need to be given priority? Are any of these laws more central to the "big" issues—what Jesus called "the more important matters of the law" (Matt 23:23)?

It's one thing to ask such questions, but how do we begin to answer them? Well, one way is to think about the core list that seems to stand at the head of the whole Old Testament law—the Ten Commandments, or the Decalogue ("Ten Words"), as it is sometimes called. The order of the commandments seems to reflect—in a broad sense—a scale of values. Now, of course, they are all important! But do some have priority above the others? It seems so.

The Ten Commandments

The Ten Commandments begin with God and end with the inner thoughts of a person's heart. In a sense the tenth commandment (against covetousness) and the first commandment (against worshipping any god other than the LORD God) correspond to one another. That is because covetousness by its nature puts other persons or things in the position that should be occupied by God alone. As Paul put it, "greed [which is the New Testament equivalent of 'covetousness'] which is idolatry" (Col 3:5).

- *First commandment*: God comes first and above all: no other gods

And that is reinforced by the next two commandments:

- *Second commandment:* no making of idols
- *Third commandment:* no wrong use of God's name

Then comes one that is both for God's sake and for the sake of family and society life:

- *Fourth commandment:* keep the Sabbath day holy and take rest

After those four, which focus on God, come the remaining six, which focus on relationships in human society. Once more, the order seems important.

- *Fifth commandment:* protecting the stability of the family through honouring parents
- *Sixth commandment:* protecting the sanctity of life — do not murder
- *Seventh commandment:* protecting the sanctify of sex and marriage — do not commit adultery
- *Eighth commandment:* protecting personal property — do not steal
- *Ninth commandment:* protecting the integrity of justice and trust in society — do not bear false witness
- *Tenth commandment:* getting at the root cause of many of the above problems — do not covet things or people in your heart

The order of the commandments gives us some clues about Israel's scale of values. Roughly speaking, the order was:

- God
- Family
- Life
- Sex
- Property

Does that challenge you at all when you think about what is treated as most important in your country or culture? Fortunately, many parts of the world have not gone the way of Western society—yet. They still honour God in some way, and they still treat family as very important. Long may that continue. But when I think of the Western society that I live in, it feels as if that order is turned exactly upside down. Money and sex matter more than almost anything else—if you just look at the greed and immorality of so much of our media, politics, advertising, and so on. Human life is valued less and less—especially when it comes to the very elderly and the unborn. Families are breaking down at an ever-increasing rate, both in relations between the sexes and between parents and children. And God is left out of most people's thinking and values; in any meaningful sense, God is irrelevant. Preaching and teaching the Ten Commandments in today's world—in my part of the world anyway—is profoundly counter-cultural.

What about the Death Penalty?

Thinking about the Ten Commandments and Israel's scale of values can help us in one other way, I think. We can be easily troubled by the severity of some of the laws in the Old Testament. The death penalty is prescribed for a number of offences that would certainly not be capital offences in our societies. Why is that? Here are a few things that put it in perspective.

First, Israel was a theocracy. That is to say, their nation was founded on their covenant with the LORD God. God was therefore the highest authority in the land, way above any king, judge, priest, or other leader. Even those high offices of the state were subject to God as the supreme authority. So any offence that threatened that covenant relationship with God was treated very seriously. For even if the offence were committed by only one individual or their family, it could endanger the whole society by breaking the covenant.

Second, when we study those laws that do have a death penalty attached, we find that all of them are either direct violations of one of the Ten Commandments or very closely related to one of them. That in itself shows how important those Ten Commandments were for Israel. They were like boundary markers for the covenant. If you broke these, you were putting yourself outside the covenant with God—and that could lead to death.

Third, therefore, the death penalty was attached to offences that, for Israel under the covenant, were considered the most serious of all. They show something of their scale of values. Any society punishes most severely the things they think are most dangerous to the health of society as a whole. Israel's penalties show us what *they* thought was dangerous for their whole society. That included:

- Actions that took people away from worshipping only the living God—like making idols. Such actions would bring the wrath of God on the nation.

- Actions that damaged society for everybody—like breaking the Sabbath.

- Actions that damaged the fabric of healthy family life on which the whole society depended—like rebelling against parents and ruining sexual integrity through marital adultery.

Fourth, however, not all breaking of the Ten Commandments was treated as a capital offence. The scale of values that we saw above in the order of the commandments is also reflected in the penalties. So, if a person flagrantly broke any of the first six commands—from idolatry to murder—the penalty was death. For the seventh (adultery), the death penalty was indeed available, but there is no record of it ever being carried out. And the eighth (theft) was definitely *not* a capital offence. You could not be put to death for stealing property in Old Testament Israel under normal law. Theft in war was different (Achan, Josh 7); and theft of *people* (kidnapping for slavery) *was* punishable by death (Exod 21:16; Deut 24:7). The ninth (lying, or false witness) would not be punishable by death unless you were caught falsely accusing somebody of a crime which would have gotten them executed if your accusation had been believed. Perjury was treated very seriously (Deut 19:16–21). And the tenth, since it was a matter of the heart and mind, could not have had any penalties in a law court.

Covetousness is a sin, not a crime (though of course it can lead to all kinds of crime).

So then, if we are dealing with some laws in the Old Testament that seem very severe and puzzling to us, we should not just dismiss them as irrelevant. Nor, of course, should we be pushing to have them enforced like that in today's world. We are not ancient Israel under the old covenant, and God did not intend the law he gave them to be applied unchanged to every society for all time. History changes. Cultures change. God knows that too! Rather, we should ask what the severity of some laws tells us about the moral priorities God was trying to teach. Why was this so important at that time? Does it express a value that we may have lost? Even if we do not, and should not, apply that kind of penalty today, what can we still learn from Israel's scale of values that can challenge our societies?

BUILDING A BRIDGE FROM OLD TESTAMENT LAW TO THE WORLD OF TODAY

The task of preaching and teaching the Bible involves building a bridge from the world of the Bible into the world in which we live today. That is a *culture bridge*. It also involves building a bridge between the particular Bible text that we are going to teach from and the message that we eventually deliver. That is a *communication bridge*. I'm thinking here about the first of those. How can we move from the world of Old Testament law to the world of today in such a way as to be both *faithful* to the original text and *relevant* to our contemporary context?

Now, what is one of the very first principles of understanding and interpreting the Bible? We should not ask, "What does this text mean for me now?" until we have worked very hard to find out "What did this text mean to them then?" We have to put ourselves back into the Bible itself and think about: Who wrote this text? When? Where? And to whom? Why did they write it? What were they talking about (the general subject)? And what were they saying about what they were talking about (the actual content)? What is the main point? Well, when we read Old Testament law, we have to do the same thing. We ask questions!

But what sorts of questions should we ask about Old Testament laws? Think about how laws work—in your society or in any society. Laws in any society are made for a purpose. Laws protect people from violence or unjust treatment. Laws restrict the power of some people in order to protect others. Laws try to balance the rights and responsibilities of different groups in society. Laws promote social objectives—that is, a government will have some political vision of what kind of ideal society they would like to see and will pass laws that try to move society in that direction. Sometimes laws are passed in order to stop a bad situation from getting worse. For example, when I was young, cars in the UK did not have seat belts at all. People got killed when cars crashed head-on. So car manufacturers put seat belts in the front seats, but wearing them was voluntary. Eventually, the government passed a law that made it compulsory to wear seat belts—in the front and back of the car. Why? The *objective* of that law was to reduce the number of deaths in road accidents. It *compelled* people to make themselves safer. It was a law, but it was for the good of everybody and society as a whole.

Now think about ancient Israel. God gave them a system of laws. It did not cover everything in life, but it certainly provided a kind of constitutional framework for key areas such as economic, political, judicial, military, and family life—as well as their religious practice, of course. So as we read and study that system of law we should be thinking of its social objectives. What kind of society was it trying to produce? What kind of society was it trying to prevent or replace?

Remember when we were thinking about how to preach and teach from Old Testament stories I said that we need to ask not only, "What is this story about? What happens in it?" but also, "*Why* is this story here in the Bible at all? What is the *reason* why the writer has selected and included this story and put it in this place?" We need to do something similar with Old Testament law. It's not enough just to ask, "What does this law say?" We also need to ask, "Why is this law there in the Bible? What was the *purpose* of this law in Israel's society?"

Checklist

Here are some questions you could ask about any passage in the legal sections of Old Testament law. Remember—you are asking them about Old Testament Israel, not about any society today. This is about them, not about you!

☐ What kind of bad situation was this law trying to prevent?

☐ What kind of better situation was this law trying to promote?

☐ Whom was this law aiming to protect?

☐ Who would have benefited from this law and why?

☐ Whose power was this law trying to restrict, and how did it do so?

☐ Whose needs was this law trying to provide for, and how did it do so?

☐ What rights and responsibilities were embodied in this law?

☐ What kind of behaviour did this law encourage, and how did it do that?

☐ What kind of behaviour did this law discourage, and how did it do that?

☐ What vision of society can be seen in this law?

☐ What would Israelite society have been like if they had fully obeyed this law?

☐ What moral principles, values, or priorities can you see embodied in this law?

☐ What reasons (if any) were included to encourage people to keep this law?

☐ What sanctions or penalties (if any) were attached to this law? And what does that show about how serious and important it was?

Let's be honest. There will be times when no matter how many questions you ask or how hard you work to think of good answers, you will still end up a bit frustrated and say to yourself, "I really haven't any idea why this law is here and what its purpose was!" Let me tell you right away that there are some parts of the Old Testament that I don't understand very well. There are some laws that even the world's greatest biblical scholars have never explained beyond any possible doubt. But that only happens in a few cases and in laws that seem fairly obscure anyway. I really don't mind having a few unsolved cases on my shelf when the overall message and point of so much of the law is very clear. As we have seen, Moses, Micah, and Jesus could summarize it in a few primary principles. And I can promise you that often the simple exercise of *asking questions* like those above does indeed lead to a better understanding of the Old Testament law. We begin to see not just *what it says* but *why it is there*. We begin to grasp what kind of society God wanted Israel to be—even though they failed.

As we build up that picture of what God wanted in Old Testament Israel, it prepares us to take the next step—to cross the bridge to our own world.

So here you are. You have done your exegetical homework. You have asked the questions and written down your answers. As far as you can, you have tried to understand a section of Old Testament law within its own context—ancient Israel at that time. What next?

Stand back. Take a deep breath. Very deliberately step out of the Old Testament world and back into your own world—wherever that is. You are no longer thinking in the Old Testament context but in your own context. So as you "cross that bridge" back from the world of the Old Testament to your own world, what you must do is *change the context but preserve the objective.* That is, in thinking about your own context—your church, your culture, your country, the society around you—how could the objectives that you have found there in the laws of the Old Testament be achieved today?

And once again, the best way to work that out is to ask questions (by now you should be very used to me saying that the key to good Bible preaching and teaching is to start by asking good questions!).

Checklist

We can ask a parallel set of questions to the ones we asked about Old Testament Israel but ask them about *our own context*. We can look for similar situations, problems, needs, powers, rights and wrongs, good and bad behaviours, and so on that need to be addressed in our own society. Then in that new context, the context of our own contemporary world, we ask how the objectives of Old Testament laws can be achieved.

☐ What kinds of situations in our society are similar to those in the Old Testament laws, and in what ways?

☐ What kinds of people in our society are facing needs that are like the needy in Israel, and why?

☐ What kinds of people in our society have the most power and influence, and in what ways does that need to be restricted?

☐ What kind of protection and provision do some people need?

☐ What should be our objectives in our society if we want to make it more like the kind of society that God wanted Israel to be, according to the laws he gave them?

☐ What could we do in practice, or encourage our people and society to do, that would reflect the values and priorities of God that we see in Old Testament law?

☐ How could the principles found in Old Testament laws be applied in practical life today—in my own life, in the church, in wider society?

☐ Does the New Testament make any reference to this Old Testament law, and if so, what does it say? Does the New Testament see the basic intention of this law as something that we also need to follow in our Christian commitment?

☐ In Christian terms (that is, in the light of Christ and the gospel), what is our motivation now for responding to God's law?

☐ How, then, can I preach and teach this part of Scripture in a way that is faithful to its original context and purpose but also relevant to my own people now? How can I make this text "speak again," so that people today see its relevance and are moved to obey God in response?

As you work toward a sermon or lesson from Old Testament law with such questions in mind, also keep in mind all the key points we've made in this chapter and the previous one:

☐ God's grace must always be the starting point, and whatever we do or encourage others to do must be in response to what God has done for us.

☐ God's people are called to live for the sake of God's mission, which is to bring blessing to all nations.

☐ Israel's law was meant to be a model for other societies in other cultures and other times of history, so it will always be "useful" and relevant.

☐ Always look for what the text teaches about the character of God.

☐ Remember the law was given for human well-being, so don't turn it into a legalistic burden.

☐ Major on the really important requirements of the law—as Jesus taught them: love for God and for our neighbour, justice, mercy, and faithfulness.

☐ And remember the reality of sin and failure in our fallen world and that both the preacher and the congregation alike are sinners in need of repentance and forgiving grace.

QUESTIONS AND EXERCISES

Choose one or more of the following passages and work on them using the two checklists above: that is, asking questions about the objectives of the laws in their Old Testament context and then asking questions about your own context today and what you can learn and apply from the Old Testament laws.

- Exodus 21:12–19
- Exodus 21:28–36
- Exodus 23:1–9
- Leviticus 19:33–34
- Deuteronomy 24:6, 10–13
- Deuteronomy 24:14–15

SAMPLE OUTLINE

God's People in Society
Leviticus 19

This is the chapter from which Jesus took his "second greatest commandment in the law": love your neighbour as yourself. That command is surrounded by many others which would be transforming in any society. But I begin by emphasizing that the chapter is not just an essay on social ethics or economics. It begins and ends with God: the holiness of God (v. 2) and the salvation of God (v. 36). You might not be able to preach or teach this whole chapter in one time. It might be easier to split it up over several. But each time, make sure you emphasize the context of saving grace.

Who Are We?

It is important to approach the content of the chapter through the "lens" of the story in which Israel's law is set. These laws were given to people who were redeemed and sanctified by God and who had been put in the world to serve God's mission to the nations. Those truths still apply to us in Christ.

- *People who are redeemed (v. 36).* The important motivation of the exodus as God's redeeming grace in action.

- *People who are sanctified (v. 2).* Holiness is both a fact and a duty. It is something God does ("I have set you apart") and something we are then called to live out ("be holy"). The two sides of this truth are combined in Leviticus 20:26. And the practical effect is seen in Leviticus 18:1–3—distinctiveness from the surrounding culture and its idolatries.

- *People with a mission (Exod 19:4–6).* This is not explicit in the text but implied in the phrase "be holy." That is necessary for Israel to fulfil their mission of being God's priesthood in the midst of the nations.

All three themes are found in 1 Peter, applied to Christians: we are *redeemed* (1:18–19), *sanctified* (1:2, 14–15), and *on mission* for God among the nations (2:9–12). So we are called to live in the world redemptively, distinctively, and attractively. A community of people who are being transformed by God can have a transforming influence in society.

How Can We Make a Difference?

Leviticus 19 is quoted often in the New Testament (e.g., Matt 22:39–40; Rom 13:9; 1 Pet 1; Jas 2:8). If you have a cross-reference Bible, check out the related passages also in Exodus 21–23 and Deuteronomy 22–25 especially. Think what society would be like if these laws were practised today! How can Christians be advocates for these principles and values in society?

- *Transforming the family (vv. 3, 20–30, 32).* Note the balance of duties of children to parents and parents to children. And care for the elderly.

- *Transforming poverty (vv. 9–10).* This is one part of Israel's welfare system. See also the third-year tithe for the needy (Deut 14:28–29) and the seventh-year release of debt and slaves (Deut 15). Note also the concern for the disabled in v. 14 (compare Deut 27:18 and Prov 17:5).

- *Transforming the workplace (v. 13b).* Deuteronomy 24:14–15 is even stronger. A challenge to Christian employers? Relevance to employment law and practice in your country?

- *Transforming the marketplace (vv. 35–36).* Honesty in commerce and trade—from local market stall to international trading relations. God detests dishonesty in business—it is put in the same category as sexual immorality. Do we have the same standards? Compare Deuteronomy 25:13–15.

- *Transforming the legal system (vv. 15–16).* Old Testament law was passionate about preserving the integrity of the justice system and rooting out corruption and bribery. This is emphasized even more in Exodus 23:1–9. We need to pray for judges and lawyers and encourage more Christians to be salt and light in that arena.

- *Transforming social relationships (vv. 11–12, 17–18).* It would be better not to have to go to court at all! So work for relationships in the neighbourhood that foster harmony, reduce conflict, and promote honest, truthful speech. Verse 17 is full of subtle insight—hatred can be as damaging as violence, as Jesus and John later pointed out (Matt 5:21–22; 1 John 3:15). Have the courage to point out wrongdoing. Avoid even grudges. Tough words. Love your neighbour as yourself—toughest of all and unlimited in its scope (Luke 10:25–37).

- *Transforming race relations (vv. 33–34).* Note the amazing parallel between v. 18 and v. 34—"And you shall love …" That phrase occurs four times: Deuteronomy 6:5 (God); Leviticus 19:18 (neighbour); Deuteronomy 10:19 and Leviticus 19:34 (both, the foreigner). Practical love for the outsider, the landless, refugees, asylum seekers. Illustration: Boaz's protection for Moabite Ruth. Note also: equality under the law for all ethnic groups in society—equal treatment for the foreigner as for the native born. We still fall far short of that.

- *Transforming worship (vv. 4–8, 26–28, 30–31).* Only a few laws in the chapter are about religious rituals. They aim to keep Israel's worship not only pure but also socially inclusive. No idolatry (v. 4). Share the food! (vv. 5–8—to eat the meat in one or two days would involve inviting a lot of people to share it). Avoid pagan customs (vv. 26–28)—these were features of Canaanite rituals, occultism, and body cutting. What are the marks of idolatry around us today? Consumerism?

Can we see a transforming vision of society in Leviticus 19? What would the world be like if there were:

- Respect and responsibility in the family
- Practical and accessible help for the poor
- Fairness in the workplace
- Honesty in the marketplace
- Justice in the legal system
- Love in the neighbourhood
- Equality in race relations
- Purity in our worship?

This is not a utopian dream. This is God's idea of "holiness." Should we not be seeking such things wherever we can in our own societies?

How Can We "Fulfil" Old Testament Law Today?

We are not "under the law" in a legalistic sense, as Paul made clear. But Jesus said he did not come to abolish the law but to fulfil it. Paul speaks of us "fulfilling the law" in two places:

- *By living according to the Spirit (Rom 8:1–4).* Being saved by Christ and filled with the Holy Spirit, we are enabled to live in ways that fulfil God's original purpose for the law.

- *By loving our neighbour (Rom 13:8–10).* Paul echoes Jesus' use of Leviticus 19:18. We obey God's law when we love, when we seek the best interests of others around us, when we are "eager to do good" — not as a way to achieve our own righteousness but as the way to make the gospel attractive (Titus 2:9–14).

CHAPTER 11

Meet the Prophets

W hat do you think about people who are supposed to have "great prophetic ministries"? There are a lot of them around in some parts of the world. They make a lot of noise and they make a lot of money. But are they "prophetic" in any way like the prophets of the Old Testament? Or, to put it the other way round, were the prophets of the Old Testament in any way like some of the famous "prophetic preachers" today? Well, I think there are some pretty important differences! My hope is that this chapter will help you to preach better from the *biblical* prophets, not make you imagine that you can imitate those who claim to be "prophets" today. Maybe also it will help you evaluate these modern "prophets" in the light of the Bible—which would be a good thing.

WHO WERE THE PROPHETS?

So who were the prophets in the Old Testament? The first thing to do is distinguish between a large number of *people* who were prophets in Israel, and the small number (fifteen) of *books* named after prophets that have been included in the Bible.

God gave prophets to the people of Israel throughout the period of the Old Testament, and most of them do not have books named after them. Moses was a prophet. So was his sister Miriam (Exod 15:20; Mic 6:4). In fact, Moses was in some ways the model for all the later prophets (Deut 18:18). Then there were prophets like Samuel, Nathan, Elijah, and Elisha, and there were many others who are mentioned in the history books but not named. Some of the most notable prophets were women. Five women are named as prophets in the Old Testament (Miriam, Deborah, Huldah, the wife of Isaiah—who might actually have been Huldah—and Noadiah).[1]

Then there are the fifteen books in the Old Testament that contain the words of particular named prophets. There are the three large books: Isaiah, Jeremiah, and Ezekiel, and then the so-called "Book of the Twelve." Those are sometimes referred to as the "Minor Prophets"—the twelve prophetic books that are listed in your Bible from Hosea to Malachi. But that word "minor" only means that their books are short not that they themselves were minor or unimportant in the work they did for God in their own day. Some of them were very significant indeed.

In our Bibles, Daniel comes between Ezekiel and the Book of the Twelve. So that makes sixteen books. But in the Hebrew collection Daniel is not listed among the Prophets but among the Writings. That's why I mentioned fifteen books above: the three "Major Prophets" plus twelve "Minor Prophets."

What all these prophets had in common—whether they got a book by their name or not—is that they were *men and women who spoke out for God*. So that is where we need to start. Let's think of the different parts of their bodies as a convenient way to remember some key things about the prophets.

Prophets Had Mouths: They Spoke for God

Quite simply, prophets were messengers. They were God's mouthpiece. God spoke his word, through them, directly into the ears and minds and hearts of his people at different times. What the prophet said was what God wanted to be said. When they spoke, they began or ended with words like "This is what the LORD says."

So even though we are thinking now about how we can preach and teach from what is *written down* in the Bible of the words of some of the prophets, we should remember that the prophets first of all *spoke* to the people. People listened to a prophet's preaching long before they were able to read a prophet's book. It's important to keep that in mind when we read their books. Try to imagine what it was like to be *hearing* these words and how you would

---

1. Interestingly, the New Testament mentions five women prophets as well—Anna and the four daughters of Philip—though Paul refers to other women in general who were exercising the gift of prophecy in the churches.

have responded to them. Read Jeremiah 36 and you'll see how God instructed Jeremiah to turn his spoken words (spoken over twenty-three years) into a written scroll. But even then it had to be read aloud (three times in one day, before it got burned!).

Now the words "prophet" or "prophetic" are sometimes used today about foretelling the future. "I'm not a prophet," we might say, meaning, "Don't ask me to predict what's going to happen." And some people have the idea that all the Old Testament prophets did was sit around predicting the future all the time. Well, certainly the prophets did sometimes speak about the future and predict certain things ahead of their own time. However, we should see that kind of thing as secondary to their main purpose and actually serving their main purpose.

Their main purpose was to speak God's word directly to the people around them — their own generation. They told the people of Israel what God was thinking and saying about the *present* situation, in the historical circumstances of their own time. So at any point when they *did* speak about something in the future, it was in order to make people think and act differently in the present. Future predictions, in other words, when they happened, were intended to affect the present (their own day), not just leave people gazing into the distance. It has been said that the prophets should be thought of as "forth-tellers," not "fore-tellers." We'll come back to this point shortly and explain further how to handle the predictions concerning the future.

Prophets Had Ears: They Heard God's Word

In order to speak God's word, prophets had to receive it first of all. They were above all instruments or agents of God's word. That's what it means to talk about "inspiration." It does not mean they were wonderfully inspired or inspiring people, like great painters, musicians, or athletes. It simply means that what they communicated was what God wanted to be said — God's word came through their words.

We are not told a lot about how they knew what they were supposed to say. Jeremiah talks about how true prophets had stood in the presence of God and heard his word, whereas false prophets had never done that — had never really heard what God said. So all *their* words were just made up out of their own heads.

Sometimes prophets received a message from God in a vision. Sometimes it was just by seeing something ordinary around them (like a blossoming almond tree, two baskets of figs, or a potter working). Sometimes it felt like an almost physical pressure. Jeremiah says that when he decided *not* to speak any more for God, the word was like a fire burning him on the inside. Isaiah and Ezekiel speak of feeling God's "hand" on them. Ezekiel speaks of "eating the scroll" of God's words—meaning that whatever he spoke was the "digested" word of God from within him. Both Isaiah and Jeremiah had the feeling of God "touching their lips." God told Jeremiah, "I will put my words in your mouth." Hosea heard God's message through the very painful experience of his broken marriage.

The main point to remember is that *what they spoke is what they had heard from God* (by whatever means). So whenever the Israelites listened to the prophets, they were listening to God. When they refused to listen to a prophet whom God had sent, they were refusing to listen to God. God made that very clear from the start (Deut 18:15–20). And that means, in turn, that when *we* listen to the prophets by reading their words in the Bible, we too are listening to God through those words now stored in Scripture.

However, we need to be careful! This does not mean that when we *preach a sermon* from one of the books of the prophets *we* are speaking the words of God directly. The word of God is what we are preaching *from*. And we certainly do want our people to hear what God is saying to them now, today, *from* God's word. But we must always make a clear distinction between the words of *Scripture*—revealed, inspired, and authoritative—and the words we speak in our *sermons*. Of course I must try to be as faithful as I can to what God *said* in the written word. And of course I do want God to speak to people from his word by his Spirit. But when I preach I should never claim that God *is saying now* exactly the words I am using as I preach. The *Bible* is God's word. My sermon is *not* in itself God's word, though it seeks to communicate as faithfully as possible what God wants to say through his word today. In fact, we should encourage our people to constantly check what we preach. They should check our preaching in the light of the Scriptures to see if what *we say* in our sermons is faithful to what *God said* in his word. That's what the Bereans did even with the Apostle Paul's preaching, and it is a good example (Acts 17:11)! Encourage your people to follow it.

Prophets Had Eyes: They Saw Things from God's Point of View

One of the early words that was used in the Old Testament for prophets was "seers." It means what it says. They were "see-ers." Sometimes this meant that, by God's mysterious power, they were able to see something others could not. For example, Samuel could tell Saul and his servant where their lost donkeys were (1 Sam 9). Elisha could see the army of angels protecting Israel (2 Kgs 6:15–17). This was not by some occult power of clairvoyance but simply because God showed them things others could not see.

But in a more serious sense, the prophets were given insight into what God was doing in the events of their own times. They could *interpret* events and see the hand of God at work. And they could see what God was planning to do in the future as a result of what the people were doing right now. That was usually very uncomfortable, but sometimes it could bring great hope.

- So, for example, when the people broke God's covenant, they thought that it didn't matter how they lived. So long as they went on worshipping God in the temple, they thought they would be safe. But Jeremiah *saw* it from God's point of view, and it was very different. "I have been watching!" says God through Jeremiah (Jer 7:9–11). They were far from safe! God's judgment was coming, and the prophet saw it coming.

- On another occasion, when enemies were threatening Judah, Isaiah told Ahaz not to panic because he could *see*, from God's point of view, that Israel's enemies would soon be destroyed. Isaiah told Ahaz to trust God, but Ahaz refused (Isa 7:1–12).

- When some of the people of Judah were taken off into exile, those left behind in Jerusalem thought that those carried off into exile were finished and discarded, while they (the ones still left in Jerusalem) would be safe and flourish. Jeremiah said that God's opinion was the exact opposite (Jer 24). He could *see* a very different outcome for the two groups.

- When Jeremiah wrote to those exiles of Judah in Babylon, he showed them how to think of their situation differently. They thought it was Nebuchadnezzar who had carried them off (and at a human level it was). But God said, "It was I, me, who carried you into exile, so settle down there with me and seek the welfare of Babylon where I've put you." That was God's point of view, and it took a prophet to tell the people that. Jeremiah *saw* their situation from God's perspective and what God wanted them to do about it.

- When the people had been in exile a long time and many had lost all hope for the future, the prophecies of Isaiah told them that God was going to bring them back to their land and continue his purposes for them, and through them for the whole world. The prophet gave people hope because he *saw* God at work already planning their future.

So when we preach and teach from the prophets, quite often we will find that their message ran counter to the popular thinking of their own time. They stood out. They pointed in a different direction from the way everybody was running. They saw things from God's point of view, and that was challenging and often unpopular. Sometimes we have to do the same in our preaching and teaching, and the prophets can help us have the courage to do it.

Sometimes the prophets could "see" what God was going to do at some unspecified time in the future. Often they would say things like "In that day ..." or "in the Day of the LORD." Of course, they could not know how long into the future that might be. We can look back now and see that some of what they "saw" happened eventually when Jesus came. But some of what they saw pointed even further ahead and still lies in the future—even for us. Later on we'll think about these different "horizons" of the prophets' vision.

Prophets Had Heads: They Had Minds of Their Own

We said above that what the prophets heard was God's word and what they spoke was God's word. But that does not mean that a prophet was just like a dictation machine. They did not stand there with blank staring eyes, mindlessly spouting words that came from above without their minds being engaged. Nor were they speaking in an empty trance induced by drugs or transcendental meditation.

Have you ever seen a ventriloquist with their dummy? Or a puppet show? The dummy or puppet moves its lips and it looks as if you are watching the dummy speaking or the puppet acting. But all the time, of course, it is the ventriloquist or puppet master who is doing the talking or action. The dummy or puppet has no mind or voice of its own. It is a mechanical toy manipulated by the human being holding it. The prophets were *not* like that at all. They were not dummies or puppets. They were not just mouthing words with no thinking in their brains.

On the contrary, when you read each of the books of the prophets carefully, you can see that they were all different. Each one had a style of speaking and writing that was very much their own. Each one had issues that they were very concerned about and spoke about most often. They emphasized different things. They concentrated on different aspects of Israel's past or future. It is very clear that they were *thinkers* as well as *speakers*. Each of them had what we would now call a "theological perspective." So we can speak of "the theology of Isaiah" as distinct from "the theology of Ezekiel." I don't mean they were contradictory—of course they had many points in common—but simply that each had a mind of his own, and God used it.

So whenever they preached a message—even though it was presented as *God's* word—it was very much their own message too. They passionately believed and wrestled with the messages they brought to the people and sometimes engaged in argument and discussion with people over what they were saying.

When, therefore, we preach or teach from any particular prophet, we need to visualize an individual person with a mind of their own. We need to read the whole of their book and find out what made them distinctive. What was their style of speaking? What themes occur again and again? What theological issues are prominent in this prophet's book? How did this prophet *think* about God and Israel?

When God gave his message to a prophet, he engaged that prophet's *mind* in the midst of their circumstances, relationships, and experiences. So that means that the more we try to enter into the mind of the prophet in that context, the better we will understand the word of God that came through them.

Prophets Had Hearts: They Felt What God Felt

> Oh, that my head were a spring of water
> and my eyes a fountain of tears!
> I would weep day and night
> for the slain of my people.
>
> *(Jer 9:1)*

Jeremiah was so distraught by the suffering that he saw coming on his own people that he felt his tears could never end, like a spring of water. That is deeply emotional language. It shows us that the prophets had feelings too. They did not just *speak* a message. They did not just *think* about their message. They *felt* their message passionately.

In fact, just as their words communicated the word of God, so also their emotions expressed the emotions of God. We human beings are made in the image of God. So although of course God does not have wild and uncontrollable emotions the way we sometimes do, God does *feel*. And the words we have to use for our own feelings are what the Bible also uses for God. God loves and longs for people. God is angry at sin and evil—especially at injustice and cruelty. God is compassionate and cares for the poor, needy, and vulnerable. God is grieved when he is rejected. God is filled with joy when people and creation are blessed. Those are emotional words. They are human words. But they speak about something real and true in God's own being.

Naturally, therefore, when the prophets speak about things that generate such emotions in the heart and mind of God, they themselves express the same emotions in their preaching. In fact, in that quotation from Jeremiah above, it is God himself who is speaking through the prophet. The language of "I," "me," and "my" between Jeremiah 8:21 and 9:3 can all refer back to God himself (as it certainly does at the end of 9:3)—using very human language. God is in tears! And so is Jeremiah, therefore. Sometimes Jeremiah is called "the weeping prophet." That is because he spoke on behalf of the weeping God—God who was deeply sad and grieving because of the tragedy that was about to fall on Israel for their sin and wickedness.

And for some of the prophets, the task of bearing the words of God and feeling the emotions of God took a terrible toll on their lives. For Jeremiah it brought loneliness and intense suffering, bordering on suicidal depression. For Hosea it brought the heartbreak of a broken marriage. For Ezekiel it brought the grief of bereavement for his wife. These men were human beings. Try to keep that in mind as you read their words. Think of a living voice behind the words on the page.

So when you read the prophets, look for the emotions in their speech and describe them specifically. Often you will find anger, of course, because they were talking about the anger of God against sin and rebellion. But here are some other emotions to look for:

- Longing: "if only you had listened."

- Nostalgia for the past: "I remember when you used to love me."

- Tenderness, like that of a parent: "How can I give you up, Ephraim, my son?"

- Faithfulness, like that of a husband: "I have loved you with everlasting love."

- The feeling of being baffled or puzzled: "Why do you go on doing this? How can you behave like this? Even animals are better!"

- Excitement about future blessing: "Be amazed at what I am going to do!"

- Comfort: "Comfort, comfort my people …"

Then, when you come to preach, think about how you might reflect the emotion of the prophet in the way you preach. The trouble with a lot of preaching today is that it can easily become just one big long shout. The tone is always the same. But it should not be. If our text speaks of God's anger and rebuke, we may reflect that. But if it is filled with tears and sadness, we should help people feel what God and the prophet felt. If it is filled with tenderness and love, show that. If it is filled with comfort and hope, let people feel that.

Prophets Had Hands: Sometimes They Turned Words into Actions

Today we sometimes use visual aids. Children love them, of course. At a more technical level, we might make use of pictures on a screen or PowerPoint presentations. We all know that when we see something as well as hear a message, we will remember it a lot better. God knows that too (he gave us eyes and ears!). So sometimes God instructed his prophets to deliver a message along with an action or sign that would reinforce it. Sometimes this might be a simple, everyday kind of thing that, in the circumstances, demonstrated great faith—such as Jeremiah's purchase of a field in Jeremiah 32. Sometimes it might be very dramatic—as when Jeremiah took a huge clay pot and smashed it to pieces outside the city in the presence of the political leaders (Jer 19). Other examples of acted prophecies include the following:

- Ahijah tore his cloak into twelve pieces and gave ten to Jeroboam to symbolize Jeroboam tearing ten tribes of Israel away from King Rehoboam in Jerusalem (1 Kgs 11).

- Isaiah went around naked in Jerusalem to portray the shame of captivity that lay ahead (Isa 20).

- Jeremiah bought and wore a new linen sash; then he buried it till it was rotten and useless to show what Israel had become like in God's sight (Jer 13).

- Jeremiah put an ox-yoke on his shoulders and burst into an international diplomatic conference in Jerusalem to tell the ambassadors of other nations to submit to the "yoke" of Nebuchadnezzar because God had raised him up for the moment (Jer 27).

- Ezekiel lay on his side "besieging" a model of Jerusalem on a large clay brick to show the first exiles in Babylon that the city would soon be captured and destroyed (Ezek 4–5).

- Jesus threw out the money changers in the temple—a prophetic action that was probably interpreted as meaning that the temple itself would be destroyed (Matt 21:12–13).

If we preach from any passage where there is an action that symbolized or reinforced the message, we will need to explain it. It is a good way to bring the message to life and help people remember it—which was why it happened in the first place, of course!

Checklist

So, as you work on a passage in a prophetic book, think of the body parts of the prophet and ask the following questions:

☐ *Mouth:* What was the prophet actually *saying* here? What was the point he was making?

☐ *Ears:* What had the prophet *heard* from God? What was it that God was wanting to say?

☐ *Eyes:* What did the prophet *see* about God and the world that was different from how people at the time thought? What insight or discernment did the prophet have into his own times?

☐ *Head:* What was in the *mind* of the prophet? What were his distinctive concerns and ways of speaking?

☐ *Heart:* What was the prophet *feeling* as he spoke these words? How did his emotions reflect God's?

☐ *Hands:* What did the prophet *do* (if anything) to reinforce his message?

KNOW THE HISTORY

We must always read any passage in the Bible within its own historical context before asking how it speaks to us today. In the case of the prophets this is probably more important than almost anywhere else. Quite simply, it is impossible to understand them properly unless you understand the historical background of their messages—at least broadly, if not in detail (though the more detail we know, the better).

This point follows, really, from the whole of the last one. The prophets were people whom God sent to speak his word very directly to the people of Israel right in the midst of the things that were happening at any given time. They were speaking to their own people against the background of those events and circumstances. Remember: the words we read on the page of a prophet's book were written *for* us (that is, for us to read and learn from much later on), but they were not written *to* us or *about* us. So as we study any particular passage, we have to find out, as much as we can, to *whom* these words were spoken or written and *what* these words were written about. What was going on?

Now here's a piece of good news. The fifteen books of the prophets (or sixteen, if you include Daniel) are concentrated into a period of Israel's history of approximately three hundred years (only!). If you think of the whole Old Testament, leaving out the stories between Genesis 1–11, it is a history that lasted at least 1,500 years. So the *books* of the prophets arose within only a fraction of that time. Even though there were prophets sent by God throughout the whole Old Testament period, the ones that ended up in named books lived within a period of three hundred years.

Amos is the first prophet whose words were recorded in a book with his own name. His ministry was around 760 BC, that is, in the middle of the eighth century before Christ. Malachi is the last recorded prophet, and he lived around 460 BC, in the middle of the fifth century before Christ.

Can you think of a reason for this concentration of prophetic books in that three-hundred-year period? The most likely reason, I think, is that these were the most turbulent centuries in Israel's history. About two hundred years after David and Solomon and one hundred years after Elijah and Elisha, the northern kingdom of Israel became riddled with social and economic injustice and idolatrous worship of Baal. God sent Amos and Hosea to warn them of his coming judgment and that Israel would be destroyed. That happened when the Assyrians destroyed Samaria in 721 BC and the northern tribes were scattered. After that, Judah in the south became even worse, and God sent prophets like Isaiah, Micah, Zephaniah, Habakkuk, and especially Jeremiah to warn them that unless they changed, Jerusalem too would be destroyed and the people scattered in exile. The warning was not heeded. God did what he threatened. In 587 BC Jerusalem was captured, the temple was burned, and the people carried off into exile in Babylon. That was the most traumatic moment in the whole Old Testament. However, God did not abandon his people. Prophecies from Isaiah, Jeremiah, and Ezekiel (who was with the exiles in Babylon) told them that God would bring them back. And God did, after two generations in exile. And then, when the people of Judah came back to Jerusalem and rebuilt the city and the temple, God sent some more prophets during that post-exilic period— Haggai, Zechariah, and Malachi.

So the books of the prophets relate to the years leading up to the destruction and exile of both kingdoms, the period of the exile of Judah in Babylon, and the years immediately after their return home to Jerusalem. It was an overarching story of God's judgment and God's forgiveness, grace, and restoration. And it was the prophets who explained the reason for the judgment and helped the people trust in God's grace. The word of the prophets accompanied the events of history and interpreted them as the actions of God. The prophets helped Israel (and us) to *understand* that crucial period of Old Testament history and to see how it fitted in with the character and purpose of God.

What all this means is that, in order to understand the prophets well enough to preach and teach from them faithfully, you need to make yourself familiar especially with that three-hundred-year period of Israel's history. It's not really too difficult. You can do at least three things for certain, and a fourth if you have access to more resources.

1. Study the summary of Old Testament history in Appendix 2. Try to fix in your mind the names of the *major* kings of Israel and Judah and the centuries in which they reigned (there's no need to remember every single one — some of them only reigned for a few weeks!). Then try to fix the names of the prophets who lived and spoke in each century. That way you should at least have a broad idea of the order of the prophets and where they fit in the history of Israel.

2. Read through the book of 2 Kings and maybe also 2 Chronicles (which tells the same history but with additional details). The book of 2 Kings starts in the ninth century BC, at the time of Elisha. But from 2 Kings 14 onwards you are into the eighth century, and the narrative runs on until the fall of Jerusalem and the exile. That tells you the big picture. In 2 Kings there is no mention of the prophets since it concentrates on the lives and deeds (good or evil) of the kings, but it provides essential background reading for the prophets from Amos to Ezekiel. And then you can read Ezra – Nehemiah as background for the early years after the exile when the people of Judah had come back to Jerusalem. That is the background for Haggai, Zechariah, and Malachi.

3. Some of the prophets actually dated their messages, telling you when they were given — sometimes quite precisely.

That may be in the form of an editorial introduction to the whole book—naming the king or kings who were on the throne of Israel or Judah when the prophet brought God's word. Or sometimes within the books particular messages are dated. When that happens, try to find out whatever you can about what was happening at that time so that you can understand the prophet's message better. After all, that is why the information is there!

4. All of the above you already have in your hands—your Bible and this book! But if you are able to get and use other resources, they can be a great help. A study Bible will give you good information about each prophet. A Bible handbook or introduction will also help. And of course, good-quality commentaries on each book would be the most helpful of all.

The basic point is this: *the more you can find out about the historical background of each prophet and their message, the more faithfully you will be able to preach that message today.*

QUESTIONS AND EXERCISES

1. Choose one or more of the passages listed below and study them using the Checklist at the end of section 1 above on the "body parts" of the prophets:

   - Isaiah 40:12–31
   - Jeremiah 2:1–13
   - Jeremiah 5:1–17
   - Jeremiah 13:1–11
   - Ezekiel 37:1–14
   - Ezekiel 37:15–28

2. Do the study of Old Testament history in Appendix 2, as suggested in point 1 in the numbered list above.

CHAPTER 12

Preaching and Teaching from the Prophets

O K, so now you've done as much homework as you can — thinking about the background to the book of the prophet you are going to preach or teach from and trying to find out if there were any particular historical circumstances that were the context in which this particular word was delivered. It's time to get down to the text itself. Well, I'm sure you will do all the basic tasks of biblical exegesis that you have learned, observing the text carefully by reading it again and again and asking all the key questions that will help you find its structure and main point.

However, in the case of passages from the books of the prophets, there are a few extra things to keep in mind that should help. Here are some things you can do.

SIMPLIFY THE MESSAGE

Basically, the prophets were sent by God to remind the Israelites of the *covenant relationship* that existed between them. In that sense, there was nothing radically new about the message the prophets brought. Rather, they were recalling, reinforcing, explaining, and applying what the people should already have known on the basis of all that God had done for them and said to them in the past — and especially in the covenant and law that God had made with Israel at Mount Sinai after the exodus.

In chapters 9 and 10 we looked hard at that covenant law, and we need to remember here what we found there — for the prophets knew all this too.

What did the *covenant between God and Israel* involve?

- First, there was a *history*. God had acted to redeem Israel by delivering them out of slavery in Egypt. Later, of course, he had also kept them safe in their wandering in the wilderness for a generation and then brought them into the land he promised. God had done so much for them in his love and grace. That was the foundation of the law in the Torah and also the foundation for the message of the prophets.

- Second, there was a *commitment*. In the covenant, God committed himself to be Israel's God, to bless and protect them, and to make them his instrument for bringing blessing to all nations. And on the other side, Israel committed themselves to obey God's law and live as a whole society in the way God wanted—ultimately for their own good and as a model to the nations. That *mutual commitment* was at the heart of the relationship between God and Israel in the Old Testament.

- Third, there were *sanctions*. If Israel would live in God's ways and obey his law, they would continue to enjoy his blessing. But if they would not, if they rebelled, disobeyed and went after other gods—they would cut themselves off from his blessing and experience God's curse instead. In a world that was already under God's curse ever since the fall, Israel would be no different from the rest of the nations under God's judgment.

One of the best ways to get these key points clear in your mind is to read the following summary chapters. They show how God's covenant included history, commitments, and sanctions (promises and warnings), and they also provide a very strong background for understanding the message of the prophets. I encourage you to take the time to read these passages right now.

- Leviticus 26 (read the whole chapter)
- Deuteronomy 4:23–40
- Deuteronomy 26:16–19
- Deuteronomy 28–30 (this is long, but make sure you read right to the end)

When the prophets came along, they essentially *reminded* Israel of these things. So there was a certain simplicity to their message—even though it took all kinds of forms and all sorts of specific content. Underneath all the variety, the message of the prophets was:

- *To remind Israel of their history.* God had done so much for them in the past. But they were behaving now in a way that was utterly ungrateful and inconsistent.

- *To remind Israel of their commitments.* They had promised to obey God but were utterly failing to do so. In all kinds of ways (specified in different messages), they had broken the covenant.

- *To remind Israel of God's threats and promises.* The covenant had been very clear in warning them of the consequences of disobedience. So unless they changed their ways, those consequences would happen. The curses of the covenant would fall on them. Be warned! But equally, the covenant included promises and blessings—even beyond judgment. So there could be long-term hope, even in the face of immediate disaster. Return to God!

Of course, every prophetic passage is different in some way. But at least start by asking if it fits into one or another of the three "reminders" above. Some passages, of course, fit in all three. Some have other emphases, but if you keep those three "reminders" in mind, it will often help.

To make it even simpler still, see if the text you are reading fits into either of the following *two* basic categories. There are many variations, but very often the message of the prophets was:

- *Either:* Giving an individual or all the people a *warning or threat* of judgment to come—and then calling them to repent and change (messages of judgment).

- *Or:* Giving an individual or all the people a *promise* of salvation and blessing to come—and then calling them to hope and trust in God (messages of hope).

As I said, that doesn't cover all the prophetic messages. There are so many! And there are many variations. But it is a good starting point. Which of those two basic types does your passage most closely fit? That will give you a sense of general orientation before you go into more specific detail. It will also help you decide what will be the basic thrust of the message you will preach or teach from that text.

QUICK EXERCISE

Read the following passages and consider which of the above categories applies best to them, whether the first three or the last two above. Remember, some of them may include more than one element.

- Isaiah 1:10–20
- Isaiah 5:1–7
- Isaiah 42:18–25
- Isaiah 43:1–7
- Jeremiah 2:1–13
- Jeremiah 7:1–15

- Jeremiah 31:1–14
- Ezekiel 18
- Hosea 1
- Amos 2:6–16
- Amos 5:1–15

SPOT THE METHOD

It will also help if we learn to recognize some of the common ways that the prophets gave their messages. Here are some of the most common forms of speech in the prophets.

"This Is What the Lord Says": The Messenger

This is by far the commonest. The prophet simply delivers a message from God. These messages are as varied as whatever God wanted to say to people.

"Guilty As Charged!": The Lawsuit

Sometimes prophets present their message as if they were in a court of law. God is the judge, but he is also the prosecutor. The people of Israel are the accused. Sometimes even the heavens and earth are called as witnesses to complete the scene. Then the prosecutor reads the charge sheet. Here are the things Israel is accused of. After that, the judge pronounces the verdict: guilty. Then comes the sentence—the terrible things that lie ahead because of God's judgment on their rebellion and sin. This way of presenting their message is a strong echo of the covenant relationship.

Examples

- Isaiah 3:13–26
- Hosea 4
- Micah 6:1–8

"We're Doomed!": The Woe

Sometimes prophets cry out "Woe!" on the people. It speaks of God's curse and judgment. But it also has the flavour of a lament. Terrible things are going to happen and people are going to suffer so much, so the prophets express their grief and pain because of that. It is the opposite of the lovely word "Blessed!" Instead of the happiness that comes from living God's way and under his smile, there will come the misery of bringing down the consequences of sin and folly on oneself. So the prophets cry out "Woe!" and lament.

Examples

- Isaiah 5:8–22
- Amos 5:18–20
- Habakkuk 2:6–20
- Micah 2:1–5

"Surprise, Surprise!": The Promise

It would be easy to think (and many in Israel *did* think) that once the covenant was broken there could be no future for Israel. They would simply die out under God's judgment in just punishment for their sins. So when the prophets speak words of *promise and hope*, it is *always* with a sense of amazement and surprise. There is something illogical and unexpected when the prophets speak of the future with the vision of hope beyond judgment or restoration beyond destruction. It is so unexpected that Ezekiel could say it was like preaching to the dry bones of people long dead and seeing them come to life again—a resurrection hope, no less. Nevertheless, such messages are there in many of the prophets, and we should rejoice that they are, and recognize, of course, that they could only be fulfilled ultimately through Jesus Christ.

Examples

- Amos 9:11–15
- Hosea 2
- Hosea 13
- Isaiah 40–55, everywhere
- Jeremiah 31–33
- Ezekiel 37

Once again, of course, we have to say that these categories do not cover all the messages of the prophets. Sometimes they spoke personal messages to individuals—particularly the kings of Israel and Judah. Sometimes they were talking to God out of their own pain and suffering.

HEAR THE LANGUAGE

One difficulty that we are bound to have when reading and teaching the prophets is that their language often seems very strange to us. I don't just mean that they spoke in Hebrew! Even when their messages are translated into our own languages, it is not always easy to grasp what they are talking about. Here are three things to remember as you try to understand a passage.

They Aimed at Persuasion

The prophets were deadly serious in what they preached. They saw that the people were in real danger if they did not change their ways. They also faced a lot of opposition. Sometimes they were rejected and hated. So we should not imagine that they were involved in polite discussions or academic debate. It was a life-and-death struggle sometimes. They were out to *persuade* people to believe what they were saying and act accordingly. Sometimes that meant that they had to *shock* people into paying attention. So don't be surprised when sometimes the language of the prophets seems exaggerated, clashing, and controversial. They could use sarcasm and mockery. They could be disgusting and offensive too. They would say whatever it took to get the people to listen to them. Sadly, as we know, the Israelites mostly chose to ignore the prophets' words and went their own way to their own destruction. But they could never say they had not been warned. So don't be so shocked at the prophets' language that you ignore their message too! If you are faced with a shocking passage, ask what it was that made the prophet talk that way, and what he wanted the people to understand and do, by using that kind of language.

Examples

- Isaiah 1:10–15
- Isaiah 3:16–24
- Jeremiah 2:22–28
- Jeremiah 19:1–13
- Ezekiel 23

They Used Poetry

A lot of the words of the prophets are in the form of Hebrew poetry (though Ezekiel, for example, seems to have spoken mostly in prose). We will explain how Hebrew poetry worked in the next chapter, on the Psalms, so I will not go into the details here. But what it means is this: often the prophets spoke in short bursts, using very graphic terms, with unusual phrases and images. That's the nature of poetry. It nearly always says a lot in very few words. And poetry also tends to use language in special ways—figures of speech, comparisons, metaphors, symbolism, and so on. Probably the main reason the prophets spoke so much in poetry is that it makes it easier to remember their words. But it can also make it harder for later readers in different cultures to understand their message! The main thing is that poetry has a way of speaking that should not usually be taken literalistically—that is, as if every word referred to something in the real world, rather than as an image—e.g., when the Psalmist says "God is a rock" or "a shield"—we know that is a picture, not a statement of literal fact. Rather we need to search for the intention, the feeling, the message behind the form of the words and recognize that poetry makes those things even more powerful. In some of the books of the prophets, especially Jeremiah, there is an intriguing blend of poetry sections with prose sections. Usually the prose sections state in more simple, straightforward, and direct ways what the wild and vigorous poetry sections say in their own far more imaginative ways. That is very helpful. And that is why it is good to read large chunks of the prophetic books and not get stuck in just a few verses here and there.

Examples

Read **Jeremiah 2**. It is full of poetic imagery and rhetorical questions. It swings wildly from one picture to another, portraying Israel's unfaithfulness and rebellion against God. The language is colourful and vivid. It helps to read it aloud, with passion, pausing with the searching questions and scathing comparisons. Now turn to **Jeremiah 11:1–13**. It is in prose. But can you see that it is basically the same message—the broken covenant? That is, Jeremiah 11 summarizes in *prose* what Jeremiah 2 proclaims in *poetry*. The language is sober, simple, and direct. It uses almost no pictures or questions. It is straightforward description of the situation and what has happened and what God thinks about it. When you compare these two passages you can see clearly how different the poetry is. You need to understand and interpret all its special ways of speaking and keep asking, "What is the prophet saying? What is his point?"

They Loved Pictures

The prophets loved pictures as much as Jesus loved parables. Of course, I don't mean actual pictures painted on paper or canvas, but *word pictures*. The prophets "painted" all kinds of images in the mind to express what they meant. They drew graphic comparisons from life around them, from nature—plants, animals, birds and insects, the sun, moon and stars, wind and fire, earthquake and volcano—from music and buildings, and from all human relationships. These word pictures are often called *metaphors*.

Turn back again to **Jeremiah 2**, now that you have already read it once! Count how many *word pictures* Jeremiah uses to make his points. By that I mean images or comparisons—like his picture of a bride (v. 2), firstfruits (v. 3), a spring and a cistern (v. 13), lions (v. 15), a vine (v. 21), soap (v. 22), camels and donkeys (vv. 23–24)—and so on. I reckon there are about fifteen or more distinct images in that one chapter. Jeremiah just leaps from one picture to another—engaging our imagination and making his message memorable.

So when you read the prophets, look out for these vivid picture comparisons. They are not meant to be taken *literalistically*. You need to think *what point the prophet was making by using that mental picture*. Sometimes you may need to know a bit about the cultural background to make sense of it. And when you preach or teach, you may need either to explain what the image meant or find a modern image that means the same thing—or both.

Examples

a) Jeremiah 2:13

Jeremiah says the people of Israel have committed two sins. He means apostasy (turning away from YHWH their living God) and idolatry (worshipping other gods). He could have just said that. But instead he paints an unforgettable picture. Imagine the stupidity of a farmer who blocks up or abandons a perennial spring of water on his farm in a dry land like Palestine. Imagine the futility of him then hewing out an enormous underground cistern to catch the rainfall—only to find that it is cracked and the water drains away. What is Jeremiah's point? Apostasy and idolatry are stupid and a wasted effort. When you know the living God, why on earth swap him for useless idols? What picture would you use from your own culture to make that point? What would be an illustration of doing something very stupid and very futile?

b) Isaiah 52:7–10

The prophet wants to express the wonderful good news that God is coming back to Jerusalem with his people—the exiles returning home. So he imagines Jerusalem itself looking out anxiously to the east, waiting for news. Then a single runner appears (the bringer of good news in v. 7 is singular)—though all we see are his "beautiful feet"!—announcing the good news that God has won the victory and is returning to redeem his people. Then the sentries on the ruined walls of Jerusalem join in the song (v. 8). Next the ruins of Jerusalem itself burst into songs of joy too (v. 9)—and finally all the nations and the ends of the earth are in the picture as well (v. 10), as "the arm of the LORD" is laid bare (yet another picture of God's saving strength).

We'll look at both Jeremiah 2 and Isaiah 52:7–10 in the sample outlines at the end of the chapter, so it's good to be reading them both now!

HANDLE PREDICTIONS WITH CARE

Back to the future. How should we handle passages in the prophets that do speak about something future (future, that is, from the point of view of the prophet)? We do need to be very careful here, for all kinds of weird and fanciful theories and predictions are pulled out of texts in the Old Testament prophets. People are easily misled into false ideas and hopes. Let's make sure our preaching and teaching does not do that!

Predictions As Warnings

The first thing we need to understand is that quite often when a prophet says something will happen in the future, there is a conditional aspect—either expressed or implied. That is, they were not making merely a flat *prediction* about some future event, but giving a *warning* about something that *would* happen *unless* the people changed their ways. So the implication is, *if* they would respond and change their ways, the predicted future *need not* happen. The word of God is not some kind of impersonal fate or destiny that can never be changed. God is personal, and God responds to how we respond to what he says—by way of warning or promise.

The place where this is most clearly expressed is **Jeremiah 18:7–10.** Read it carefully. God says that he can declare a certain future for a people (e.g. judgment). But if they take heed, repent, and do what is right, he can suspend that judgment and do something different. The story of Jonah illustrates this perfectly. Jonah's prediction of judgment brought Nineveh to repent. So God spared them, and the book makes it plain that that was God's purpose all along.

Think of it like this. Suppose you are a parent, and you go into your child's room when they are supposed to be doing their homework and studying hard. But instead they are watching TV or are outside playing with their friends. You know this has happened many times before, so that night you speak sternly to your child and say: "*You are going to fail your exams!*" Now that statement is in the form of a prediction. It is in the future tense. But what is the real point of it? What is implied?

What you really mean is: "You are going to fail your exams, *unless* you change your ways, stop wasting so much time playing, and work harder. *If* you change your ways, you will not fail. But if you go on the way you are going now, you *will* fail the exams and you will only have yourself to blame." So the "prediction" is really a warning.

And note something else: the "prediction" is *not what you actually want to happen.* You are not saying: "You are going to fail your exams because I say so, and I'll be glad when you do!" No, you tell your child what will happen if they don't change *because you don't want it to happen.* You want them to behave differently *so that your prediction* need not *come true.*

Now think of it like that with God and Israel (or God and Nineveh, for that is exactly what happened in the book of Jonah). Again and again God told them through many prophets what would happen to them if they went on rebelling and sinning against him. Again and again he appealed to them to change their ways and avoid that judgment. So the predictions were not just "fated." They could have been avoided. But Israel persisted in disobedience until the covenant was so shattered that God's judgment became unavoidable.

So be careful not to read all the predictions in the Old Testament as if they were just "bound to come true" no matter what. Think about *why* they were spoken and what God's purpose was.

Predictions in Poetic Pictures

Second, remember the point we made above about the way the prophets used vivid language. They often used graphic ways of speaking that we should not read literalistically. There were accepted imaginative ways of talking about certain things that people understood. Sometimes the imagery was "stereotyped" — that is, it was a conventional way of describing something that everybody knew was not to be taken literalistically. It is similar to the way we might talk about an event as "earth shaking," not meaning that the earth literally shook, but that the consequences of the event were very serious. Or we might say that one football team "annihilated" the opposition. We don't mean that they killed all the other players but simply that they won the match with a lot of goals! But we use a sporting metaphor that everybody understands.

Example

In **Jeremiah 50–51** we have a very long prophecy from Jeremiah about Babylon. Essentially it has a very simple message: Babylon will eventually fall, and the people of Israel will come back to their land. But if you skim through those chapters you'll see that again and again the prophet speaks of Babylon being invaded, attacked, overthrown, and destroyed by combined armies in a great battle. The pictures are all very vivid and pretty horrific. Well, in historical fact, nothing like that actually happened. The Persians captured Babylon without a fight. But we should not therefore blame Jeremiah for "false predictions." He was using standard pictures for the defeat and ending of an empire. His language uses graphic images that everybody understood. His point was: Babylon is going to fall and will never rise again. That certainly did happen. The *prophecy* was true. The *details* were poetic and imaginative, not literalistic prediction.

SCAN THE HORIZONS

The horizon is the limit of what you can see in the distance from wherever you are standing. The distance of the horizon depends on how high your eyes are from ground level. Now, think of the prophet's "eyes." As we said above, the prophets could "see" things from God's point of view. That included seeing the truth about their own day and also looking further ahead into the future. When the prophets spoke about what God was enabling them to "see," we can describe three major horizons of their words. That is to say, we can see three places where their words "landed," three places where their words were relevant and fulfilled.

Horizon 1: The Old Testament Era

This is the horizon of the prophet's own world, the Old Testament era itself. By far the greatest number of things the prophets said applied to their own times. And most of what they predicted happened either in their own lifetimes or at some point within the history of Old Testament Israel. We should start out assuming that this was the case before we look for other horizons or imagine that some future fulfilment still lies ahead. This is fairly easy to see in some cases. For example, Jeremiah predicted that the false prophet Hananiah would die (Jer 28:15–16) because he had prophesied falsely in the name of the LORD (a capital offence; according to Deut 13:1–5). That prediction came true two months later. We don't now go around looking for somebody called Hananiah and tell him he's going to die within a year because Jeremiah predicted it! Jeremiah's prophecy was fulfilled at Horizon 1. It has no further fulfilment waiting in the future.

In the same way, many prophets predicted that God would send Israel, and then Judah, into exile because they persistently broke the covenant and rebelled against him. That was fulfilled within the Old Testament period itself, in 721 BC for the northern kingdom of Israel and in 587 BC for the southern kingdom of Judah. Those prophecies were fulfilled at Horizon 1.

Several prophets also predicted that God would bring the exiles of Judah back to their land. He would restore their fortunes and bring their exile to an end. The covenant would be renewed and they would rebuild the temple. That also was fulfilled within the Old Testament period. After the edict of Cyrus, king of Persia, in 538 BC, several waves of exiles returned to Jerusalem. Those prophecies also were fulfilled at Horizon 1.

Do you remember in chapter 2 that we talked about how *promise* is greater than *prediction*? A promise may go on being fulfilled in new and different ways as life goes on. So sometimes we will find that an Old Testament prediction that was made and fulfilled at Horizon 1 can also "carry forward" and have even more significant fulfilment later. A good example is Isaiah's "sign" to Ahaz in Isaiah 7. Since it was a "sign," we have to assume that a child was indeed born (many scholars believe it was Isaiah's own next child, with the code name "Maher-Shalal-Hash-Baz"), and that what Isaiah predicted about Israel's enemies did indeed come true—all at Horizon 1. In the midst of the danger and threat of those months, God was indeed with them ("Immanuel"). That is where we must start as we read and understand that text. Isaiah was speaking to Ahaz in his own day and his words must have had some application and fulfilment at that time. However, we also know, of course, that Matthew finds an even greater level of fulfilment of that "Immanuel" prophecy in the birth of Jesus. And that brings us to Horizon 2.

Horizon 2: The New Testament Era

Prophecy, like the rest of the Old Testament, moves ultimately toward Christ and toward the great central gospel events of the biblical story—Stage 4 in our "Bible on the back of an envelope" diagram. We thought a lot about that in chapters 2 and 3, so I don't need to repeat it here. Remember: we are not saying that every verse in the prophets is *about* Jesus (remember chapter 4!). Rather, we mean that whatever the prophets said in their own day was part of a journey that led to Jesus. And so we can look at everything they said *in the light of Christ*, even when they were not specifically thinking about a longer-distance future.

Sometimes, however, prophets spoke about the future in ways that we now know could only be true in and through Jesus Christ and the gospel of salvation through his death and resurrection.

Sometimes this is called "messianic prophecy," but the word "messiah" does not often occur. It is not just that the prophets spoke about a coming one, but rather that they described things that could only be perfectly true through Jesus. For example, when Jeremiah speaks about God making a "new covenant" (Jer 31:31–33), much of what he says is *similar in principle* to the Sinai covenant. But when he says that part of that new relationship will include the complete forgiveness of sins, we know that was accomplished only by Jesus Christ. Similarly, when Isaiah speaks about the "servant of the LORD," there are several things said about the Servant that are also said about Israel (chosen and loved by God, given as a light for the nations). But when he speaks of the Servant bearing the sins of many and dying vicariously for us (Isa 53), then we can only see such words fully embodied in the Lord Jesus.

So when we read or preach or teach from a passage in the prophets (after we have carefully seen what it meant at Horizon 1), we need to ask if it has dimensions that need to be seen at Horizon 2. We need to ask how this passage connects with the gospel of Jesus Christ revealed and accomplished in the New Testament. You'll remember that in chapter 5 we explored some ways such connections can be made. And you'll also remember, I hope, that even when we *do* see such a connection between a passage in an Old Testament prophet and the Lord Jesus Christ, we must also make sure that we do not immediately jump to teach that text as if it is just "all about Jesus." Make sure that you check what the prophet was actually speaking about to his own people at the time.

Horizon 3: The New Creation

Sometimes a prophet speaks of the future in terms that go beyond anything we have ever seen in history itself. This may be in relation to God's judgment. We know that the prophets can speak about God judging Israel and also other foreign nations. But sometimes they describe God's judgment engulfing the whole earth and all nations in cataclysmic destruction of all that is wicked and evil (e.g., Isa 24). We can only relate that kind of vision to the ultimate horizon of the second coming of Christ and the final judgment.

But more often such "exalted vision" is in relation to God's future blessing. It is described in words overflowing with joy and excitement. We find ourselves imagining a world in which everything is perfect. Nature is full of abundance. The earth itself seems to rejoice in its Creator. Human life is safe, fulfilling, and free from violence, injustice, hunger, and danger. War and violence are no more. People and animals live in harmony and peace. People never again turn away from God in disobedience. People from all over the world and all nations reject their false gods and turn to the living God and worship him with joy and gifts (e.g., Isa 25:6–9; 35; 65:17–25; Jer 32:37–41; 33:6–9; Joel 3:17–18).

When we read such words, we know that they were certainly not fulfilled at Horizon 1. Much that God promised Israel *did* come true at that horizon—in their return to the land. But they were still sinners and far from perfect—as books like Nehemiah, Ezra, and Malachi show. And although Christ accomplished the redemption of the world in his death and resurrection (at Horizon 2), we have not yet seen the fulfilment of all that we and the prophets long for. And so we are driven on to the ultimate Horizon 3—or the "eschatological horizon," to use technical terms. The Bible ends in Revelation 21–22 with a picture of the new creation that very deliberately echoes many of the themes in the prophets (read Isa 65:17–25 and then Rev 21). Their ultimate vision will only be fulfilled when Christ returns and the earth is cleansed and renewed to be the dwelling place of God with us.

Example

Read **Jeremiah 32:36–44**. This is God's answer to Jeremiah after he had bought a field at Anathoth (read the rest of the chapter if you can). It was a great act of faith on Jeremiah's part, since he was in prison in Jerusalem just before it was captured by the Babylonians, and the Babylonians were trampling all over that field. Buying that field was a signpost to a future when people would once again buy and sell fields in the land after they had returned from exile. Now, you can immediately see that verses 43–44 are looking to Horizon 1. They describe exactly what did in fact happen. It was still future when Jeremiah spoke those words just before the fall of the city, but it was a prediction that came true within the Old Testament period itself. The people of Judah returned to the land after two generations in exile, resettled their towns, and started farming their fields again.

But read verses 38–41 again. These describe a perfect future in which there will be an everlasting covenant between God and his people, in which there will never again be any sin or disobedience. It will be a time when God's presence and blessing will be complete and when people will live in complete security forever. That goes way beyond anything the little community of Judah was like after the exile. And it goes beyond the experience of the church too (unless your church is as perfect as verse 39 and the end of verse 40 describe!). This is a picture of that perfect relationship between God and his people that we know will only be finally complete in the new creation. Horizon 3.

Checklist

So when you are studying and preaching passages from the prophets that speak about something that was in the future (from their point of view), ask questions like these:

☐ In what ways did this prophecy address the prophet's own people and speak about their immediate future? In what ways was it fulfilled within the Old Testament period itself (Horizon 1)? Remember: always start with this question. For some passages, it is the only one that will have a clear answer. This question will apply to *most* prophecies.

☐ Even if it was fulfilled in the Old Testament period, are there ways in which the prophecy was further fulfilled by Jesus and in the New Testament church? Or are there ways in which it was given deeper or additional meaning in the light of the coming of Christ (Horizon 2)? This question will apply to *some,* but certainly not, all prophecies.

☐ Are there any ways in which this prophecy points toward a final fulfilment in the perfection of the reign of Christ in the new creation (Horizon 3)? This question will apply only to a *few* prophecies.

☐ Is this prophetic text quoted anywhere in the New Testament? If so, what purpose did the New Testament speaker or writer have in quoting it? Does the New Testament speaker or writer connect the prophet's words to Horizon 2 or Horizon 3, or both?

As I've said, there are some passages in the prophets that seem to include all three horizons, and this may feel confusing at first. We'll look at an example in the sample outline at the end of the chapter. But remember that the prophets were looking into a future which, as far as they could see, was all one single vision. They did not (could not) know that it would be centuries before Horizon 2 came along and unknown centuries further before Horizon 3 would come (it still lies ahead). *We,* with our perspective, can now see that their words have stretched over a long period of time. *They* saw things "from the front" and saw things near and far as if they were all part of one big single picture.

If you look at a range of mountains from a distance, they may all look close together in line on the far horizon. But when you get into that range, you discover that there may be great distances between the nearer and farther peaks. Or imagine looking at a train coming toward you straight down the line. From that angle you can only see the locomotive and the train is compressed or foreshortened behind that. It's only when you move round to the side that you can see the length of the train from a different perspective. What was a single shape from the front becomes a long line of carriages stretching over a huge length of the track. So it is in the Old Testament: some prophecies may have a "single shape" from the "up-front" standpoint of the prophet, but a much longer range over time when looked at in relation to Christ and the new creation. Once again, I hope you can see how important it is to read any passage of Scripture in the light of the whole-Bible story line.

Example

Read **Isaiah 52:7 – 11**. Can you see all three horizons in this wonderful vision? Basically, this text is "good news." That is what verse 7 announces. And it is good news at all three horizons. Indeed, that is how I would preach it (see the sample outline at the end of the chapter).

- *Horizon 1.* The prophet wants to encourage and motivate the exiles to get ready to go home to Jerusalem. God has won the victory (he reigns), and God is already returning to his city and taking them with him. As at the exodus, God is redeeming his people. So they can rejoice and go home. And indeed, that did happen. The prophecy was fulfilled at Horizon 1.

- *Horizon 2.* Every dimension of the good news that the messenger announces is good news through Christ. Verse 7 speaks of the God who *reigns*. Verse 8 speaks of the God who *returns*. Verse 9 speaks of the God who *redeems*. All of those are true in Christ. He preached the kingdom of God. He went to the temple, as God had said he would. And he is the Redeemer and Saviour, through his death and resurrection. At Horizon 2, Jesus is God reigning, God returning, and God redeeming.

- *Horizon 3.* As is so often seen, the prophet broadens out the vision. He started with one messenger bringing good news to the ruined city of Jerusalem so the exiles could return and rejoice (v. 7). But in verse 10 he moves to the global stage — to "all the nations" and "all the ends of the earth." This goes beyond anything that has happened yet. But through the mission of the church, the gospel of "the salvation of our God" is indeed going to "the ends of the earth." So the ultimate vision of the prophecy lies at Horizon 3. It will be finally fulfilled when the Lord Jesus Christ returns to reign over all the earth and to redeem his people forever.

BUILD THE BRIDGE

What about today, then? Perhaps you are wondering if we ought to talk about a *fourth horizon* — the world of today. After all, our goal is *to preach and teach* from the words of the prophets, and that means building the bridge from the world of the Bible into today's world. We want to see how the words of the prophets can relevantly apply to our own world and our own people. And of course it is very important to do that. In some ways, finding and applying the message of the prophets for today is similar to doing the same for the law. Below you will find a checklist of questions that reflects what we did in chapter 10. However, here are a few words of caution to think about first.

- Do not make dogmatic identifications of persons, places, or events in modern times based on Old Testament prophecies. There is a whole industry of people manufacturing fulfilments of prophecies — especially about the "end times." They take a word or phrase from an Old Testament text and tell us that it clearly refers to something that has happened, or is about to happen, in the world today. One example was the prediction that was very common in the 1970s that the words of Ezekiel 38 – 39 about Gog and Magog would be fulfilled in a great invasion of the modern state of Israel by the forces of the Soviet Union. People made lots of money writing books about that. But they were wrong (though they never apologized or accepted they were wrong). That kind of confident attaching of an Old Testament prophecy to a modern event is nearly always questionable and mistaken. So be very careful. Don't be gullible, even when those who preach or write such stuff sound very persuasive.

- Be careful not to promise to hearers today something that was promised only within the historical period of the Old Testament. God made promises to Old Testament Israel that he kept when he delivered them from their enemies or brought them back from exile. We can take encouragement from these fulfilments, since they teach us about the faithfulness of God. But we cannot expect that God guarantees to do exactly the same in the present or immediate future for anybody in similar circumstances today. We should not use an Old Testament prophecy to promise refugees, for example, that they will soon go back to their own land. We can certainly point to God's salvation through Christ (at Horizon 2) and that God will ultimately put all things right (at Horizon 3). And we can certainly work for justice in the present for all suffering and oppressed people—we know God wants that. But we cannot turn prophecies to Old Testament Israel at Horizon 1 into guarantees for everybody else today.

- No nation today stands in covenant relationship to God as Old Testament Israel did. So we should not preach to society as if they were in the same position as Old Testament Israel. No state today is a Christian theocracy—that is, truly honouring God as supreme King, Law-giver, and Judge. The covenant people of God today are those from every nation, Jews and Gentiles, who are believers in the Lord Jesus Christ, scattered throughout all nations. Nevertheless, we can certainly use the *principles* that we find in Old Testament prophecy (as also in Old Testament law) to critique and challenge what goes on in the secular world of nations and governments. Like the prophets, we can expose injustice and oppression—we can point out the terribly damaging effects of cultural idolatries of all kinds. And like them also we can speak out on behalf of the poor, the marginalized, and vulnerable and condemn those who profit from keeping them like that.

- We should not preach and teach only from the "nice" parts of the prophets. It is easy to take wonderful promises like

Jeremiah 29:11 or Isaiah 43:1–2 and preach and teach them without attention to their context. We need to let God's people hear the whole message of the prophets— including when they exposed wrongdoing and warned of God's judgment. The church (not just secular society) needs to be challenged about idolatry, injustice, lack of compassion, disunity, compromise, and so on—things the prophets had plenty to say about. If we touch on such things, of course, we are not likely to be popular, any more than the prophets were. But "prophetic preaching" should tackle such things.

Checklist

Building the bridge means that we start with the way the prophet challenged his own people in their context at that time. Then we move across to the ways in which his message challenges our contemporary context today in the church or society. So we follow a similar list of questions to those for the Old Testament law at the end of chapter 10.

☐ What was the historical situation (so far as we know it) into which the prophet was speaking?

☐ What was the purpose or objective of the prophet's words? What primary point was he making?

☐ Who was he condemning or praising, and why?

☐ What was going on and what was the prophet saying about it, and why?

☐ What issues or priorities can you see in what the prophet says again and again?

☐ Was the prophet's message in this passage mainly a threat and warning or a promise and hope? In either case, what did the prophet want the people to do in response?

☐ How would you summarize the word of God through the prophet for the people of Israel *at that time?*

Now cross the bridge from the world of the prophet to the world of today:

☐ What would the prophet want to say to us today?

☐ What comparisons can you make between what was happening in Israel at the time of the prophet and the church/world today?

☐ What would the prophet condemn or praise today, and why?

☐ For what reasons do we need to repent?

☐ For what reasons do we need to have hope and faith?

☐ What will be the tone of a sermon or lesson that reflects the tone of this passage? Encouragement? Rebuke? Warning? Hope? Challenge to change? Promise? Strengthening faith?

Then try to preach in a way that expresses the central thrust of the passage and with the same tone. If Jeremiah or Amos (or whichever prophet you are preaching from) were listening to your sermon, you would want them to be thinking, "Yes, that's what I meant (more or less). Preach it!"

SAMPLE OUTLINES

I have chosen two passages to illustrate the two major themes of the prophets: judgment and hope. The aim of the first is to help people see that some of the sins Jeremiah condemned can also be seen in the church today and then to encourage them to repentance. The aim of the second is to help people see that the good news (gospel) of Jesus was anticipated in the Old Testament and that God gave a message of hope to the exiles that would eventually be good news for the whole world.

Broken Promises, Broken Cisterns
Jeremiah 2

Context: Jeremiah 2 is probably some of his earliest preaching. The reformation of King Josiah was in full swing. But Jeremiah saw no real change in the hearts and lives of the people. God saw people who were a disappointment to him (vv. 1–8), who were being disloyal to the covenant (vv. 9–13), and who were deluding themselves (vv. 14–37). They were heading for disaster.

Disappointment (vv. 1–8)

God remembers with nostalgia Israel's early years (vv. 1–2) and contrasts it with their behaviour later (vv. 5–8).

The Honeymoon! (vv. 1–3)

But it's all in the past. Compare Hosea 9:10; 11:1.

Their Ingratitude (vv. 4–8)

They had forgotten what God had done for them. Jeremiah points out three features of what Israel were doing—each of which have modern equivalents.

- They were going after what is worthless (v. 5b).
- They were wasting what is precious (vv. 6–7).
- Their leaders were failing at every level—religious, legal, and political (v. 8).

Disloyalty (vv. 9–13)

"I bring charges" (v. 9). This uses the picture of a law court, with Israel as the accused and God as the prosecutor and judge. Israel was breaking the covenant. Jeremiah condemns their disloyalty:

It Was Unnatural (vv. 10–12)

Other nations had other gods, which were really no-gods. But those other nations were at least loyal to their no-gods, whereas Israel knew the one true living God—and swapped him for worthless idols! What a shock. It was appalling.

It Was Unprofitable (v. 13)

The picture of an abandoned spring of living water and a useless, cracked, leaking cistern. A very powerful picture of futility. When you turn your back on God and try to work out your own solution, it can be both stupid and a waste of effort.

Some of the things that Israel were doing included:

- Political alliances (vv. 14–18, 36–37)—trying to find security in military and political alliances that were basically evidence of lack of trust in God.

- "Prosperity" religion (vv. 20, 28)—the worship of health, wealth, sex, and fertility.

All these things have modern equivalents when Christians try to find their security or happiness in all kinds of attractive alternatives to trust in God.

Delusion (vv. 14–37)

The worst thing about Israel's condition was that they denied it! They protested that they were doing nothing wrong. So:

Their Sin Was Unacknowledged (vv. 23, 35)

Amazingly, they went on saying they were innocent.

Their Guilt Was Unhidden (v. 22)

"An abundance of cleansing powder" may refer to the reforms of Josiah. But Jeremiah sees it all as only external, cosmetic. Their guilt remained.

Conclusion: The only remedy: call to repentance (chs. 3—4:4).

The honeymoon (2:1–3) ended in divorce (3:1). But was there any possibility of restoration? Jeremiah urges Israel to turn round and come back in chapters 3 and 4. We can't preach those whole chapters in this sermon, but when we face up to the truth of what God exposes in chapter 2, we must show that genuine repentance and change is the only answer.

Challenge: In what aspects of our lives is it possible that:

- We are a disappointment to God—in spite of all his loving and giving?

- We are being disloyal to God by going after idols of the culture around us?

- We are deluding ourselves that it doesn't really matter?

Return to the fountain of living water.

Our God Reigns! The Running Shoes of Mission
Isaiah 52:7–11

Heartbeat: The gospel of the reign of God is good news! It was good news that brought hope to the exiles; good news that is fulfilled in Jesus; and good news that we can hang on to with hope, in the problems of the world today. Good news to share!

Context: Israel in exile. Jerusalem in ruins. Hopes and longings. Would they ever return? The prophet pictures someone in the ruins of Jerusalem looking out to the east, longing and waiting to see if God and the exiles will come back. Then he sees a single runner bringing good news! God has won the victory! God is on the way home!

Good News for the Exiles (The Text in Its Old Testament Context — Horizon 1)

God Reigns (v. 7)

- "Peace"
- "Good"
- "Salvation"

Each of those words has rich Old Testament significance that can be brought out. When God reigns, there will be peace, life will be good (as God intended at creation), and we shall be saved. The messenger was bringing "gospel" news to the exiles — summed up in the climax "Your God reigns!"

God Returns (v. 8)

The voice of the single runner is joined by the shouts of the sentries because they can see God himself returning to his city.

God Redeems (vv. 9–10)

The prophet makes the ruins of Jerusalem join the singing! God is comforting and redeeming his people — more rich Old Testament words. Then verse 10 opens the text up to the world: "all the ends of the earth"! Surprising. But it fits with the whole-Bible story. What God did for Israel was always ultimately for the blessing of all nations (Gen 12:1–3).

"The arm" of the Lord—verse 10, but this picture for God in action is also used in 40:10–11 and 53:1—and the rest of that chapter.

- Power with compassion
- Victory in battle
- Suffering and death

Good News in Jesus Christ (The Text in Its New Testament Context—Horizon 2)

There is a Christmas song, "Go, tell it on the mountain, that Jesus Christ is born."[1] It was probably inspired by this passage. And it is right to see this text as good news, not just for the exiles of Israel in the Old Testament, but also as describing what Jesus came to be and to do. The language of "good news," "peace," "salvation," "redemption," and "kingdom of God" are all terms that resound in the New Testament because they are all true in Jesus Christ.

Jesus Was and Is God Reigning

He announced the arrival of the kingdom of God.

Jesus Was and Is God Returning

Jesus fulfilled the prophecies of Malachi 3 and Zechariah 9: God returning to his temple and his people. And he will return again.

Jesus Was and Is God Redeeming

The Lord's "holy arm" was stretched out on the cross for the salvation of the world.

Good News for Us and the World (The Text in Today's World, with Future Hope—Horizon 3)

What Does It Mean for Me to Say That:

- Jesus is the *reigning* God? It means seeking to discern the signs of the kingdom of God at work in the world. "Jesus is Lord" (not Caesar). I look at the world with eyes of faith.

---

1. John W. Work, Jr., 1907.

- Jesus is the *returning* God? The "waste places" will be put right (Ps 96:10–13). I have hope.

- Jesus is the *redeeming* God? The ends of the earth will see the salvation of our God. I have joy in anticipation of that.

That's what it means to me and, I hope, to us all as Christians. BUT...

What Do These Truths Mean for the People Around Us?

What does it mean to people in the streets of our land that Jesus is the reigning Lord of history, the returning King of creation, and the Redeemer and Saviour of the world?

NOTHING!!—unless someone tells them.

That's why our text comes echoing back in **Romans 10:12–15**. "How beautiful on the mountains are the feet of *those* who bring good news" (Paul makes the singular runner of Isa 52:7 plural). All of us can be messengers of the good news. There is nothing very beautiful about feet—except when they are wearing the running shoes of the gospel and taking it to the world.

"Go, tell it on the mountain, that Jesus Christ is born"—and is reigning, returning, and redeeming.

CHAPTER 13

Getting to Know
the Psalms

o you like preaching and teaching from the book of Psalms?
I expect the answer is "Yes!" I certainly do too. Well, that
puts us in good company. Jesus used the Psalms more often
in his preaching and teaching than any other Old Testament book.
And most of the writers of the New Testament quote Psalms often.

Psalms is such a central and important book. Not only is it
the place where our Bibles tend to fall open if we open them at
random, coming right in the middle. It is also the book where
millions of believers—Jews and Christians—down through many
centuries have found words for every possible occasion and experience: words of faith and hope, of pain and comfort, of joy and
sorrow, of thanksgiving and lament, of confession and forgiveness,
of encouragement and peace. It speaks about God as he truly is,
and about life as it often is. It speaks to our hearts and lets us speak
from our hearts. No wonder it is a wonderful source for preachers.
It can seem very straightforward to take the words of some psalms
and preach and teach them fairly simply and directly. I hope by the
end of this chapter you will still be able to do that but with perhaps
more depth, understanding, and appreciation.

SONGS IN POETRY

The first thing we ought to know already is that the Psalms
were basically songs that were sung by Israelites, and like most
songs, they were composed in poetry. Today we call the words
of our songs "lyrics." The Psalms also have lyrics, and they were

designed to be sung to some kind of music. Some of the Psalms actually have little headings with musical suggestions about the instruments or tunes to use. Mostly we don't now know what those terms referred to, but they do remind us that we must read, sing, and preach the Psalms for what they are—poetry.

Poetry takes different forms in different languages and cultures. In English, a lot of poetry until more recent times made use of two basic elements—metre and rhyme. Metre means the number of stressed words or parts of words in each line—setting up a rhythm and pace for the words. Rhyme means that the words at the end of the lines sound similar—either one line after the other, or alternating, or in some other pattern.

In Hebrew poetry they did not bother with rhyming at the end of lines, but they did seem to like metre. So you often find that the lines of their poems have a pattern of three stressed syllables followed by another three or sometimes two (3 + 3 or 3 + 2). That happened in the original Hebrew, of course, and it is not always possible to show it in our translations. Nearly always we have to use more words in English translation, for example, than are there in the original Hebrew poetry.[1] But as you read a psalm, you can see that most of the lines are roughly the same length—showing that the underlying Hebrew has this metrical, rhythmic pattern.

Let's think about some important features of biblical poetry.

Hear the Echo

There is one very common and typical feature of Hebrew poetry. We find it not only in the Psalms but also in other parts of the Old Testament that were written in poetry, such as Proverbs, Job, and many of the messages of the prophets. That feature is known by the technical word *parallelism*. It is the trick of saying more or less the same thing twice (in parallel) but with minor variations so that it does not merely sound repetitive.

I like to think of it as the *stereo effect*. God has given us two ears, so when we listen to something in stereo, we are hearing two soundtracks in parallel, as it were—from each side of our head. But the combined effect is to create a single, almost three-dimensional

---

1. For example, Psalm 23:1 has eight words in English—"The LORD is my shepherd, I lack nothing"—but it only takes four words in Hebrew.

sound in our brains. So the Hebrew songwriters used this technique of parallelism as a way of "rounding out" and emphasizing what they were saying or singing by giving it greater depth.

In our Bibles, Hebrew poetry is set out in lines. The first line is set to the left hand margin, and then the second line (and sometimes a third) are often indented a bit to the right. Usually (though not always, of course — the Hebrew poets were quite free and informal in the way they wrote!), that second or third line stands in some kind of parallelism to the first or connects to it in a fairly obvious way.

Here are some of the different kinds of parallelism, with a few examples of each.

Same Again

We could call this *repeating* parallelism.[2] This is probably the commonest and most familiar. The psalmist makes a statement and then makes the same point again but using slightly different words or filling out some of the "flavour" of what he has just said. For example:

> The heavens declare the glory of God;
> > the skies proclaim the work of his hands.
> Day after day they pour forth speech;
> > night after night they reveal knowledge.
> > > *(Ps 19:1–2)*

> Do not fret because of those who are evil
> > or be envious of those who do wrong;
> for like grass they will soon wither
> > like green plants they will soon die away.
> > > *(Ps 37:1–2)*

In this kind of parallelism, you need to understand that the writer is making a single main point, even though he may spread it out over two or more lines. We need to connect the pieces together to get his full meaning. So, in that first example, the heavens and the skies are not proclaiming two separate things. No, the glory of God is seen in the work of God's hands. And they are not doing one thing by day and something else by night. No, the universe reveals truth about God all the time.

---

2. The technical word for it is "synonymous parallelism."

Take a moment now to read a few psalms at random and see if you can spot this kind of parallelism. Notice how it enriches and deepens what is being said.

Pairs of Opposites

We could call this *contrasting* parallelism.[3] This is where the second line reinforces the first line by saying the opposite in a negative way. For example:

> You have granted him [the king] his heart's desire
>   and have not withheld the request of his lips.
>   *(Ps 21:2)*

> For I have kept the ways of the LORD;
>   I am not guilty of turning from my God.
>   *(Ps 18:21)*

> You save the humble
>   but bring low those whose eyes are haughty.
>   *(Ps 18:27)*

This form of parallelism is even more common in the book of Proverbs. It is, again, a way of strengthening a point by making us think of the contrast with its opposite.

And Another Thing

We could call this *supplementing* parallelism.[4] This is where a second or third line *adds* to the point of the first with significant further content. The lines are all pointing in the same direction and combine together to express all they want to say. But the parallels are not simply repeating the first line but substantially filling it out or adding a further dimension to it. Once again, we should not isolate each line but see how they all work together to make their point complete. For example:

> Praise the LORD, my soul,
>   and forget not all his benefits—
> who forgives all your sins
>   and heals all your diseases,

---

3. The technical word for it is "antithetical parallelism."

4. The technical term for it is "synthetic parallelism." You don't need to remember the technical terms, and you certainly shouldn't use them in the pulpit!

who redeems your life from the pit
and crowns you with love and compassion.
(Ps. 103:2–4)

For the word of the LORD is right and true;
he is faithful in all he does.
The LORD loves righteousness and justice;
the earth is full of his unfailing love.
(Ps 33:4–5)

Sometimes the words are piled up like steps and stairs—repeating and then adding a bit more each time.

The LORD reigns, he is robed in majesty;
the LORD is robed in majesty and armed with strength;
indeed, the world is established, firm and secure.
Your throne was established long ago;
you are from all eternity.
The seas have lifted up, LORD,
the seas have lifted up their voice;
the seas have lifted up their pounding waves.
Mightier than the thunder of the great waters,
mightier than the breakers of the sea–
the LORD on high is mighty.
(Ps. 93:1–4)

Why are we observing this feature of the Psalms—this characteristic parallelism? Well, it certainly is not in order to encourage you to repeat everything you say in your sermon! Some preachers do that too much as it is! Rather, it is so that we get a *feel* for the texture and depth of the poetry of the Psalms. The language is so cleverly and beautifully put together. And when we preach or teach from the Psalms, even though we don't speak in poetry, we should help our audience to appreciate not just *what* the text says but *how* it says it. The language of the Psalms is resonant and "echoing." And that helps us to remember it more easily too.

Pause and read a few short psalms right now, preferably aloud. Try to feel this feature of their poetry and appreciate how it strengthens what they are saying. Hear the echo. Listen in stereo.

Watch the Pictures

Poetry is a vivid form of expression. Poetry likes to use mental pictures and striking comparisons. Often a single image can set the imagination racing. A strong metaphor can be more powerful than a thousand words.

One day David was thinking how glad he was that God cared for him, guided him, protected him in trouble, and provided for his needs. He could have just said all that and then expanded each of those statements with more theological truths about God and a few practical illustrations from his experience. He could have written a whole essay about God—or maybe a long letter, like the Apostle Paul.

But instead he took a look at the sheep he was guarding, and he said just two words (in Hebrew), "The LORD is my shepherd." And with that simple image David began the most loved and memorable psalm in the whole book, creating a whole world in our imagination.

That statement is, of course, a metaphor. It uses one reality (the life and work of a shepherd with his sheep) to describe another reality (the way God cares for people). The second of those realities is the one he is actually talking about (the target of the metaphor). The first is the one he is using for comparison (the source of the metaphor).

The Psalms are brimming over with metaphors like that—all kinds of mental pictures.

Many of them speak about God. What do you think of when psalmists describe God using the following pictures: a rock, a shield, a fortress, a strong tower, a roaring lion, a chariot rider, a father, a king, a builder? Of course, God is not *literally* any of those. But each of them is a metaphor that speaks powerfully and imaginatively about God. They convey truth in a way that abstract descriptions can't quite match.

Some metaphors speak of human experiences. Psalmists speak of sinking in mud or being washed away in a flood. They feel surrounded by wild beasts or pinned to the ground. They can compare themselves to a wineskin dried up in the smoke or a worm in the earth. Or they can frolic like calves or have their horns lifted high like a victorious bull. They may be standing on a rock or hiding under the wings of a large bird. They can flourish like a palm tree or trample on lions and snakes. All of these, of course, are pictures that speak of different kinds of experience.

Some psalms picture creation responding to the acts of God. Mountains melt or skip like lambs. Trees dance. Rivers clap their hands. Fields rejoice.

When we preach and teach from the Psalms, try to let these images do their work. Sometimes they will need explanation. But don't just "explain away" every vivid image. Let them appeal to the imagination of the hearers.

Just a few words of caution:

- Don't try to squeeze everything into a single metaphor. For example, although Psalm 23 begins with the picture of a shepherd and sheep, it does not persist with that metaphor to the end. At verse 5 it shifts to another picture — a host preparing to entertain his guests for a good meal. Shepherds don't lay a table for their sheep, anoint their heads with oil, or give them drink from cups. That's what a host does. So David is comparing God *both* to a caring shepherd *and* to a generous host. He blends the pictures together very nicely — but they are separate pictures.

- Don't push a metaphor too far or go beyond its main point of comparison. Just because Psalm 23 describes God as a shepherd does not mean that we should behave in all the ways sheep do. It certainly means that we should follow our shepherd and trust him. But sheep typically wander off on their own, and that is a bad thing (Isa 53:6)! Be careful to stick to the intended point of the metaphor as the Bible uses it in that particular context and don't extend it with uncontrolled imagination.

Feel the Emotion and Share the Experience

Poetry is the language of experience, and poetry gives voice to all the feelings that surround different experiences. And the range of experiences and emotions in the book of Psalms is simply vast! Here is just a sample of the emotions that we find. You could easily write down references in the Psalms for each of these:

- Joy and happiness
- Gratitude and thanksgiving
- Awe and wonder
- Pain and hurt
- Anger and bitterness
- Remorse and sorrow
- Puzzled questioning
- Longing
- Agony
- Hope
- Trust
- Relief

The psalmists describe all kinds of situations. Again, you could find psalms that mention these:

- Being alone
- Being with lots of others
- Being falsely accused
- Being in acute danger or distress
- Being sick, even close to death
- Suffering loss or injury
- Being rescued from danger
- Feeling guilty for doing something sinful
- Being thankful for God's gifts or actions
- Travelling to worship God in Jerusalem
- Going into battle
- Coming back from battle
- Enthroning a new king
- Giving testimony in public worship
- Seeing their city and temple destroyed
- Going into exile

One interesting point about the book of Psalms is that originally these songs were written by people and addressed to God or to other people (calling on others, for example, to praise God). They are *human* words spoken (mostly) *to God*. And yet now we read them as part of the Bible—that is, as *God's* word *to us*. That is why we are able to *preach and teach* them. When we preach or teach from any part of the Bible, we are saying to our people, "This is what I believe God wants to say to us now from what he said in this passage of the Bible." So, in that sense, the Psalms have become part of God's message to us, not just human words to God.

I think there are several reasons for that "shift" (i.e., words that were written back then as human words to God, which we read now as God's word to us).

First, of course, it is because *that is what God wanted to happen.* While these songs came from the real hearts and minds of their human authors (they really did feel, think, and say these things for themselves), it was God's plan that what they wrote and collected would become part of his inspired word. In that sense, the Psalms are no different from other parts of the Bible — human words that God inspired to be part of God's word.

Second, I think it is because of *the way God himself is so deeply involved in the experiences and the emotions that fill the Psalms.* God was right there in those situations that the psalmists faced. So those who collected the Psalms for later generations of Israelites to sing recognized that, through the words of the original writers and the circumstances they faced, *God could continue to speak* to them again and again. And in the same way, through having these songs in our Bible, *God also speaks* to all of us who ever face the same kinds of situations or feel the same kinds of emotions.

That is what happens when we preach and teach them faithfully. And in order to preach and teach them faithfully we need to *try to enter into the experience and the emotions of the writers.* Don't read the Psalms "cold." Don't read them merely as "doctrine in verse." They do indeed contain wonderful truths about God, the world, and ourselves (to which we'll come below). But they are first of all songs in poetry, filled with real life and real emotion. Try to see, hear and feel that. Identify the *mood* as well as the *message* of each psalm as part of your preparation for preaching or teaching it.

SONGS IN VARIETY

In our Christian worship we have different kinds of songs to sing. We know the difference between a traditional hymn with regular verses and a familiar tune and a short modern worship song or chorus or something performed by a group or soloist. We have songs for different occasions, like Christmas carols, Easter hymns, harvest thanksgiving hymns, Communion hymns, hymns associated with weddings or funerals, and so on. The Old Testament's hymnbook also has its different categories of psalms, and it is worth knowing some of the main ones and their features.

This can help us when we come to study a psalm for preaching or teaching it. We can think about not only what the words say but also *what kind of psalm* it is. That may help us discern the structure of the psalm and its flow of thought.

Here are the major categories.[5] Take a moment to look at the examples listed in the footnote for each one. Read through a few of those listed under each category in order to get a feel for the typical form and structure of that kind of psalm. Spending a bit of time reading a few of the different kinds of psalms in each category will really help you to understand the differences between them.

Hymns of Praise[6]

"Praise" is the strongest element in the Psalms. In fact, the title of the whole book, in Hebrew, is simply "The Praises." Praise does not just mean saying how happy you are. Praise can include lament, as we will see below. But there are many psalms that are what we might call "pure praise." And they are, of course, praise of God. The shortest psalm gives us a perfect example of the key elements in such hymns of praise—Psalm 117:

> Praise the LORD, all you nations;
> extol him, all you peoples.
> For great is his love towards us
> and the faithfulness of the LORD endures for ever.
> Praise the LORD.

The structure is:

A Summons to Praise

This may be very general or addressed to other Israelites or (as here) to the rest of the world. It may be short or expanded. And sometimes it is simply assumed as the psalm launches into its praise of God.

The Reasons for Praise

This is the central element. Often (but not always) it is introduced by the word "For." The psalmist is saying: "I am calling you to praise the LORD God, and here is why you should do so." All kinds of reasons are given in the hymns of praise, but they usually

---

5. Biblical scholars have come up with several other kinds of psalm, and they subdivide some of these categories into even smaller ones. But I'm trying to keep things simple.

6. Hymns of praise include psalms such as 8, 33, 47, 65, 66, 100, 103, 104, 111, 113, 117, 145–150.

do one of two things (or both): either they *describe* what God is like — his greatness, character, goodness, faithfulness, etc. — or they *declare* what God has done — his great acts in creation and redemption. Israel's praise was always filled with content and substance. The psalmists were not just whipping up happy feelings and loud noise. They had *reasons* why people should praise God — all the reasons you could think of.

A Renewed Call to Praise

This again may be short (just a quick "Hallelujah" to finish off!), or more extended and reflective. Sometimes it may lead to a call to *trust* God for the same reasons that we were called to *praise* him. For example, look at Psalm 33. It begins with a call to praise (vv. 1–3). And it ends with an affirmation of trust and hope (vv. 20–22). And in between it gives the reason for praise and the foundation for hope. That is a classic hymn of praise.

In some ways, the hymns of praise are the most straightforward of the psalms for preaching. Their main focus is on God himself, and they have the same aim as biblical preaching — encouraging people to know God and worship him for who he is and what he has done.

Here's a small tip for "getting inside" the praise psalms. When you read what the psalmist says about God, put yourself back into their situation — as an ancient Israelite centuries before Christ — and ask the question, "How do you know this about God?"

Example

Go back to **Psalm 33**. The psalmist says:

> For the word of the LORD is right and true;
> he is faithful in all he does.
> The LORD loves righteousness and justice;
> the earth is full of his unfailing love.

When I preach this psalm, I say: "Let's ask the psalmist, 'How do you know those things about YHWH, the God of Israel?'" Then I imagine the psalmist saying: "Let me tell you our story. Our God proved his faithfulness, justice, and love in the great events of the exodus and wilderness. That's how we know what God is like and that's why we praise him."

But that raises another question (and again, in our preaching we can ask the psalmist in our imaginary conversation): "You say that the whole earth is full of the love of God. But how can that be? How can the whole earth experience what Israel knows about the transforming faithfulness, justice, and love of God?" The psalmist answers that question by pointing out that the God who redeemed Israel also created the whole universe. The stars, the seas, and the earth all come from him, so he has the power to rule the earth (vv. 6–9). And he *does* rule the earth. For the psalmist then goes on to say that the God who created the earth also controls history (vv. 10–11). He holds all people on earth accountable to himself (vv. 13–15). So the best place to put your trust is not in human resources but in God alone (vv. 16–19). And that is what the singers of the psalm do at the end of the psalm (vv. 20–22).

Can you see that by putting yourself back into the world of the author you are led to understand his perception of God from the things he knew at that time from the story of Israel? Now, of course, we know still more. We know that it is through Christ that God created the world, redeemed the world, and rules the world. Christ is Lord of heaven and earth and Lord of history. So we can connect the great truths in the New Testament to the praises in the Old Testament. That's good biblical preaching!

Thanksgivings[7]

Thanksgiving is similar to praise but more focused on a particular thing that God has done in the experience of the author of the psalm or the people he wants to sing it with him.

Most of the thanksgiving psalms are written by individuals, referring to an act of God for which they are thankful. This may be deliverance from enemies, illness, or death; victory in battle; or forgiveness of sins. They often include other elements, such as bringing a thank-offering in fulfilment of a vow or giving testimony within the worshipping congregation.

Some are community thanksgivings, when the whole people give thanks to God for a good harvest, or for deliverance from enemies (e.g., Pss 65, 124).

Gratitude is not only an emotion. It is a very important spiritual discipline. We can use these psalms to encourage our people to give thanks sincerely and regularly to God. That is an essential part of a healthy Christian life.

---

7. Thanksgiving psalms include 18, 30, 32, 34, 40, 66, 92, 116, 118, 138.

Laments

This is in fact the largest single category of psalms. About two-thirds of the Psalms include some lament, and a few are almost nothing but lament! These are songs of protest, songs in distress, songs out of suffering and pain. Many of them are individual laments,[8] while others are community laments sung by the whole people in moments of terrible distress.[9]

Is this not a bit surprising? Here we have a book that bears the title "The Praises," yet the largest group of "Praises" are actually *laments*! This may seem contradictory to us, but that is because we usually think of "praise" only as something we do when we feel happy and joyful. But for Israel, praise was something far deeper than that. Praise could happen even in the darkest moments — in fact, *especially* in those darkest moments.

For Israel, praising God meant *recognizing God's reality and presence*. Praise meant affirming that the LORD God of Israel is the one and only true and living God. Praise described the character of God and declared the acts of God. Praise was, essentially, God-talk. Praise is to bow down in God's presence (no matter what the circumstances) and affirm, "God is alive, and God is here, and God is like this, and God has done that."

But more than that, praise meant bringing the *whole of life* into the presence of God in that same way. Not just the nice bits of life for which we want to say "Thank you very much." But also all the tough and baffling bits of life, about which we want to cry out, "What's going on here?" The point is, the psalmists came into God's presence to acknowledge God's reality no matter what they were feeling — and that was a form of praise. They brought the whole of themselves into the whole of what they knew about God. So when life was painful, unbearable, or simply beyond understanding, they threw all that up to God and cried out to him. Notice that they cried out *to him*. They did not cry out *about him* to other people, as we so often do with our complaints. No, they brought it all into the presence of God — and stood there, or kneeled there, weeping, wondering, waiting.

---

8. Individual laments include 3, 6, 13, 22, 31, 39, 42, 57, 71, 73, 88, 142.

9. Community laments include 44, 74, 80, 91, 94, 137.

I think we have lost something in Christian worship because we hardly ever allow ourselves or others to do this. We ignore the psalms of lament. And instead we try to pretend that everybody is, or should be, happy. We even imply (or actually say) that if you are not happy and joyful in your worship, there is something wrong with you, or with your faith. We do not encourage or allow people to be *honest* in worship and truly engage with God in the midst of their struggles.

Something that really annoys me in some church services is when the worship leader starts off saying something like: "Well, we've all got many things on our minds and in our lives this week, all sorts of problems and maybe things that are sad or tough. But let's just lay them all aside, let's forget about ourselves, and let's just come into God's presence and worship him." But what good is that? All it means is that you put your troubles down at the church entrance as you come in and pick them all up again as you go out. You have not thrown them up before *God* and asked God the tough questions that are really bothering you. *Your reality has not touched God's reality.* And for that reason, whatever you did or sang in church was not really "praising God"—at least, not in any way that the psalmists would recognize as praise. For they did not "just lay their troubles to one side." No, indeed. They let God know all about their troubles in no uncertain terms. They cry and scream and complain and protest and get angry and struggle—but they do so in God's presence and with trust in God's faithfulness and power.

The lament psalms also have a typical structure. It goes basically like this:

- God, I'm suffering pretty badly here.

- God, everybody is against me or laughing at me. It's horrible and it isn't fair.

- God, you aren't doing anything to help right now, and I desperately need you to.

- How long will this go on, please? Must I wait forever?

- But God, I still trust you and will go on praising you, no matter what.

That last element is found in most of the psalms of lament. There is a shift from the misery and pain of the lament to some expression of hope, trust, or the expectation of deliverance and renewed praise. In Psalm 73 it comes at the point when the psalmist goes to worship with other believers and that helps him get things into their right perspective (Ps 73:15–28). Occasionally, though, the lament lasts right to the end of a psalm and the psalmist seems to find no comfort at all. That is true in Psalm 88, which is probably the darkest of all the psalms of lament—indeed it ends in darkness. I'm sure it speaks for many down the ages who have found no end to their sufferings—at least in this life.

Take some time to read through a selection of the lament psalms listed in the footnotes. Try to *feel* them. Try to enter into the variety of situations that caused such language. Notice the typical sequence above, and particularly notice how the shift into renewed faith and praise happens only after the singer has fully expressed how terrible are his sufferings or distress.

Then let me ask you two questions:

- First, if you are a pastor, do you allow people to think and say the kinds of things that the psalms of lament say? Or do you tell them that Christians shouldn't say such things? If God put these psalms in the Bible, surely we should encourage people to know them and use them for those times when they feel exactly the same as the psalmists. Let's not stifle God's own words when people need to say them. Let's not force people to be dishonest in the things they sing and pray.

- In your preaching and teaching, have you ever taught from a single psalm of lament or preached a series on several of them? If not, I think you are depriving your people of a very important part of Scripture and a valuable resource for times of suffering and need. God has put them in the Bible. In fact, he put *a lot of them* in the Bible, as if to give us plenty of words for every situation. Let's give them to our people.

Psalms of Zion

Israelites knew that they could pray to God anywhere (as Jonah discovered). But the centre of their worship was the temple in Jerusalem. That was the place where God had made his name dwell, as the Bible puts it. And when the temple had been dedicated by Solomon, what he stressed most about it was that it was a place of prayer (1 Kgs 8).

For that reason, some psalms celebrate the place itself—the temple, the city of Jerusalem, or Zion as it came to be known. These psalms of Zion originally were composed about that city and the things that happened there.[10] But Zion also stood for the people of God themselves, gathered in their covenant worship and commitment to him. So a number of the Zion psalms are clearly talking about the people, not just the place. They talk about God's love for his people, his protection of them, and his dwelling among them. And we can preach and teach them with that same basic message, since in Christ we have become that temple, the dwelling place of God through his Spirit (Eph 2:21–22).

Israelites would go up to Jerusalem from other parts of the land, especially for the great annual festivals. They would eagerly look forward to arriving in the city, going to the temple, and joining in the worship of their God. So a number of songs were composed to accompany their journey to Jerusalem. These are songs of pilgrimage.[11] They express a longing to be in the presence of God, the difficulties and dangers of the journey, and the joy of worshipping with God's people. It is not hard to translate these things into a Christian framework. Indeed, Hebrews tells us that, through the Lord Jesus Christ, we "have come to Mount Zion," by faith (Heb 12:22), to worship the living God along with all his saints and angels.

Royal Psalms

Since David, the author of many of the psalms, ended up as king over all Israel in Jerusalem, that city became not only the place of the temple but also the "City of David." It was where the kings had their palace and throne. First of all, David and Solomon reigned over all the tribes of Israel, and then the kings of Judah reigned in Jerusalem after that. That lasted until the end of the line came for the descendants of David. In 587 BC the city and the temple were destroyed by Nebuchadnezzar of Babylon. The last king who reigned in Jerusalem was Zedekiah. And the last king in the line of David, Jehoiachin, died in exile in Babylon, where he had been taken as a captive even earlier in 597 BC. But up until that time, many songs were written about the king or for the king.

---

10. Psalms of Zion include 46, 48, 76, 84, 87, 122, 125.

11. In the book of Psalms they are called "Songs of Ascents" because people literally had to go "up" to Jerusalem since it was set on a hill. They include Pss 120–134.

Some of them were possibly composed at the time of a coronation. Some were written to support the king when he went to battle. They are known as Royal Psalms or Kingship Psalms.[12]

The human king on the throne of David represented, in one sense, the fact that God was the true King of Israel (and the world). So some of the psalms present an idealized picture of what the king should be and do in order to reflect the kingship of God and God's character. The clearest of these is **Psalm 72**. It is a psalm of (or for) Solomon, and it paints him in very glowing terms indeed.

However, once the line of kings descended from David came to an end, who could these psalms then be sung to or sung about? From the time of the exile onwards they were interpreted *messianically*. That is, they expressed the hope and expectation that God would one day raise up a king in the line of David who would be Israel's true King. He would be God's anointed one through whom God would truly reign as King.

We know that that hope was fulfilled by Jesus Christ, the Son of David. And that is why the New Testament can take many of those royal psalms and apply them in different ways to Jesus — especially Psalm 110, which is the most quoted psalm in the New Testament. So when we preach and teach them we can and should connect them appropriately with Jesus. But we must also remember that they were *first* written for, or about, one of the kings of Israel in the line of David. A good example of this point would be Psalm 22 — a psalm of David.

Example: Psalm 22

Jesus quoted the first verse of Psalm 22 on the cross. "My God, my God, why have you forsaken me?" Clearly, Jesus felt himself in the same situation as David in his distress. His sufferings could be described in the same way, especially verses 6–18. So Jesus cried out the opening words of the psalm as if to say, "All that this psalm says is where I am right now." For that reason, the psalm has often been taken as prophetic — pointing toward the suffering of the Messiah and especially the cross itself.

I don't disagree with that. After all, it was Jesus who claimed it for himself. But we need to be careful. As we discussed in chapter 4, we should not simply say: "Psalm 22 is all *about* Jesus" — as if it were simply a prediction. It was written originally by somebody suffering terribly who describes

---

12. Royal psalms include 2, 18, 20, 21, 45, 72, 89, 101, 110, 132.

their suffering in a series of pictures, which would have been *mainly metaphorical*. He is surrounded by enemies attacking him (vv. 12, 13, 16). He is feeling paralysed with fear (v. 14). He can't speak in his own defence (v. 15). It is as if he is pinned to the ground and can't move (v. 16b). He feels vulnerable and exposed to public shame (v. 17). He is being treated as if he were already dead and his belongings are up for auction (v. 18).

Some of the pictures that the writer of Psalm 22 used to describe his own suffering did become vividly and literally real for Jesus (thirst, piercing, and the dividing of his clothes). But some did not (bulls, lions, and dogs). So we should see this psalm as a remarkably vivid and perceptive description of suffering—suffering that Jesus endured infinitely more than the original writer ever did. But it was not simply a "prediction" that "came true" on the cross (otherwise we have to explain the absence of those bulls, lions, and dogs which were not "fulfilled").

What is actually more significant about the connection between Psalm 22 and Jesus is the way the psalm turns amazingly to deliverance and praise (vv. 22–31). The psalmist trusts God for deliverance and links that to God's ultimate salvation of the whole world (what a vision!). Jesus, of course, did not pray to be delivered *from* the cross. But though he died in agony, he did not die in despair. He trusted that God would raise him from the dead and that his death and resurrection would be the ultimate victory that would lead all the ends of the earth to praise God (v. 27). So his final cry, "It is finished," probably also echoes the last line of Psalm 22—"He has done it!"

So when you preach or teach Psalm 22, don't dwell only on the first half and how it can point us to Jesus on the cross. Make sure you move on to the second half and how it points to Jesus' victory and the plan and mission of God to bring the whole world to worship and praise him.

SONGS IN A COLLECTION

Have you ever wondered why the book of Psalms is divided up into five books? (I won't embarrass you by asking if you actually *did* know that already!) It is. Check it in your Bible and you'll find the following:

- Book I: Psalms 1–41
- Book II: Psalms 4–72
- Book III: Psalms 73–89
- Book IV: Psalms 90–106
- Book V: Psalms 107–150

The first thing that this shows is that the book of Psalms is not a random mixture of worship songs. Somebody at some time edited it into this shape and put it together in this way as a structured collection. Unfortunately, they did not also write down the reasons behind why they did it, so we have to think that out for ourselves. All sorts of ideas have been offered, but three of them seem helpful to me.

Reflecting the Torah

One possible reason is that it reflects the five books of the Torah—the Pentateuch (Genesis to Deuteronomy). This idea is strengthened when you look at Psalm 1. Here's an interesting thing. The book of Psalms, as we said above, is called "The Praises" in Hebrew. But it starts with a psalm about the Torah![13] Psalm 1 is a kind of preface to the whole book. It seems to be saying: "In this book we will be worshipping God in all kinds of ways. Here is a whole collection of songs for every occasion. But before we start, remember that worship is for *life*, not just for Sabbaths and festivals. And there are only two ways to live your life: the *way of the righteous* or the *way of the wicked*. Here's the difference."

Psalm 1 then describes how blessed and fruitful is the person who delights in "the law of the LORD"—that is, the Torah. And then, as if to prove the point, we find that the whole book of Psalms has five books, just like the law of Moses, and serves the same purpose. Worship is guidance for life. Worship keeps us walking in the way of the LORD.

Moving from Lament to Praise

A second thing to notice about this structure of five books is that each of the five books ends with doxology—words of praise

---

13. Actually, what is even more interesting is that this call to observe and meditate on the Torah of the LORD comes not only here at the start of the book of Psalms (Ps 1), but also at the start of the book of Joshua. That's the only other place that talks about "meditating on the law of the LORD day and night" (Josh 1:8). In the Hebrew Bible there are three sections: *the Law* (or Torah: Genesis to Deuteronomy), *the Prophets* (starting with Joshua; they called the historical books "The Former Prophets"), and *the Writings* (starting with Psalms and including Job, Proverbs, and the other books). So at the very start of the Prophets (Josh 1) and of the Writings (Ps 1), readers are reminded of the foundational importance of the Law. Remember, of course, that the Torah included the story of creation, God's promises to Abraham, the redemption out of Egypt, and the covenant at Sinai—as well as the laws themselves.

to God and double "Amen" (look at the final verses of Pss 41, 72, 89, and 106). In fact, the fifth book ends with five whole psalms that begin and end with "Hallelujah!" We were thinking a few moments ago about the psalms of lament and how many there are. But notice that almost all of the psalms of lament are found in Books I–III and most of them are *individual* laments. Once you get into Books IV and V the note of thanksgiving and praise is far more dominant and the emphasis is on the community at worship. In other words, taking the book as a whole, there is a gradual shift from lament to praise and from individual to community. Almost certainly this is not accidental. It reflects what we actually find in Psalm 73, where an individual Israelite who is struggling with his faith because of the prosperity of the wicked comes to worship with all God's people and turns again to trust, praise, and deeper understanding. So the book as a whole carries the message: there are many reasons in life why we will lament and protest to God, many things that cause us pain and suffering, but in the end we will find that God meets our greatest needs and can be trusted. Together we can continue to bring him praise, and at the end of the day praise will fill the whole of our life. Hallelujah!

Following the Story of Israel

Third, it seems that the psalms have been organized in a way that, in a broad and general sense, accompanies the story of Israel in the Old Testament. It goes like this:

- In Books I and II we have a number of psalms that are connected to David's early life and then his rise to becoming king—the anointed "son of God" (Ps 2). Book II ends with a picture of the ideal king—in the prayer for Solomon in Psalm 72.

- But Book III begins ominously with a very contrary picture (Ps 73). The wicked are still prospering—as they did throughout the reigns of the kings that followed Solomon. Psalm 78 recounts the failure and rebellion of Israel over many generations. Psalm 79 clearly portrays the destruction of Jerusalem and the temple in 587 BC. Then Book III ends in Psalm 89 with the people remembering all that God had promised to David but how it has all gone horribly wrong in the ending of the line of David and the exile.

A huge question mark hangs in the air—just as it did for the exiles, and just as in the book of Lamentations.

- Book IV begins soberly with the reminder that the only safe place is to trust in the LORD himself, as Moses did (Ps 90 is called "A prayer of Moses, the man of God"). And in the middle of the book there is a concentration of psalms that proclaim that YHWH, the LORD, is king (93, 96–99). Even if there is no son of David on the throne in Jerusalem, God is still on the throne of the universe, and so Israel must learn to trust him again. But the book ends still remembering Israel's historical record of failure and rebellion—they desperately need to be saved (106:47)!

- Book V opens with a celebration of God's redemption, describing the first exodus as a way of telling Israel that there will be a new and greater exodus (as in Ps 114 also). The exiles will prove "the loving deeds of the LORD." The songs of pilgrimage up to Zion will again be the joy of those who are returning to their God and have proved his saving power. And so the whole collection can end in an outpouring of praise to God.

Now, as I said, this is "broad and general," and we mustn't try to squeeze every individual psalm into this scheme. But there does seem to be a sense of some historical flow through the whole book that matches the great moments of Israel's Old Testament history. Israel's worship was linked to Israel's story. They were "tracking" with God through the centuries and their songs reflect that.

"What is the point of all this for preaching and teaching?" you might ask. I don't expect that you will bring all this out in one sermon, but if you were doing Bible studies and teaching with your church, it might be useful there. But I think it always helps to see any book in the Bible *as a whole*. And when we do that for this huge book of Psalms, these are some of its features and their possible significance. So, of course, we still have to study and preach each individual psalm on its own, but when you see where the psalm comes within this overarching structure of the whole collection and the way it has been arranged, it may give you a deeper appreciation of its message.

CHAPTER 14

Preaching and Teaching from the Psalms

Why do we preach the Bible at all? Surely it's because we want people to *know the faith they have* by understanding more fully all that God is and all that God has done for them and also because we want them to *keep the faith they profess* by going on with God, even in the midst of difficulties and suffering. We preach in order to *teach* the faith and to *strengthen* faith. Well, if that is so (and I hope you agree), the book of Psalms should be on your preaching programme regularly. For the Psalms do both of those things over and over again.

SONGS FOR FAITH

Declaring the Faith of God's People

It's been said that the book of Psalms puts the whole theology of the Old Testament into worship. I would go further. I think the book of Psalms expresses the theology of the whole Bible. Of course it comes from Stage 3 of the Bible, before Jesus was born, lived, died, and rose again (the gospel story of Stage 4). And it comes before Stage 5, the great missionary expansion of the church from Acts onward. But even so the book of Psalms anticipates that great New Testament story. And those who were part of the New Testament story—Jesus and his disciples—frequently used the Psalms to help people understand who Jesus was and what the events meant.

Think again of the single, great Bible story along that line of six stages that we drew in chapter 2. The Psalms are relevant to all six stages, as shown in the table. So, if you plan to preach or teach over a period of time (several months at least) from all six stages of the great Bible story, you could bring in at least one or two psalms for every section. And when you do preach or teach the Psalms (even if not as part of a series like that), make sure you show those connections to the great Bible story. People need to know that their *personal faith* is connected to *The Faith*—the great truths from the whole Bible that God's people have received and passed on from one generation to another. We share the faith of the psalmists because we share their story too.

Stage 1	Creation	Creation and the Creator feature often in the Psalms.
Stage 2	The fall	The realities of sin and evil are vividly exposed. The Psalms have a lot to say about wickedness in all its forms.
Stage 3	The promise—Old Testament Israel	The history of God with Israel, since Abraham, is remembered often in the Psalms. God's character as Redeemer is prominent. The exodus motif comes often. God's "mighty acts" are celebrated.
Stage 4	The fulfilment in Christ	The Psalms anticipate the identity of Jesus (Son of David) and the coming of the kingdom of God. Jesus used the Psalms often to show who he was and God's purpose for him.
Stage 5	The mission of the church	Some psalms emphatically proclaim God's saving purpose for all nations and the expectation that all nations will come to worship God (see below, Stage 6).
Stage 6	The new creation	Some psalms speak about the reign of God and anticipate the joy of all creation when God will put everything right (e.g., Pss 96, 98).

Think again of the ancient Israelites singing these songs over and over again. What were they learning? What were they remembering? What were they declaring about God, the world, themselves, and the future? Israel's worship was a constant *education* in the essentials of their whole faith and understanding. And there can be no doubt that this was exactly what God intended for them. As they sang and sang these songs, they *learned* the substance of their faith.

That is why it is important to preach and teach the Psalms and encourage our people to read them regularly for themselves. Incidentally, it is also why we should pay attention to what *we* sing in our worship times. People unconsciously come to believe what they sing often enough. Let's make sure those words and songs express the breadth of our biblical faith. Many modern worship songs seem very shallow and empty in comparison with the Psalms!

Sustaining the Faith of God's People

But faith is tested. The Old Testament is full of stories that show that. And the Psalms want to encourage God's people to go on trusting and obeying God, even in tough times or when they are tempted to go off in other directions. Sometimes the Psalms do this in a very positive way—simply calling on the worshippers to remember how great God is and to go on trusting him (Ps 46). Or an individual will give testimony about how God supported him in trouble or rescued him from danger (Ps 40). These are psalms that *encourage* hope and *strengthen* faith. Sometimes they do it more negatively by recounting times in Israel's history when the Israelites rebelled against God and suffered for it (Ps 106). These are psalms that *warn* against unfaithfulness and rebellion.

Such experiences and testings are common to God's people in every age. So we can certainly preach and teach from these psalms in order to sustain people's faith—especially in the midst of challenges or suffering. That is what Peter did. Read 1 Peter and see how many times he quotes from the Old Testament, and especially the Psalms, to encourage his readers in their suffering.

Checklist

Here are some questions that will help you when you set out to preach or teach from a psalm you think will instruct or strengthen people's faith. But remember: the *first* thing you need to do (as with every passage of Scripture) is to read the psalm very carefully for itself. Each one has its own main theme and its own structure. You need to study it until you are able to summarize the psalm's main point and to outline the flow of thought within it. Then think about these things:

☐ What does this psalm teach about God? What pictures are used for God? What characteristics of God are mentioned? What actions of God are described — past, present, or future? How do you think the writer knew all that about God? Where did he learn such things?

☐ What events in the story of Israel are mentioned, if any? What was Israel supposed to learn from those events?

☐ What truths about the world, the people of Israel, or other nations are mentioned or implied?

☐ What reasons does this psalm give for trusting God, or for obeying him, or for not giving up in faith?

☐ In what ways does this psalm connect with the New Testament, with Christ, the gospel, or the church?

☐ Is this psalm quoted in the New Testament, and if so, for what reasons?

☐ In what ways, then, should we respond to this psalm in our *understanding* of our faith and in *persevering* in our faith? What can we learn that increases our knowledge of God and our confidence in God?

SONGS FOR LIVING

In the last chapter we noticed how **Psalm 1** functions as a preface to the whole book of Psalms and reminds the Israelites that worship is not just about how well we can sing but about how well we are living.

Go back and read Psalm 1 slowly a few times. Can you see the poetic combining of pictures? There is the agricultural contrast between a fruit tree planted by water and the useless chaff that is blown away from the grains of wheat. There is the metaphor of "two ways." And there is the sober picture of two destinies: the righteous will stand safely under God's judgment, but the wicked will be destroyed. It is a short, but very powerful, encouragement and warning combined.

The righteous person delights in and meditates on "the law of the LORD." The word "meditates" (in Hebrew) does not just mean silent inner thinking (as it does in English). In Hebrew it usually meant reading aloud (alone or in company), or reciting or even singing, the words of Scripture again and again. It was an active engagement with the text, "chewing it over," as we might say. But the word "delight" means exactly what it says in both languages — to take pleasure in something, to enjoy and relish it. We are delighted by good friends, by a loving gift, by a good meal, by a beautiful day. And the righteous person, says the very first psalm, takes that kind of pleasure in the teaching of God in his word.

Now let's notice, first of all, that these two words (delights and meditates) do not mean that the psalmist is involved in just an emotional or intellectual activity. Rather, this person loves God's law because they are *living* that way. They are putting it into practice. This psalm, at the very head of the whole book, shouts out a blessing on those who *live* their faith in God by *following* God's instructions. That is the only kind of person who can worship God acceptably (as Pss 15 and 24 explain further).

But, second, notice that this blessed person does not see the law as a stern, heavy burden of requirements that they must legalistically carry out to the letter. They *delight* in the Torah! And their life is fruitful because of it. This is not a code of religious slavery but a recipe for responsible freedom and joy in living life in the presence of the living God. The same message comes in **Psalms 19 and 119** (again and again!).

Worship, then, is a learning experience — or should be; and not just learning in the head but *learning for living*. Many of the psalms offer reflections about life, wisdom for times of trouble, and good advice for living in a way that pleases God. Above all, they give constant encouragement to go on trusting God and walking in God's way, even when the ways of the wicked seem more enticing. Sometimes these are called "Wisdom Psalms," because they are similar in some ways to what we find in the Wisdom literature.[1]

---

1. Examples of these wisdom psalms, or teaching psalms, include 36, 37, 49, 73, 112, 127, 128, 133.

But even in those psalms that are simply praising God there are lessons for life. For Israel, the character of the LORD their God was their best clue as to how God wanted them to live their own lives. So whenever they sang songs about how the LORD is faithful, truthful, trustworthy, just, compassionate, loving, caring, and providing, the unspoken but very powerful implication was, "That's what we ought to be like also." Worship leads us to become like, and to want to become like, the One whom we worship.

Sometimes that implication is very clearly expressed. **Psalms 111 and 112** are a pair. They are both "acrostic"—that is to say, each line of each psalm begins with a letter of the Hebrew alphabet in correct sequence—like an A–Z. Psalm 111 is a song describing the character and actions of the LORD. And then Psalm 112 is a song describing the character and actions of those who fear the LORD and "delight in his commands" (echoing Ps 1). Read them both side by side. You will see that several of the things said about God in Psalm 111 are then echoed in what is said about the righteous in Psalm 112. Compare verses 3, 4, and 7 in both psalms and also 111:5 with 112:9. The righteous who live in the fear of the LORD will grow more and more like the God they worship.

So there is a lot of *ethical* teaching in the Psalms. As they were sung over and over again, they were rubbing into Israel's minds and consciences ways of life that were pleasing to God—and warnings against those that were not. For that reason, we can preach and teach them with the same intention—to help people not only to understand and sustain their faith but to live it out in the world outside. There is so much to discover about ourselves, about life in God's world, about the temptations of sin and evil, about what is righteous and pleasing to God. There is plenty of good preaching and teaching in these psalms!

But when we preach and teach the Psalms as songs for life— that is, helping people know how to live their lives—we should remember a few things:

- First, remember that the ethical teaching of the Psalms was (and still is) for those who know the great story of God's salvation and belong to God's people. As we saw with the law itself, we must always preach the Bible's instruction and teaching on the basis of God's grace—not as a means of earning credit with God. We live in *response* to who God is and what God has done. That must always be our emphasis.

- Second, remember that the psalmists saw God's law as a gift, a joy, and a delight (check out Pss 1 and 19 again), not as a burden. So use these psalms to help people *love and enjoy and delight in* living in obedience to God. Don't preach them in a way that generates the burdens of legalism.

- Third, while some of these psalms speak of the good things that come to those who live in obedience to God's ways, we should never preach them as heavenly guarantees and promises. That is what some Prosperity preachers do. They twist verses like Psalm 34:10, "Those who seek the LORD lack no good thing," into an assumption that if you have enough faith you will have health, wealth, and all the good things of life. But the psalmists themselves knew that, although it was right, good, and blessed to live in faithful obedience to God, sometimes those who do so still suffer terribly in this fallen world with evil all around us. Psalm 73 addresses that very problem. Don't preach the Psalms in a way that generates false or selfish expectations.

SONGS FOR MISSION

I sometimes wonder what went on in the head of an ancient Israelite as he or she sang some of the psalms. Mind you, I sometimes wonder what goes on in the heads of some Christians when they sing the words they do in our worship services—but let's not go there! But listen. Here is an Israelite, maybe a thousand years before Christ, when Israel was just a tiny dot on the world map and Jerusalem a modest-sized city on a small hill. Yet he sings out the following words (I've emphasized the words that are so surprising):

> *All the nations* you have made
> will come and worship before you, Lord;
> they will bring glory to your name.
> *(Ps 86:9)*

Another day he sings,

> The nations will fear the name of the LORD,
> *all the kings of the earth* will revere your glory.
> *(Ps 102:15)*

Then he actually calls on all the nations to give the LORD a round of applause and join the singing:

> Clap your hands, *all you nations*,
>> shout to God with cries of joy.
>>> *(Ps 47:1)*

> Sing to the LORD a new song;
>> sing to the LORD, *all the earth.*
>>> *(Ps 96:1)*

These are only a few of many verses throughout the book which extend the horizon of worship right out to all nations and the whole earth.[2]

How on earth did Israelite worshippers ever imagine such things could happen? I really don't know. But they had the faith-imagination to put such expectations into their songs of worship. Even Paul calls this "the mystery ... hidden for ages" (Col 1:26). That is, the Old Testament Israelites believed *that* God would one day keep his promise to Abraham and people from all nations would be so blessed by God that they would come to worship him. But the mystery, what they could not have known, was *how* God would do that. Now, of course, we do. For as Paul says, the mystery has now been revealed *through the gospel* (Eph 2:11 — 3:6). It is through the Lord Jesus Christ that the way has been opened for people of all nations to come to God (including you and me). Paul, in Romans 15:11, quotes Psalm 117 among a number of the Old Testament texts that celebrate in advance the missionary expansion of the church among the Gentiles (which just means "the nations").

These psalms are part of a much wider theme running through the Old Testament, looking forward to people of all nations coming to share in the blessing and salvation of God and then worshipping him as they do so. Look at the range of texts in this next footnote[3] and note especially how prominent the theme is in Isaiah. This was the vision that inspired Paul and the early church as they took the good news about Jesus to the Gentiles—the non-Jewish nations in the world of their day.

---

2. Look at the following psalms to see the same universal note: Pss 22:27; 67; 87; 96; 98; 99; 117.

3. 1 Kgs 8:41–43, 60; 2 Kgs 19:15–19; Isa 2:1–5; 12:4–5; 19:19–25; 45:22; 49:6; 56:3–8; 60:1–3; 66:19; Amos 9:12; Zech 2:11.

What was promised at Stage 3 (blessing for all nations) was accomplished at Stage 4 (the gospel of Jesus Christ) and is being fulfilled throughout Stage 5 (the spread of the gospel with the mission of the church). And it will be completed at Stage 6, when people of all nations will indeed gather to worship at the throne of God (Rev 7:9–10). That is the overarching biblical context for these psalms that picture all nations and the whole earth praising God.

Can you see how it fills out the importance and meaning of such psalms when we see them in the light of the whole-Bible story? They were not just cheerful worship songs with a bit of poetic imagination thrown in. They were not just romantic exaggeration — talking about the whole earth in the way a lover might tell his beloved she is the most beautiful woman in the whole world. No, these psalms were affirming and celebrating the mission of God to bring blessing to all nations. They were anticipating all nations coming to worship God from the ends of the earth. They are part of the Bible's gospel! We must read and preach and teach them in the light of God's promise to Abraham, in the light of the Great Commission of Jesus to make disciples of all nations, and in the light of the Bible's glorious finale in Revelation 21–22. That is their proper background and context.

SAMPLE OUTLINE

I love preaching and teaching some of these great "missional" psalms, such as 47, 67, and 87. One of my favourites is **Psalm 96**. It begins by calling everybody to "sing a new song." I make that the key phrase for the outline. I like to preach this on "World Mission Sundays."

A New Song for a New World
Psalm 96

Three questions: In today's world filled with suffering, violence, and evil,

- Is it still possible to believe the old truths of the gospel?

- Is it possible to go on believing them when we are surrounded by the gods and idols of other people, including other religions?

- Is it possible to have any hope of a new and better world?

This psalm answers "Yes!" to all three.

Structure: Notice that vv. 1–9 focus on the earth as the place of human habitation—peoples and nations. Vv. 10–13 focus on the earth itself—the creation. All will come to praise God, with "a new song." The LORD reigns over all (v. 10 is at the central point of the psalm).

A New Song That Revives the Old Words (vv. 1–3)

The songwriter starts with great enthusiasm: "Sing, sing, sing, praise, proclaim, and declare!" He wants us to "sing a *new* song." But the content of the song is full of the *old words*—what Israel always sang about:

- The *name* of the LORD

- His *salvation*

- His *glory*

- And his *mighty works*

(Ask what each of those words would have meant to an Old Testament Israelite, first of all, and then what they now mean to us through Christ.)

- What makes it a *new* song is: where it is to be sung (in all the earth), and who will join the singing (all the nations). The old song of Israel (about God and his salvation) becomes the new song of the nations. The old song becomes new when it is sung by new people in new places.

- That's what mission does with the gospel. "The old, old story it is ever new" when it is heard and believed by new people to the ends of the earth. And that is the task of world mission. Nothing can change the foundational historical facts of the gospel, but we are called to celebrate them with newness and freshness and to adapt them to every culture and to do so with joy and singing.

Mission makes the old songs new.
Mission invites the world to hear the music and join in.

A New Song That Displaces the Old Gods (vv. 4 – 9)

- This is a song *for YHWH, the* Lord—not for any other god.

- If the nations are being invited to worship the Lord, the God of Israel, they will also recognize that all other gods are false and useless in comparison with this God (vv. 4 – 6). So there has to be a radical displacement of the old idolatries. For only YHWH is great, worthy of praise, and to be feared (v. 4).

- Whatever the other gods "are" (things we fear, or love, or admire—all kinds of idolatries in the world, not just "other religions"), they are ultimately nothing in comparison with the living God (vv. 5 – 6).

- So the nations must bring their worship to the one living God alone (vv. 7 – 9). Read these verses with the emphasis on *the* Lord: ... *his* sanctuary ... *his* name ... *his* courts ... *his* holiness. There is a strong contrast (v. 5). The psalmist is not inviting the nations to accept YHWH as one of their gods along with all the others. No. He is the only real living God, so all other false gods must leave the room.

- Mission transforms the religious landscape. We do not *attack* other religions but bring people to know the only living God who is worthy of worship so that other gods simply fall away. That happens as mission brings people to know the Lord Jesus Christ.

- World mission leads to great change in individuals, families, villages, regions, and even whole cultures. It can happen very quickly or take hundreds of years. But ultimately, the new song will displace the old gods.

Mission transforms the religious landscape.

A New Song That Celebrates the End of the Old World (vv. 10–13)

- V. 10 is the climax and keynote of the psalm: "Say among the nations, 'The LORD reigns.'" YHWH has always been, is now, and will always be, the true King of the universe. Here, then, long before Jesus preached it in Galilee, is the good news of the kingdom of God.

- But the description of God's reign in these verses stands in stark contrast to the world as we know it now—the old fallen world of sin and evil. The psalm appeals to our imagination and invites us to see the world that God is creating and then celebrate it in our new song. And it is a new world that turns our old world upside down.
    - A world of *reliability*— "firmly established"
    - A world of *righteousness*— "with equity"
    - A world of *rejoicing*— "Let the heavens rejoice, let the earth be glad." When God comes to "put things right" (the meaning of "judge the earth"), all creation will be included. The gospel is holistic, not just evangelistic; ecological as well as theological.

- Our old world is the opposite of all three: a place of instability and chaos, a place of injustice and oppression, a place of suffering and sorrow—for humans and nature.

- But we look forward to the new world God is creating. World mission looks forward with a vision that transcends and transforms the present. We celebrate in advance "Mission accomplished." And in the confidence of that biblical hope, we go out to participate in the work of God's kingdom—in word and deed. The psalm calls us to look up, look forward, and celebrate what God is doing and what he will one day accomplish.

Mission proclaims and celebrates a new world.

> *Hope is the ability to hear the music of the future*
> *Faith is the courage to dance to it today*
>
> Ruben Alves

A NOTE ON THE CURSING PSALMS

There are some Psalms that are hard to preach and teach from. Indeed, it is hard to know whether we should preach or teach from them at all. Some Christians wonder why they are there in the Bible. I mean, of course, those Psalms which call for God to bring his judgment on the wicked — Psalms of cursing. Here are some of them. Don't spend too much time reading them all now or you'll end up depressed!

Psalms 7, 10, 17, 35, 55, 58, 59, 69, 83, 109.

Here are a few thoughts that may help us think more clearly about them.

> They are part of the Scriptures that Paul says are "God-breathed" and "useful" (2 Tim 3:15–16), so we cannot simply ignore them. They must be there for a purpose and we need to receive them as part of the overall message of what God has to say to us in the Bible and learn what they can teach us.

> Jesus knew them, read them, studied them as part of his years as a young Jewish boy and man, and would have sung them regularly in the synagogue. We do not have any hint that Jesus rejected them or was embarrassed by them. He did, however, at one crucial point of his life *transcend* them, as we shall see.

> We must see the context in which they were written. They come out of intense suffering caused by people behaving wickedly. That may be when the writer is a victim of unjust accusation in a court, in which his life may be at risk, or when he has been lied to or betrayed, or when he is facing violent enemies who wish to kill him. We know that David, for example, did face such situations, and many other Psalmists probably did too.
>
> But it is not only when people are suffering *personal* attack that they express such feelings. Sometimes there is a longing for God to stop injustice in the world because *others* are suffering so much — the poor, the hungry, the marginalized, etc. And most of us have had such feelings too. We are angry and distressed when people do despicable cruel things to others. We want God to stop them!

So perhaps we should not immediately jump to condemn psalmists when they let loose some angry words and call on God to act — until we ourselves have walked in their shoes. For there are many believers in our world who suffer great injustice and find that these psalms actually give them comfort, for they are able to express *to God* what they long for without seeking vengeance themselves.

And that is another important point. What the Psalmists are doing in such psalms is *obeying* God's command that we should *not* take revenge. We do not set out to "get even" with those who do us wrong. Rather we are to put the matter into God's hands and let him deal with the wicked in his way and in his time. That is what the psalmists are doing. They are asking God to do *what God had promised to do* — that is, to put down the wicked and vindicate the righteous, to put things right, to stop wrongdoers, to do justice in his own world.

Mind you, they sometimes seem impatient! They ask God to hurry up! And they suggest a few possible actions they would like him to take! However, we need also to realize that in the ancient world (and still in many traditional cultures today), there was a whole catalogue of curses that you could use. They had many stock phrases and stereotypes. They had very colourful and rather nasty lists of curses you could choose from. So when we read something like Psalm 109, for example, we should not imagine that the writer meant every word literally. A lot of the language is rhetorical and exaggerated.

Above all, of course, we have to bring these Psalms (as we do with all of the Old Testament) into the light of the New Testament revelation and teaching. And that leads us immediately to Jesus — both his teaching and his example.

Jesus was quite clear on this: those who are his disciples must bless others and not curse. We are to love our enemies, not seek to kill them or demand that God should (Matt 5:43–48). And then he followed his own teaching at the time of his trial and crucifixion. He could

have cursed his enemies then. He could have used any of
those psalms, if he had wanted to. Nobody would have
been surprised at that. But no—he surprised them and
us with his immortal words: "Father, forgive them ..."
At that moment, Jesus transcended the psalmists. He
did not say it was wrong for them to have asked God to
judge the wicked. That is part of the whole message of the
Bible, that God will do that. But Jesus had come to *save*
the wicked, and even at the moment of his death that was
what he was asking God to do.

And of course, on the cross, Christ not only bore the curse of
sin, he became a curse for us. In that way, the prayers of the
psalmists that God should judge the wicked were fulfilled.
God *did* judge sin and evil. But God did it by taking that
judgment, that curse, upon himself in the person of his
own Son.

So, like Stephen, the first martyr, we are to follow the
example as well as the teaching of Jesus and pray even for
those who do us harm (Acts 7:59–60). That is extremely
hard to do. In fact it is impossible without the transforming
love and power of Christ within us. But it is also what the
Apostle Paul commands: "Bless those who persecute you;
bless and do not curse" (Rom 12:14, 17–21).

What then are we to do with those Psalms?

I believe we can help people to understand them carefully in
the way I've outlined above. We should *never* use them as a way of
directly cursing any particular person or group of people. We are
forbidden to do that. But we *can* pray them in a very general sense
of longing for God to bring justice to the world and stop evildoers bringing so much pain and suffering on others. Like Jesus,
however, we should not pray for God to judge them without also
praying and longing that they should come to repentance and be
forgiven by Christ who died for them.

Remember, every time we pray the Lord's Prayer, we pray,
"Your kingdom come." That is a prayer for God to put the world
to rights, and when God's kingdom is finally established at Christ's
return, it will include the final judgment and destruction of those
who have remained unrepentantly wicked. The cursing Psalms are

not there for us to imitate now in the sense of preaching and praying them against our enemies. But they are still there to remind us that there is real suffering in the world, especially for persecuted believers, and we should pray for them and pray that God delivers them from the hands of evildoers. And they also teach us about the seriousness of God's reaction to sin and evil and that we can trust him ultimately to do justice in all the earth.

CHAPTER 15

Preaching and Teaching from the Wisdom Literature

We've covered a lot of ground so far, haven't we? We've thought about the stories in the historical books, the books of the law, the prophets, and the Psalms. Is there anything left? Well, there are several small books that I'm afraid we won't have space to deal with (like Ruth, Esther, Lamentations, Song of Solomon). But there is one more group of sizeable books that we really need to say something about: Proverbs, Job, and Ecclesiastes. They are usually grouped together and given the name "Wisdom literature." Sometimes that term includes the Song of Solomon and a few psalms as well. But we'll concentrate here on the big three.

WISE BOOKS FROM WISE PEOPLE

In Israel, and in the ancient Near Eastern nations that surrounded them, there was a special class of people who were known as "the wise" or "the sages." These were people who were renowned for their knowledge and wisdom. People went to them for advice on all kinds of matters. Sometimes this was at a fairly local level—older men or women in the community who were respected for their experience of life. They could be trusted to give wise advice to the youth—like parents to children. Sometimes, though, "the wise" seem to have been an educated elite of royal advisors, more like government "think tanks" and administrators. Through archaeological discovery, we know of such people in

Egypt and Babylon also. There are manuals of instructions for government servants full of advice for success in public life. There are also some philosophical texts reflecting on the meaning of life and the questions of evil and suffering. So, the Wisdom literature that we find in the Bible is part of a class of literature that is common across a wide spectrum of ancient Near Eastern culture, stretching back a thousand years even before Israel settled in Canaan. We'll come back to this international dimension of wisdom and what it means for our preaching and teaching a little later.

Read **Jeremiah 18:18**. Some of Jeremiah's enemies are out to kill him. And they say to themselves, "It won't matter if we kill Jeremiah. We will still have the priests to teach us the law. And we'll still have the prophets to give us God's word. And we'll still have the wise to give us their counsel. One less prophet won't make any difference." What this shows us is that they clearly distinguished between these three groups — *priests*, *prophets*, and *wise* people. They were like separate professions.

So just as we have the books of the law (which the priests were supposed to guard and teach) and the books of the prophets, so also we have the books of the wise people of Israel. They come in the third part of the Hebrew canon, known as the Writings, which includes Job, Psalms, Proverbs, and Ecclesiastes.[1] Of these, it is Proverbs, Job, and Ecclesiastes that we are considering here. So when we use the term "wisdom" in what follows, we mean those books — the Wisdom literature.

As Jeremiah 18:18 shows, the wise were a separate group of people from the priests and the prophets. So let's see how their books are different too.

WISDOM WAS DIFFERENT FROM THE LAW

Here's a little exercise.

> Read Exodus 20:14; Leviticus 20:10; and Deuteronomy 22:22.
>
> Now read Proverbs 5 and Proverbs 6:20–35.

---

1. The Writings include the following books of the Hebrew canon: Psalms, Job, Proverbs, Ruth, Song of Song, Ecclesiastes, Lamentations, Esther, Daniel, Ezra, Nehemiah, 1 & 2 Chronicles.

I'm sure you can see that all the passages are about adultery—sexual unfaithfulness in marriage. And they all condemn it. But the style is very different. The laws are blunt and to the point: "Don't do it! The penalty is death if you do." It is a straight command from God backed up by a severe legal penalty. But Proverbs gives not so much a command as a strong warning backed up by pointing out some of the disastrous results: "It can ruin yourself and your family. Even if you aren't caught and actually put to death, there's still far too much to lose. Think again!"

This example illustrates one important difference between wisdom and the law.

- The law commands. Wisdom advises, warns, and persuades.

- The law stands on the foundation of God's authority and his covenant requirements. Wisdom speaks from experience and points out the probable results.

- The law points a finger directly in your face and just tells you what not to do. Wisdom puts an arm around your shoulder and urges you to think twice.

As Christians in our various societies we have opportunities to discuss all kinds of social, political, and moral issues with people around us—sometimes people of other faiths or people who say they follow no religion. Sometimes we get the opportunity to speak at civic occasions in the presence of community leaders. I think the Wisdom literature enables us to do that without appearing to "lay down the law" or impose legalistic demands on people. We can stand up for what is wise and prudent. We can point to the good or bad consequences that will follow certain policies or actions. We can hold up biblical values and priorities and invite others to see that they make sense and are for the common good.

So remember the difference between the law and the wisdom books if you want to use the book of Proverbs for preaching and teaching. *The proverbs are not laws.* They are not absolute commands, or rules, or statements of what will *always* happen. They are short, pithy statements about all kinds of situations in life. They are designed to get our attention and make us think. They offer insights, perspectives, and guidelines, not hard-and-fast rules. They tell us that certain kinds of behaviour will usually produce good results and other kinds of behaviour will usually produce bad results. Wise people choose the first. Foolish people choose the second. And the results *usually* follow. But we can't turn these observations either into unalterable laws or into guaranteed promises. Life is more complicated than that. Things don't always work out in the way the proverbs put it in their simplicity. And the wise men and women who collected the book of Proverbs knew that too—which is why they also gave us Job and Ecclesiastes, as we shall see below.

WISDOM WAS DIFFERENT FROM THE PROPHETS

Here's another little exercise.

Read Jeremiah 22:13–17; Ezekiel 34:1–6 ("shepherds" is a metaphor for kings in Israel); Amos 7:10–11; and Isaiah 10:1–4.

Now read Proverbs 8:12–16; 16:10, 12–13; 20:8, 26; 25:2–5; 31:1–9.

Both groups of texts are about kings, government, and political leaders. What differences do you see? Well, on the one hand, the prophets are far more hostile and personal in their attacks. They specifically denounce corrupt and failing leaders, even naming some of them in person. They are very sharp and particular. The wise men, on the other hand, state principles and expectations. They are more optimistic, laying out the ideals of good government in general terms. This is how political leaders ought to behave. They are very general.

Once again, there is no conflict in principle between the prophets and the wise, even if there is a clearly different tone of voice. Proverbs describes what ought to be, while the prophets describe what actually is—the situation "on the ground," as we say. And we need both perspectives. You can't criticize *the way things are* unless you have some vision of *the way things ought to be*. The Bible gives us both.

The table shows some other marked differences between the prophets and the wise.

The Prophets	The Wise
"Thus says the LORD …"	"Listen to my advice …"
Challenge to hear and decide	Invitation to learn and understand
Focus on God's redemption and judgment	Focus on God's creation and providence
Frequent use of the history of Israel	No use of the history of Israel
Very specific and particular context	General and universal relevance
Addressed to specific individual or nations	Addressed to any and all who will listen
Direct and imperative style	Reflective and persuasive style

We saw in chapters 11 and 12 that when we preach or teach from the prophets, we cannot really understand them unless we know something of the historical background of their messages. We need to answer the questions "Who?" "What?" "When?" "Where?" and "Why?" as clearly as we can. However, when we preach or teach from the Wisdom literature, it is already much more general. It does not depend on specific historical contexts in the same way. It is somewhat "timeless." Of course, it was still written in the cultural context of Old Testament Israel, so we will need to know about their culture and way of life in order to understand some of the proverbial sayings and idioms. But in other respects, these books can speak in a more general sense at any time.

WISDOM EMPHASIZED GOD AS CREATOR

Ready for another little exercise?

Read the following texts from the law. As you read each one, notice not only what the law says but also the reason that it gives. *Why* should Israelites keep these laws? **Exodus 23:9; Leviticus 19:33–36; 25:39–43; Deuteronomy 15:12–15; 24:14–22.**

> I'm sure you saw that they are all about justice and compassion for those who are in need—foreigners, debtors, slaves, the poor. And in each case God refers back to the exodus, reminding the Israelites of how they had been foreigners and slaves in Egypt—an oppressed, immigrant ethnic minority. But God had been kind to them and delivered them. So they should do the same for people in similar circumstances.
>
> **Now read the following texts from the Wisdom literature: Proverbs 14:31; 17:5; 19:17; 22:2; 29:7, 13; Job 31:13–15.**
>
> Once again, they are all concerned with how we relate to those who are poor or in need. We should treat them with kindness and respect and deal with their grievances with justice. But how do the wisdom writers back up their point? *They go back to creation.* God is the Creator of all of us, whether rich or poor. We have one Maker and so we share one common humanity. So if we mock or insult a poor person, we are effectively doing that to God, their Creator. And if we are kind to the poor, it is like "lending to the Lord."

So both the law and the wisdom books (and also the prophets, of course) teach about social justice and compassion. There is no difference in their objectives. They all want the same thing. They all want people to do what is just and kind in society. But there is a significant difference in how they go about *motivating* people to do those things.

The law and the prophets point back to the history of Israel. They remind Israel that they are a people whom God had redeemed out of slavery in the exodus. They remind Israel of the covenant. We saw this already in our chapters on the law and the prophets. They were speaking to redeemed people who should have known how to live in a way that was consistent with what God had so graciously done for them.

But the wisdom writers do not refer to the history of Israel at all. They don't make any use of the great historical traditions of Israel's faith—the promise to Abraham, the exodus, Sinai, the wilderness wanderings, the conquest of the land. They don't refer to the story of redemption that we know so well from the early books of the Bible.

It can't be that the wise men and women of Israel did not know of those traditions. They lived in Israel — they *must* have known them! And of course, by using the divine name YHWH, the LORD, as they repeatedly do, they showed that they knew him as the God of redemption and covenant. But they also knew (as all Israelites did) that the same God who was the Redeemer of Israel was also the Creator of the world and all nations. So they reckoned that if God was morally consistent, then his standards should apply to all people. They saw that there are moral principles built into creation itself. There are ways of living that are good for people anywhere, and other ways of living that will be damaging for human life everywhere. In other words, while the law and the prophets were addressed to Israel in particular as God's redeemed people, the wisdom literature has a more universal human appeal.

However, there is no contradiction. For, as we saw in chapter 10, God had created Israel from the very beginning to be the means of blessing the nations. God gave them his law partly in order to shape them to be a model for the nations. So the teaching that we find in Old Testament law could be used as an example or paradigm for others. And that is what the wisdom writers do. They see the general principles behind the specific laws, and they turn them into advice, guidance, proverbs, and pictures that can be understood and taken to heart by anybody.

I think it is helpful to remember this point if we are preaching or teaching from these texts. The wisdom of the Bible is not just for Christians but for anybody. We are all human beings, made in God's image, living in God's world. That means that we must show respect for all people, no matter what ethnic or cultural background they come from, what religion they follow, or what social status they have. There is a fundamental equality of all human beings because all are created by God. The Wisdom literature affirms that, and it is a good place from which to teach that message. In a moment we'll think more about how this can also help build a bridge for the gospel.

WISDOM ASKED THE TOUGH QUESTIONS

Can you manage one more little exercise? It comes in two parts. In each one, you'll read two passages side by side and contrast them.

Read Psalm 146:5–9.

What does it say about YHWH—the Lord God? It is heartwarming, isn't it? That is the God Israel knew and worshipped.

Now read Job 24:1–12.

Now that's a massive contrast! Job sees what really happens to the poor and needy in our fallen world, and it is heartbreaking. But worst of all, what does Job say about God in verses 1 and 12? God seems to do nothing and say nothing about the tragic injustice and suffering of our world.

Read Leviticus 26:3–5, 14–17; and Deuteronomy 30:15–18.

These texts express the straightforward "logic" of the covenant between God and Israel. If Israel walked in obedience to God, they would continue to enjoy his blessing. But if they became unfaithful and wicked, then they would suffer greatly under his judgment. That seems simple enough.

Now read Ecclesiastes 8:14—9:4.

There's another huge contrast! The writer of Ecclesiastes (often he is given the name that he calls himself in the book—Qoheleth, meaning "The Preacher") points out that sometimes life throws up the opposite to what we should expect on the basis of Leviticus and Deuteronomy. What people deserve seems to go to the wrong people! And in the end, everybody dies anyway. Where's the sense in it all?

As I just said, the wise men and women of Israel knew the Torah and the Psalms. So it seems that sometimes they pick up some of the strong affirmations that we find there and hold them up for question. It's as if they do what you've just done in the exercise above. They say, "Look at what this text says. Now look at the world around you. They don't match up very well, do they?"

It's important to say that they are not *denying* the truth of the Scriptures. They were believers, not atheists. But they are willing to *ask tough questions* about the way life doesn't always work out in a neat and logical way or just the way the Bible says it should. But even in the midst of those questions, they go on believing and trusting God to make things right eventually. So even Ecclesiastes ends with strong advice.

> ... fear God and keep his commandments,
>> for this is the duty of all mankind.
> For God will bring every deed into judgment,
>> including every hidden thing,
>> whether it is good or evil.
>>> *(Eccl 12:13–14)*

"That is what I *believe*," he seems to say, "but this is what I *see* in the world. Why? Why?"

It is important when we preach and teach from the wisdom books to keep the same sense of balance that wisdom itself does. We could become very optimistic and naïve if we only read Proverbs and think life will always be like that. But we could become very pessimistic and depressed if we only read Ecclesiastes and think there is no point in living at all since life is so futile, frustrating, and short. There is a kind of self-correcting mechanism in the wisdom tradition that prevents us going to one extreme or the other. It's like a conversation between the books that goes something like this:

Proverbs: "Here are guidelines for life. Follow them, and your life will be long and happy."

Job and Ecclesiastes: "We did, and it isn't."

Proverbs: "Nevertheless, we live in God's world, and even in the midst of suffering and frustration it will always be better to follow God's instructions, even if life is tough or unfair."

The book of Job wrestles with the problem of the suffering of good people who don't seem to deserve it. It is a brilliantly written drama in which we see a man who is as righteous as can be imagined (both the narrator and God himself say so, 1:1, 8; 2:3) but who suffers the worst that can be imagined. The speeches of his friends explore all the possible reasons for his suffering — especially the theological reason that he must be suffering because of sins he has committed. But they are completely wrong. We know it (because we've read the opening chapters), God knows it, and Job knows it. Still he suffers. And the worst of it is not just his suffering but the *silence of God*. Job cannot "get through" to God in order to state his case and be vindicated. In the end, when God speaks, God does not "answer the problem of suffering." Rather, God restores his relationship with Job and in effect asks him to trust the God who is greater than we can begin to imagine, the God who ultimately controls the very forces of evil that we don't understand.

The book of Ecclesiastes wrestles with the problem of how futile life seems. He knows that life is full of good things—food and drink, work, marriage, family, and so on—and that these things are gifts from God that we should enjoy. But so often even the best things in life end up destroyed or wasted or going to the wrong people. And in the end, death seems to make it all pointless anyway. He knows it is better to be wise than to be a fool, but when you're dead, what does it matter? A dead wise man is just as dead as a dead fool, and both are as dead as a dead dog. What's the difference in the end? It's all meaningless, frustrating, pointless (that's the meaning of the Hebrew word that used to be translated "vanity").

I think Ecclesiastes is the best Old Testament commentary on **Genesis 3**. It shows us the results of the fall in human life. It looks hard at the dust of death that God said would be our destiny. Only **Romans 1:18–32** goes further in describing the terrible results of sin. Ecclesiastes faces up to harsh realities. He knows *some* of the truth about God and he goes on trusting in God, but he is simply baffled, grieved, and depressed by what happens in our world. Aren't we all, sometimes? I think Ecclesiastes speaks out what many people think, feel, and ask. And that makes it a bridge for the gospel, as we shall come to in a moment.

But for now, what does the Wisdom literature do for our biblical preaching and teaching? I think God has put these books in the Bible for the same kind of reason as for the psalms of lament. They give us *permission* to ask hard questions, face up to appalling problems and suffering, wrestle with the things that trouble us, and sometimes even complain and protest about things that just aren't the way they should be. But, like those psalms, the Wisdom literature does all this *from a position of humble faith and trust*. And that is the clue for our preaching and teaching, I think. We must stay humble and not try to know everything—or pretend that we do. I think that will protect us from two opposite dangers:

- On the one hand, some preachers can be very *dogmatic.* They must be seen to have all the right answers to every question. Whatever the pastor says must be the final truth on everything. I hope you are not tempted to be like that, but you probably know some preachers who are. They can explain everything and insist that their interpretation must be accepted. The trouble is, that's exactly what the friends of Job were like. They had the right answers—they thought. But they were completely wrong and pastorally cruel. And God condemned them in the end for speaking *wrongly* about him and Job.

• Or, on the other hand, some preachers can be very *naïve*. They preach as if everything will turn out exactly as the Bible says in this or that single verse. They make glowing promises and raise unrealistic expectations. And they ignore that the Bible itself shows that life does not always work out like that in our fallen world.

Surely the Wisdom literature encourages us to be *humble* in our preaching and teaching (as in life generally). There are times when we have to say: "I do not know the answer to this problem. I do not know why these things have happened. I do not know why God allows things that seem so contrary to all that we know about him. And there are *people in the Bible* who did not know the answers either. But they asked their questions and struggled and wrestled in their pain and sometimes in anger. God *allows* us to do that—to feel that way and say those things. It's OK to be not OK. God even gives us examples of people doing it (in the lament psalms and books like Jeremiah, Job, and Ecclesiastes) so that we can make their words our words. But let us hold on to God even in our struggles, as they did. Let us go on trusting him even when we can't understand him. "The fear of the LORD is the beginning of wisdom."

WISDOM AS A BRIDGE FOR THE GOSPEL

At the start of this chapter I mentioned that the Wisdom literature in the Old Testament is part of a whole range of writings from the world of the ancient Near East at that time. The wise men and women of Israel belonged to a kind of international class that was found across different cultures. And they knew it. The Old Testament refers to the wise men and women of several other countries around them—sometimes in admiration and sometimes less generously! They knew, for example, about the wisdom traditions or schools of Egypt (Gen 41:8; Exod 7:11; 1 Kgs 4:31), Edom (Jer 49:7), Tyre (Ezek 28; Zech 9:2), Assyria (Isa 10:13), and Babylon (Isa 44:25; 47:10; Jer 50:35). And we have the example of the Queen of Sheba who came, like other cultural tourists, to visit Solomon and admire his wisdom (1 Kgs 4:29–34;

10:1–9). It seems as if Jerusalem had become an international university city!

A lot of the writings of these other cultures have been found — especially from Egypt and Mesopotamia (the land of Assyria and Babylon). It is interesting to see that their wisdom books address some of the same issues that we find in the Old Testament. For example, they give advice on basic social and relational skills — how to behave with family and friends. They are concerned about moral order, social stability, and good government. They give advice about how to achieve success in political life. They talk about how to have a good marriage and family. And they also reflect on more philosophical things like divine justice (Do the gods act fairly?) and the problem of undeserved suffering.

It is clear that the wise men and women of Israel not only knew about the wisdom of these other cultures, but they were even happy to make use of some of them in their own writings. There is an Egyptian text, *The Wisdom of Amenemope*, which has so many similarities with Proverbs 22:17—24:22 that it is pretty clear the writer of Proverbs had a copy of it. There is a remarkable openness to recognizing that God had given wisdom to people of other nations too.

However, the Israelites realized that they should use the wisdom of other nations with care. For although they could respect and benefit from the wisdom of others, the Israelite authors did not just take it over unchanged. They were not guilty of simple plagiarism. There are some clear differences as well as similarities.

For example, there were things in those foreign wisdom texts that are completely absent from the Old Testament ones, such as polytheism (having many gods), occult practices and interest in the "underworld" after death, the use of magic, and fatalism (just accepting whatever happens as impersonal unchangeable fate).

And on the other hand, the Old Testament writers affirm their faith in their one, true, living God, YHWH, the God of the covenant with Israel. Everything in life must be related to God and his sovereignty. And the very first starting point and principle of wisdom was to give God the respect and obedience that were his alone — "the fear of the LORD is the beginning of wisdom."

So how does all this build a bridge for the gospel?

Well, just as in Old Testament times, we live in a world in which we, as Christians, share many things in common with people around us. Ordinary people everywhere have a desire to live happily, to have a good family life, to enjoy their work, to be successful and respected, and to live in a society that sustains good order and punishes wrongdoing. These are common desires in all cultures. We also share the same problems as others. We all know about sickness, robbery, violence, and accidental deaths that seem so senseless. We wonder why such things happen and we long for a better world where they wouldn't happen. These are all topics that are found in the Wisdom literature of the Bible—and in the culture around us. Surely we can bring the two together in our conversations and sometimes in our preaching and teaching.

I have a number of friends who work as Christians in diverse cultures around the world. They say that there are many points of contact between the proverbial sayings and stories in those cultures and the Wisdom literature in the Bible. So the Wisdom literature is very useful for building contact and relationships with other cultures. The Thai Bible Society, for example, has recently published the book of Proverbs (on its own) in the Thai language because it is such a useful tool for starting conversations with others in that society.

However, a bridge is just a bridge. Something has to cross it. And that is where we need to find ways to use the wisdom bridge for the sake of the gospel. I suggest that we can do that through three simple words: *Yes. But. So.*

- **Yes** is where we can agree on many matters of common interest and desire with others. And we can show that the Bible also talks about those things in the wisdom books. That builds the bridge.

- **But** is where we have to say that so much of the brokenness in our world is caused by our own sin (even if not all of it is, it is still true that so much of our suffering is the result of human sin or folly). That is the Bible's diagnosis. And we can point that out in relation to any issue we are sharing in common.

- **So** is where we show what God has done through Jesus Christ and the big story of the Bible to give us salvation, life, and hope. There is good news to share!

I think that the best way to preach or teach from the book of **Proverbs** is probably *thematically*. The first nine chapters are fairly thematic themselves and could be preached as whole chapters. But from then on the proverbs seem to tumble over one another like a great cascade. It's not easy to preach a coherent sermon with a single main point from a whole chapter, and it's probably too much to preach a whole sermon on one single verse. So I think it's probably more helpful to pick out some of the major themes that we find again and again and then preach on those using a number of different verses. And as we do so, here's what we might do to build bridges for the gospel. I'll suggest just four fairly major themes. You should be able to find plenty more themes like these through your own study.

Wisdom and the Family: Marriage, Parents, and Children

- *Yes:* There is plenty in Proverbs that affirms marriage, the virtues of a good wife, and the importance of being faithful (Prov 5; 7; 12:4; 18:22; 19:14; 31:10–31). And there is plenty about the relationship between parents and children (1:8; 2:1; 3:11–12; 4:1–4; 13:24; 22:6, 15). Probably there are similar proverbs in other cultures. You should be able to make some useful comparisons between the biblical proverbs and common sayings in your country about marriage and parenting.

- *But:* We see the reality of the fall and human sin in all these areas. Marriages break down. Families are broken. Parents are cruel. Children go astray. And the Old Testament itself illustrates these realities in many of its stories. The Bible is terribly honest about human failure in family relationships.

- *So:* We need the gospel of God's forgiveness and grace in all these relationships. And we need to connect our preaching of what Proverbs has to say to what the New Testament teaches about how the gospel transforms relationships within the family.

Wisdom and Friends

- *Yes:* Proverbs puts a very high value on friendship (17:17; 27:6). And it sees the importance of kindness and generosity as a way of sustaining friendship (11:17, 25; 12:10; 14:31; 22:9). These things are admired in most cultures.

- *But:* The fall has made all of us selfish and greedy. We fight for ourselves, and sometimes we neglect others and betray even our friends. Once again, the Old Testament itself has plenty of stories on that theme!

- *So:* We need the gospel of God's reconciling love, which makes us not just friends but sisters and brothers in Christ. That is an even stronger bond, and it calls for even greater kindness and generosity among us.

Wisdom and Work

- *Yes:* Work is one of the good gifts of God in creation. God himself is a worker in Genesis 1 and he made human beings in his own image. So work is also highly valued in Proverbs, just as laziness is strongly condemned (6:10–11; 10:4–5; 12:11; 14:23; 26:13–16). This is a cultural value widely shared (though not everywhere followed!). Work is something we have in common with almost everybody else around us.

- *But:* Our work is corrupted and spoiled by sin in all kinds of ways. We have to toil and sweat just to survive in the world. Work can become a tool of oppression and exploitation of others (as of the Hebrews in Egypt and many places in today's world). Work can seem futile and frustrating (as Ecclesiastes shows very clearly). Sin has infiltrated the workplace in major ways.

- *So:* We need the gospel of God restoring us to our true humanity in Jesus Christ. The New Testament has a lot to say about the importance of work and also condemns laziness and idleness. The gospel transforms a Christian's work. Even Christian slaves of non-Christian masters can work "for the Lord."[2] And our work can contribute even to the new creation (Rev 21:24, 26). In Christ, our work is "not in vain." Paul's words at the end of 1 Corinthians 15 deliberately echo the complaint of Ecclesiastes. Qoheleth

---

2. This does not mean that slavery itself is simply affirmed. The Bible as a whole subverts slavery and points in the direction that led eventually to its abolition. The point here is simply that the gospel transforms *work*—even the work of a Christian slave.

moans, "Everything is in vain." Paul says, "No it isn't, not when you are in the risen Lord Jesus Christ."

Wisdom and Suffering and Death

- *Yes:* All cultures know about the realities of suffering, injustice, and death and deal with them in many different ways. The Wisdom literature wrestles with these evils too, especially in Job and Ecclesiastes.

- *But:* Although the wisdom writers knew all about the connection between sin and suffering (in the general sense that so much of the suffering in the world is caused by human wrongdoing and folly), they also knew that big questions still remain.

Job raises the problem of the innocent suffering of good people. And the book *refuses* the "explanations" that the three friends and Elihu give. So we should not join those friends and trot out the same reasons as "explanations" when we have friends or members of our congregation who are suffering in some way or have been stricken by disaster. Some preachers are tempted to say that in the end Job did commit the sin of self-righteousness. They take that from Job 32:1–2, which says that Job was "righteous in his own eyes," and they think that must be wrong and sinful. But Job was righteous in God's eyes too, and God said so twice. If Job had suddenly fallen into sin, God would have asked the three friends to pray for him, but instead God tells Job to pray for them. He was in the right; they were in the wrong. So we should not teach the book of Job in a way that ends up taking sides with the friends and accusing Job! No, in the end, God does not answer Job's question ("Why am I suffering, when I know it is not punishment for sin?"). But God does answer Job's longing—for the presence of God himself and a right relationship with God. Job is justified in the end.

- *So:* We need to bring the issue Job raises into the light of the gospel. For God longs to declare us also righteous in his eyes. But that can only happen through the One who suffered innocently—for us. For ultimately the only truly righteous One was Jesus Christ. And because he, who was innocent of all wrongdoing, suffered in the place of us sinners, we can be justified by faith and will one day see him as our living Redeemer. This does not "answer the problem" (any more than the book of Job does), but it puts it within the perspective of the cross. God has been there for us.

Ecclesiastes raises the problem of death. Life itself is baffling and frustrating enough. But even if life has been good, death comes in the end and seems to destroy all value and all hope. The book cries out for God to do something about the futility and uncertainty of "life under the sun" and to overcome the terrible curse of death itself.

- *So:* We need the gospel that tells us God has done both those things. The writer of Ecclesiastes could not know what we now know through the New Testament. He did not know that God (whom he trusted but couldn't understand) would one day enter this world himself. And in the incarnation of his Son, God would experience all the limitations and frustrations of "life under the sun." And then God himself, in Christ, would suffer exactly what one verse in Ecclesiastes describes as something "meaningless" and turn it into the means of our salvation:

> There is something else meaningless that occurs on earth: *the righteous who get what the wicked deserve,* and the wicked who get what the righteous deserve.
>
> *(Eccl 8:14; my italics)*

Did Paul have that verse in mind when he wrote, "God made him who had no sin to be sin for us, so that in him we might become the righteousness of God" (2 Cor 5:21)? Perhaps. I don't know. But I am convinced that Paul did have Ecclesiastes in mind when he finished off his great chapter about the resurrection of Christ with the words:

> Therefore, my dear brothers and sisters, stand firm. Let nothing move you. Always give yourselves fully to the work of the Lord, because you know that your labour in the Lord is not in vain.
>
> *(1 Cor 15:58)*

"Not in vain!" Not meaningless. Not empty. Not "vanity." Paul may well be thinking of the cry of Ecclesiastes — "Meaningless! Everything is meaningless!" "No!" says Paul. Not any longer,

because Christ has died and has risen again. God has defeated death. Death no longer has the victory. And in the end, death itself will be no more.

So the gospel of the life, death, and resurrection of Jesus is the Bible's own answer to the challenge of Ecclesiastes.

Now that does not mean that Ecclesiastes is "not true" or that it shouldn't be in the Bible. No, it is *very* true in describing the reality of life in this fallen world. Like Ecclesiastes, we can see so much that is good because of God's gifts in creation, but we can also see how much everything is spoiled and frustrated by sin. You could put it like this: Ecclesiastes is a reflection on *the world as we know it from Stage 1 and Stage 2 of the great Bible story.* But it was written by someone living within Stage 3 who had no knowledge of what God was going to do at Stage 4 or how the Bible's story will end at Stage 6. By God's grace we do now know all that God did through Jesus Christ, and all that God will do when Christ returns, as revealed in the New Testament. And that is how I think we should preach and teach Ecclesiastes. We can explore all that he says about life—and agree that he is realistic and right in what he observes. But we know that the only answer to the problems and evils that he sees has to be found in the gospel of the Lord Jesus Christ.

Once again (and for the last time!), I hope you can see how much it helps when we set everything we read in the Bible within the flow of its great story. The Bible *as a whole* brings us God's good news. So even when we read the "bad news" parts, we can make sense of them in the light of God's fullest revelation in the gospel. And even when a book like Ecclesiastes does not *know* it, that is where it is pointing in its unanswered questions and unfulfilled longing.

Here are some other themes running through the book of Proverbs especially. Why not read through the book, picking out verses that relate to these themes, and then compile them into a list and select the most appropriate ones for building into a sermon or a lesson on that theme.[3]

---

3. If you have access to Derek Kidner's Tyndale *Commentary on Proverbs* (Downers Grove, IL: IVP Academic, 2009), the introduction has a very useful survey of different themes in Proverbs, with many illustrating verses.

- *Righteousness and justice.* There is a strong concern for political integrity and the proper exercise of authority within the community by those who should uphold the standards of justice and fairness. Equally there is condemnation for all kinds of wickedness and inequality.

- *Kindness and compassion.* Since God's love, faithfulness, and compassion are highly praised in Israel (see especially the Psalms), these should be qualities seen among those who "fear the LORD."

- *Words and speech.* God has given us a very powerful tool in our mouths—the tongue (as James also says)! There are many proverbs about our use of the gift of speech—whether it is wise or foolish, life-giving or destructive, healing or hurtful. Gossip is particularly condemned (as it is also by Paul).

SAMPLE OUTLINES

Although I have just said that it may be best to preach thematically from Proverbs, it is possible to take a whole chapter and work on an outline that picks up some of its main motifs. Here is an example.

Righteousness for Life
Proverbs 11

Righteousness, in both Old and New Testaments, means not just being in a right relationship with God but also cultivating right relationships on earth, in society. Proverbs is full of sayings about "the righteous person" in contrast with the wicked. This chapter illustrates several aspects of what righteousness involves.

You could preach or teach a chapter like this, making the first two points relevant to society in general. But when you come to part three, you can show how ultimately our only security is in the righteousness that comes from Christ and guarantees eternal life and safety on the day of judgment.

If you present material like this, particularly to Christians, you should try to connect it both to some other relevant texts in the law and prophets, from the Old Testament, or to some of the teaching of Jesus and the apostles in the New Testament.

Righteousness in Economic Life

- Verse 1 states a fundamental principle (e.g., Lev 19:35–36; Mic 6:10–11). Dishonesty in trade is not just illegal, it is a sin hated by God.

- Verse 15 echoes the warnings of 6:1–5.

- Verse 18 shows the fickleness of wealth gained through deceit and the value of honest reward.

- Verse 26 condemns the speculator who holds back something that people need in order to make a bigger profit from higher prices later—an evil that happens on an international scale today.

- Verses 24–25 commend generosity and may have influenced Paul in 2 Corinthians 9:6–15.

Righteousness in Social Life

- Verses 10–11: In positions of social leadership (in cities or national government), integrity is a requirement and also a benefit to all.

- Verses 9, 12, 13: Among friends and neighbours, the righteous are careful about the things that are said. The slanderer, the gossip, and the tale-bearer are not only disliked and destructive, they are also an abomination to God (6:12–19). But in the end they damage themselves too (v. 17).

Righteousness and Security in Life

- Life is full of dangers and threats on all sides. This chapter affirms that the best way to be safe is to be righteous—a person of upright integrity (vv. 3, 6, 8, 19, 21, 30, 31). This is similar to the English proverb "Honesty is the best policy."

- But in experience it may not always seem like that in a fallen world. So there are hints of a more spiritual or eternal sense in which righteousness leads to "life" (vv. 19, 30).

- And even if verse 18 doesn't always work out exactly as it says, there will be a final reckoning that will put things right (v. 21).

- So don't trust in riches alone. It is not what a person *has*, but what they *are*, that will count in the end (vv. 4, 21).

The Greedy Life
Ecclesiastes 5:8 – 20

This could be a message that warns Christians about the dangers of greed (there is plenty about that in the New Testament also, especially from Jesus). But it could also be used in a gentle evangelistic way since it exposes some of the dangers and deceptiveness of wealth and greed—which is so prevalent in society—and can then lead to a gospel ending that goes beyond the positive conclusion of the passage itself.

Greed Is Oppressive When Combined with Bureaucracy (vv. 8 – 9)

- A very accurate observation about social hierarchy and the way money seems to flow upward from the poor to the rich (in spite of all the theories about "trickle down").

Greed Is Unsatisfying and Produces Stress and Anxiety (vv. 10 – 12)

- Greed feeds on itself. The more riches you have: i) the more beggars surround you; ii) the less personal enjoyment you have, other than for show; iii) the more anxious and sleepless you become. So people spend enormous amounts on security, walls, guards, alarm systems, etc.!

Greed Is Unreliable in Times of Misfortune (vv. 13 – 14)

- Wealth can lead to violent robbery. It can be lost through "bad luck." Markets collapse. Banks go bust.

Greed Is Pathetic in the Face of Death (vv. 15 – 17)

- Very gloomy verses, yet totally realistic. The consequences of Genesis 3. "Life is a pilgrimage between two moments of nakedness—at birth and at death. It is better to travel light" (John Stott).[4]

- Jesus: Luke 12:13 – 21.

BUT life is to be enjoyed as a good gift from God (vv. 18 – 20)

- A sudden turn to the positive.
- *Greed* may be destructive and frustrating, but *wealth in itself*, if it is earned honestly and received as a gift from God, can be enjoyed with productive work, joy, and satisfaction in life.
- Ecclesiastes has a positive view of the value of life and work and the good things God has given to humanity in this world. His answer to the evil of greed is not "asceticism" — withdrawing into a life of false poverty and hardship. Rather, he commends *responsible* enjoyment with contentment.

From there, you can move to New Testament teaching on the topic, e. g., 1 Timothy 6:6 – 10, 17 – 19.

---

4. As I often heard him say in his preaching and teaching.

Appendix 1

Ancestors of Israel	Slavery in Egypt	Exodus	Land	Judges	United Monarchy	Divided Kingdoms			Judah alone		Post-exilic period
2000	1400				1000	900	800	700	600	500	400 →
Abraham		Moses	Joshua	Samuel	Saul	Judah (South)		Israel (North)	587 Fall of Jerusalem		Ezra
Isaac		Sinai	Conquest; Settlement of tribes		David			721 Fall of Samaria	Babylon		Nehemiah
Jacob		Covenant Law			Solomon			Assyria	EXILE		Persia
Joseph		Tabernacle			Temple				538 BC beginning of return to land		Greece
		Wilderness									Rome

Centuries of the great prophets

Appendix 2

	10th Century BC	9th Century BC	8th Century BC	7th Century BC	6th Century BC	5th Century BC
	1000 — 900	900 — 800	800 — 700	700 — 600	600 — 500	500 — 400
	United Monarchy	Judah (South) : Israel (North)*	Judah (South) : Israel (North)*	Judah	Judah	Judah

Kings

10th Century BC	9th Century BC — Judah (South)	9th Century BC — Israel (North)*	8th Century BC — Judah (South)	8th Century BC — Israel (North)*	7th Century BC — Judah	6th Century BC — Judah	5th Century BC — Leaders
Saul	Rehoboam	Jeroboam I	Amaziah	Jehoash	Hezekiah	Jehoiachin	Ezra
David	Abijah	Omri	Uzziah	Jeroboam II	Manasseh	Zedekiah	Nehemiah
Solomon	Asa	Ahab	Jotham	Menahem	Amon		
	Jehoshaphat	Ahaziah	Ahaz	Hoshea	Josiah		
	Jehoram	Joram			Jehoahaz		
	Ahaziah	Jehu			Jehoiakim		
	Athaliah	Jehoahaz					
931 BC Division of the kingdoms	Joash			721 BC Fall of Samaria		587 BC Fall of Jerusalem. Babylonian exile	
						538 BC start of return to the land	

Prophets

10th Century BC	9th Century BC	8th Century BC	7th Century BC	6th Century BC	5th Century BC
Nathan	Elijah	Isaiah	Isaiah	Jeremiah	Haggai
	Elisha	Micah	Micah	Ezekiel	Zechariah
		Hosea	Jeremiah	Habakkuk	Malachi
		Amos		Zephaniah	

* Only the major kings of the Northern Kingdom of Israel are included. Some of the minor ones reigned only for a few days or weeks!

Bibliography

This list includes books I have found helpful — not necessarily meaning that I agree with everything in them! They are a mixture of some that are at a simple level and a few that are more academic. Some are a bit old and may not be easily available. But if you have access to a library, some of these may be helpful to you too.

Achtemeier, Elizabeth. *Preaching from the Old Testament*. Louisville: Westminster John Knox, 1989.

Bruce, F. F. *New Testament Development of Old Testament Themes*. Exeter: Paternoster and Grand Rapids: Eerdmans, 1968.

Clowney, Edmund P. *Preaching and Biblical Theology*. London: Tyndale, 1961.

Davis, Dale Ralph. *The Word Became Fresh: How to Preach from Old Testament Narrative Texts*. Fearn: Christian Focus, 2006.

Davis, Ellen F. *Wondrous Depth: Preaching the Old Testament*. Louisville: Westminster John Knox, 2005.

Duduit, Michael (ed.). *Handbook of Contemporary Preaching*. Nashville: Broadman, 1992.

Gibson, Scott M. (ed.). *Preaching the Old Testament*. Grand Rapids: Baker, 2006.

Goldsworthy, Graeme. *Preaching the Whole Bible as Christian Scripture*. Leicester: IVP and Grand Rapids: Eerdmans, 2000.

Greenslade, Philip. *A Passion for God's Story: Discovering Your Place in God's Strategic Plan*. Milton Keynes: Authentic, 2002.

Greidanus, Sidney. *Preaching Christ from the Old Testament: A Contemporary Hermeneutical Method*. Grand Rapids: Eerdmans, 1999.

Haslam, Greg (ed.). *Preach the Word: The Call and Challenge of Preaching Today.* Lancaster: Sovereign World, 2006.

Hill, Harriet and Margaret. *Translating the Bible into Action: How the Bible Can Be Relevant in All Languages and Cultures.* Carlisle: Piquant, 2008.

Holbert, John C. *Preaching Old Testament: Proclamation & Narrative in the Hebrew Bible.* Nashville: Abingdon, 1991.

Kaiser, Walter C. Jr., *Preaching and Teaching from the Old Testament: A Guide for the Church.* Grand Rapids: Baker, 2003.

Kent, Grenville J. R. (et. al., eds.). *'He Began With Moses': Preaching the Old Testament Today.* Nottingham: IVP, 2010. In the USA, *Reclaiming the Old Testament for Christian Preaching.* Downers Grove: IVP, 2010.

Roberts, Vaughan. *God's Big Picture: Tracing the Storyline of the Bible.* Leicester: IVP, 2002.

Standing, Roger. *Finding the Plot: Preaching in a Narrative Style.* Milton Keynes: Paternoster, 2004.

Williams, Michael. *How to Read the Bible through the Jesus Lens: A Guide to Christ-Focused Reading of Scripture.* Grand Rapids: Zondervan, 2012.